AROUND GOD'S ACRE
in South-western Wales

Gyda dymuniadau
goran –

Cyril Treharne
2006

Around God's Acre

in South-western Wales

*A Miscellany of Churches, Chapels,
Churchyards and Memorials*

Cyril L. Treharne

ISBN: 1-84527-087-8

Cover design: Sian Parri

Published by
Gwasg Carreg Gwalch, 12 Iard yr Orsaf, Llanrwst,
Wales LL26 0EH.
☎ 01492 642031   📠 01492 641502
✆ books@carreg-gwalch.co.uk
Web site: www.carreg-gwalch.co.uk

My sincere and grateful thanks to the writers of
all the books listed in the Bibliography. Without
the invaluable information contained within the
books that provided me with much background
information to my researches I would not have
succeeded in achieving my aim.

To my dear wife Barbara for her patience and forbearance over the years. While I disappeared into churches and churchyards, looking for anything I considered interesting, she patiently read in the car until my reappearance. I am also grateful to my daughter, Anne, for reading and correcting errors in the draft chapters with such care, and for her helpful suggestions.

*'I like that Saxon phrase, which calls
The burial-ground God's Acre!'*

Longfellow

Bibliography / *Llyfryddiaeth*

Breverton, T.D.: *The Book of Welsh Saints*
Carmarthenshire Histories, Vol. XIII, 1976
Carmarthen Journal
Davies, Aneirin Talfan: *Crwydro Sir Gâr*
Davies, D. Elwyn: *Y Smotiau Duon*
Ellis, T.I.: *Crwydro Ceredigion*
Episcopal Register of St. David's 1397-1518
Farmer, D.H.: *The Oxford Dictionary of Saints*
Havard, Robert: *Wellington's Welsh General*
Jones, G. Prys: *The History of Carmarthenshire*
Jones H.M.: Llanelli Lives
Jones, Leslie Baker: *Princelings, Privileges and Power*
Jones, Major Francis:
    Historic Cardiganshire Homes
    Historic Carmarthenshire Homes
    Historic Houses of Pembrokeshire
    Treasury of Historic Carmarthenshire
    Treasury of Historic Pembrokeshire
Laws, Edward: *The History of Little England Beyond Wales*
Mee, Arthur: *Carmarthenshire Notes*
Noakes, D: Jane Austen
Owen, G; Cambrian Register, Vol. II
Rawlings, Bert: *The Parish Churches and Nonconformist
    Chapels of Wales*
Rees, Sian: *A Guide to Ancient and Historical Wales*
Salter, Mike: *The Old Parish Churches, (1) South-West Wales
    (2) Mid-Wales, (3) Glamorgan and Gower*
Spurrell, W.: *Carmarthenshire and Its Neighbourhood*
Stephens, Meic: *The Oxford Companion to the Literature of Wales*
Tomalin, Claire: *Jane Austen – A Life*
Western Mail
Various Parish Registers
Vaughan, H.M.: The South Wales Squires – 1926

Contents/*Cynnwys*

Introduction / *Cyflwyniad*

Dai Jones, Llanilar, is well known throughout Wales as presenter of the television programme 'Cefn Gwlad' (The Countryside). On one occasion he was seen in the company of a man in Anglesey whose hobby was visiting churchyards. I, too go round churchyards as well as into churches, where one can find interesting artefacts and memorials. I am frequently fascinated by some of the inscriptions on gravestones and memorials. I can well imagine that some people, while reading this, may think that my hobby is tinged with a morbid interest. I can assure them that they would be wrong to harbour such a thought. It should be remembered that gravestones do not only record the names of people who have walked this earth before us but that they are also a rich source of interesting historical information. And, on occasions, the inscriptions can be humorous and morbid, therefore cannot be the word to describe my hobby.

In the churchyard at Strata Florida in Ceredigion, the inscription on one stone informs us that only the person's leg was interred in the grave – where the remainder of his body is buried, goodness only knows.

I wrote at the beginning that churches and churchyards provide a rich source of information for historians. I believe that future historians with an interest like mine, will not be able to find information, on the present-day, plain headstones, with their brief inscriptions, to interest them in the way we find facts inscribed on the gravestones and memorials of yesteryear.

The Victorian era, especially, provides the historian with a great wealth of information. In this book I invite you, the reader, to come with me on a journey around some of the churches and churchyards of Carmarthenshire, Pembrokeshire, Ceredigion, Glamorgan and Powys. I feel sure that you will be surprised by some of the information in the book and I hope that you will find the journey worthwhile.

In addition to being places of worship, our churches are repositories of the history of Christians down through the ages. Some churches have their origins hidden in the mists of time but, however old they may be, each one has something of interest for the visitor to see. Many have been built on pre-Christian sites and in their churchyards lie the remains of countless men, women and children who have lived within the parish and beyond. The churches are also of architectural interest, and incorporate a variety of architectural styles. Some are richly endowed with various artefacts that are priceless; these include chalices and patens that are hundreds of years old, beautiful stained glass windows and interesting memorials. Also kept in churches are parish registers of baptisms, marriages and deaths, some, like the chalices, with details dating from the sixteenth century. These registers tell the story of the people who lived within the parishes. Within these registers the historian is able to glean a great deal of information about the lives of parishioners of former times. Similarly, information can be gathered from inscriptions on gravestones in the churchyards; some telling tragic tales while some, surprisingly, can bring a smile to the reader's face.

It is a sad reflection on our society that it is necessary these days to keep our churches locked during the weekdays and only open when services are held within them. But for the person who really wants to go inside the church it is possible, by asking the local Vicar, Rector,

9

Churchwardens or Sexton, to obtain the key and gain admittance to the building. A question put to a local resident will soon help the visitor with an answer as to where to locate the above-named persons.

Visiting churches will often take the visitor to very special parts of the country, their beauty and tranquillity making the journey really worthwhile.

To those not conversant with Church administration, I feel sure that the following details will be of value. A diocese is divided into archdeaconries, deaneries and parishes. Within Carmarthenshire, there is the Carmarthen Archdeaconry covering nearly all of the county, and the deaneries of Carmarthen, Dyffryn Aman, Cydweli, Llangadog and Llandeilo, and St Clears. A few of the churches of the county are in the deaneries of either Pembrokeshire or Ceredigion.

Nearly all the churches are dedicated to various saints, most of them belonging to the period known as 'The Age of the Saints'. This period extended from the fifth to the eighth centuries AD. It was during these years that Wales was converted to Christianity and the saints were largely responsible for this. The saints were missionaries who set up cells in various parts of the country, often located in areas that were previously centres of pagan worship. As a result of their efforts, small wooden churches were erected and these later replaced by stone edifices. Over the years these early churches have been extended and restored. The end of the nineteenth century was a time of much church restoration throughout the land.

The churches of the Archdeaconry of Carmarthen are dedicated to over sixty saints, the majority of whom are British while other saints are from the New Testament. Some churches are dedicated to Christ, the Holy Trinity and to All Saints. The church of, Llanpumsaint is

10

dedicated to five saints and, according to legend, they were quintuplets – Gwyn, Gwynno, Gwynoro, Ceitho and Celynin. There is no church in Wales dedicated to four saints, and it is said that two of the five died, leaving the three remaining saints responsible for the church of Llantrisant in Glamorganshire. When there were only two remaining, they became responsible for the church at Llanddeusant. Following the death of four saints, the last remaining brother set up a church at Llansaint.

The following saints have churches dedicated to them within the Archdeaconry: David, Michael, Cynwyl, Alban, Peter, John, Twrog, Cynnwr, Anne, Luke, Cain, Cynog, Llawddog, Stephen, Teilo, Lucia, Catherine, Margaret, Lleian, Mary, Tybie, Dyfan, Mark, Edith, Edmund, Maelog, Elli, Paul, Gwynog, Non, Illtud, Cyndeyrn, Ishmael, Thomas, Paulinus, Barnabus, Sawyl, Dingad, Egwad, Cadog, Simon, Jude, Sadwrn, Cwrdaf, Martin, Odoceus, Tysilio, Cledwyn, Philip, James, Brynach, Canna, Lawrence, Cynin, Cyffig, Patrick and Geler.

Of the churches in the Carmarthen Archdeaconry, eighteen are dedicated to St David, ten to St Mary, six to St Teilo, and four each to St John and St Peter. There are six Holy Trinity churches, four All Saints, three to Christ. There are three St Margaret, two Saint Anne, St Cynwyl and St Alban, and one saint dedicated to each of the remaining churches. For those interested in these saints T.D. Breverton's book, *The Book of Welsh Saints*, is a mine of information.

Around Carmarthen

It is in the Deanery of Carmarthen that I shall begin our journey. There are twenty-seven churches in the deanery, and the first one we visit is the church of St David, at Abergwili.

The church has a long and interesting history. There may have been a church at Abergwili since the sixth or seventh century. In a twelfth century poem in honour of its Patron Saint, Abergwili church is one of six named and ascribed to the patronage of St David. As early as 1395 it is on record that there was a church at Abergwili and that it was known as St David's Church. In the Episcopal Register of St David's, (1397 to 1518) there is, for 1398, the following entry: 'On 1 February, in the year above-said, at Shrewsbury, the said Reverend Father (i.e. Lord Guy, Bishop of St David's) in consideration of charity collated by his letters patent to his beloved son, Clerk of the Diocese of Lincoln, a canonry and the prebend of Llandisilio in the collegiate church of Abergwili of the said diocese . . . ' Also in the same book there are other references to the 'collegiate church of Abergwili'. It is significant that Bishop Beck, Bishop of St David's, founded a college at Abergwili and at Llanddewi Brefi in 1287, and both churches are dedicated to St David.

In 1935 Bishop Prosser, then bishop of the diocese, in the course of a very hot, dry summer, noticed a brown streak on the palace lawn. It was arranged that the lawn be dug and, a few feet below the surface, the foundations of the college were discovered. The Palace was built in 1550, and it is highly probable that stones from the college were used in the building of the Palace. Up until the dissolution of the monasteries, abbeys and priories which

12

occurred during the reign of King Henry VIII, it is believed that Abergwili Church was under the care of St John's Priory in Carmarthen.

The proximity of the old Palace, now the County Museum, as well as the present palace to the church, has meant that many of the bishops of the diocese have had a great deal to do with the church itself.

In 1555 Bishop Ferrar was martyred for his Protestant beliefs by being burnt at the stake in what is now called Nott Suare, Carmarthen. In the Sanctuary of the Church in 1581 were buried the remains of Bishop Richard Davies. During the 1560s Bishop Davies translated the *Book of Common Prayer* into Welsh as well as large sections of the New Testament.

On the north wall of the Sanctuary is a memorial to Bishop Davies. An inscription in Welsh, reads: 'Er coffadwriaeth am y Gwir Barchedig Dad yn Nuw, yr Esgob Richard Davies, DD. Ganwyd ef ym mhlwyf Cyffyn ger Aberconwy yng Ngwynedd. Dygwyd ef i fyny yn New Hall, Rhydychen. *Codwyd ef i Esgobaeth Llanelwy, Ionawr 21ain 1561.* Bu farw Tachwedd 7fed yn y flwyddyn 1581, oddeutu 80 mlwydd oed, ac fe'i claddwyd yn yr eglwys hon.

Efe a gyfieithodd Joshua, Ruth, Barnwyr, 1 Samuel, 2 Samuel yn y Beibl Saesneg pan ddiwygiwyd yr hen gyfieithiadau o dan arolygiad yr Archesgob Parker yn y flwyddyn 1568, ac efe hefyd a gyfieithodd 1 Timotheus, Yr Hebreaid, Iago, 1 a 2 Pedr yn y Testament Newydd Cymraeg a gyhoeddwyd gan William Salesbury o'r Plas Isaf, ger Llanrwst yn y flwyddyn 1567.

Esgob oedd ef o ddysg bur a diwyd,
Diwyd oedd mewn llafur.
Gwelir byth tra'r Ysgrythur
Ol o'i ofal a'i gur wiw.

Tegid

A brief translation tells us that Bishop Richard Davies was born at Cyffyn, near Aberconwy in Gwynedd. He studied at New Hall, Oxford and was Bishop of St Asaph from January 21st 1559 until becoming Bishop of St David's on May 21st 1561. He died November 7th 1581 at about 80 years of age. He is buried in the Chancel of Abergwili Church.

Bishop Davies translated a number of books from the Old Testament in the English Bible and, with William Salesbury, translated in 1567 parts of the New Testament into Welsh.

It is said that, when Bishop Thirlwall had a memorial tablet placed above Bishop Davies's resting place, a heavy stone fell from the scaffolding and tore itself into the grave. Here was found the coffin bearing the bishop's name. The coffin lid which had been damaged later resulted in the bishop's remains mouldering into dust.

It is recorded that Bishop Laud, who was Bishop of St David's from 1612 to 1627, only visited the diocese on two occasions during his period in office – in 1622 and 1625. In his diary he reports that on September 24th 1625: 'Only one person desired to receive Holy Orders from me, and he found unfit, upon examination.' On August 21st 1625 he consecrated a chapel in the Palace. Bishop Laud was beheaded on Tower Hill, London in 1645. It is possible that it would have paid him to have resided within the See of St David's!

In 1633 he became Archbishop of Canterbury. His

support for King Charles Is unparliamentary rule, censorship of the press and persecution of the Puritans aroused bitter opposition and his strict enforcement of the statutes against enclosures and laws regulating wages and prices alienated the propertied classes. His attempt to impose the use of the *Prayer Book* on the Scots precipitated the Civil War. Bishop Laud was impeached by Parliament in 1640 and, five years later he was beheaded.

Buried under a plain raised tomb at the east end of the north aisle is Bishop Adam Ottley who was Bishop of St David's from 1714 to 1724. Prior to his death he, 'ordered out of his humility, that his body be laid in Abergwili churchyard.' Another remarkable bishop of the diocese was Bishop Thirlwall who lived in the palace from 1840 to 1874. Although a Londoner, in less than a year he had learnt Welsh well enough to preach in the language. It is said that he could read English before his third birthday and, at the age of four, could read Greek fluently. His book *The History of Greece* is considered to be a standard work. The pulpit of the church is dedicated to his memory, and the window in the west wall, which used to be in the east wall, was donated by him. It is unusual in that it contains Welsh Scripture and Hebrew characters representing the First Person of the Trinity, the figure of the Lamb representing the Second Person, and the Dove representing the Third Person.

The chalice and the paten have inscribed on them: 'Poculum ecclesioe de Abergwili, 1574'; this illustrates that they are only eight years younger than the oldest in the county, those of Laugharne which are dated 1566.

Legend has it that during the restoration work of the 1800s, the stone to which Bishop Ferrar was tied when he was burnt in Nott Square in 1555, was placed on top of the church spire.

I shall end my writing on Abergwili Church on a personal note by quoting from *The History of Abergwili Church*, issued in the 1930s: 'Until 1269, the Prior and Canon of Carmarthen possessed half only of the interest of Abergwili Church, the remainder belonging to Hywel, son of Trahaearn'. This interests me greatly since my surname is Treharne and, according to the late Norah Isaac, the origin of my name is Trahaearn, a truly Welsh name, and not Cornish as some maintain.

Leaving the church of Abergwili, we travel westwards across Carmarthen, and arrive at another St David's Church, this one situated in Picton Terrace. The church is one of two Welsh language churches in the town, the other being St. John's Church in Priory Street.

The foundation stone for St David's was originally laid on the site where Christchurch now stands but due to unforeseen problems the church was moved to its present location. The stone was relaid in its present position on November 27th 1824 by the Rt. Rev. Jenkinson, Bishop of St David's. Building work was completed by 1837, and it was opened and consecrated by Bishop Thirlwall on January 19th of that year. On November 10th 1843 the Parish of St David was founded and gazetted on the 16th February 1844.

The church stands on rising ground, well in from the road that was, until the construction of the western bypass, the main road westwards from the town. The church has a large turreted tower that appears at first sight to be separate from the main building. Surprisingly, the church was originally on a north to south axis but, as a result of the Church becoming too small, it was decided in the 1850s to build the present nave and porch at a right angle to the original church, thus running on an east-west axis, the usual form for churches in our land. During the

1880s the north-south nave was changed into the present chancel in memory of the Rev. D. Archard Williams who had been vicar for a number of years until his death. In the east wall, above the altar, there is a very large stained glass window, reputed to be the largest in any church in the Principality.

The visitor, on walking towards the point where the south and east walls of the churchyard meet, will see a rather insignificant stone resting on the east wall. The inscription reads: 'In memory of Sgt. John Samuel of the 1st Battalion, 1st Royal Regiment of Foot, who was born at Llangunnor in 1788, and died at Carmarthen on October 16th 1874. He served in the Army for 25 years, was wounded at San Sebastian on July 25th 1813 and at Waterloo on June 15th 1815. On the celebration of the Battle of Waterloo a wreath was laid on the grave by General Sir James-Hill Johnes, VC, and this stone was erected by the Vicar, the Rev. Thomas Griffiths, and D. Davies, Sculptor.'

Let me take the visitor back to January 23rd 1791. On that day, a husband and wife would have been seen making their way up the steep, narrow lane leading to Llangunnor Church. The woman, named Anne, was carrying a small child and, at her side, walked her husband, William Samuel. They were taking their boy, John, who was according to the inscription on the gravestone, born sometime in 1788, to be christened by the then vicar, the Rev. John Jones, who was assisted by his curate, the Rev. Thomas Price. Little did the parents of that boy imagine that he would one day be one of the Duke of Wellington's soldiers in both the Peninsular War and at the Battle of Waterloo.

According to the Parish Register of St David's Church, John Samuel, at 86 years of age, was laid to rest in the churchyard on October 26th 1874, his death having been ten days earlier.

John Samuel enlisted in the Carmarthen Fusiliers in 1807 at 19 years of age. Four years later, he joined the 1st Royals, somewhat surprisingly as the Royals was a Scottish regiment. He was sent to fight in the Peninsular War and took part in the battles of Salamanca and Vitoria. He was wounded in the chest during the siege of San Sebastian. He also served in the West Indies and arrived back in this country in time to join the Duke of Wellington's army once more, this time at Brussels, before moving to take part in the Battle of Waterloo. He was one of the 'letter orderlies' and, early on in the battle, he was wounded in the knee. In his disabled state he managed to crawl to the churchyard of Waterloo, and succeeded to staunch the bleeding of his wound. He remained there overnight. The day after the battle was over, he was conveyed to Brussels where he soon recovered. He was discharged from the service on the 8th of October 1833 on a sergeant's pension. While serving in the army he was regarded as a good and efficient soldier and, according to reports, he maintained the same character of sobriety and integrity up to the time of his death.

Before retracing our steps across the town to St Peter's Church, we journey westwards for approximately two miles and arrive at St Mary's Church, Llanllwch.

In the majority of cases the word that completes the place name beginning with Llan is the name of a saint, for instance, St Cynnwr giving us Llangynnwr, near Carmarthen. This, however, is not the case with Llanllwch. The word 'llwch' does not mean dust as one might imagine; ('llwch' is the Welsh word for dust) 'llwch; in this instance however, it is a Welsh version of the Scottish 'loch', the Irish 'lough' and the English 'lake'.

It is believed that at one time a lake or pool was located not far from the church and, even today, the land to the west of the church is wet and marshy, so the church in a literal translation could very well be called 'Lakechurch'.

Llanllwch Church was, until 1843, attached to St Peter's Church, Carmarthen; it was on November 10th of that year that St Peter's Parish was divided into three districts – St David's, Carmarthen forming the third along with St Peter's and Llanllwch. Fourteen years later they were formed into three distinct parishes.

The original church is undoubtedly very old; its large tower was probably built in the fifteenth century. Over the years much restoration work has been carried out to the building. It is reported that, at the beginning of the eighteenth century, the roof was destroyed and the church disused. There are a number of interesting memorials in both the church and churchyard but the main reason for the visit is in order to look at a small, insignificant looking gravestone to the right of the path leading to the church itself. On it is inscribed: 'In memory of John Davies of Llanllwch, Pensioner, died August 5th 1858, aged 82. Fought at Corunna, Cuidad Rodrigo, Salamanca, etc. Etat et vitae.'

On page 94 of the Burial Register we see the following entry: 'Name: John Davies, Abode: Llanllwch village. Buried August 9th 1858, age 82. Officiating Priest Rev. Thomas Williams.' So what else is there to discover about this old soldier who, like John Samuel of Carmarthen, fought in the Duke of Wellington's Army in the Peninsular War.

From the 1851 Census we learn that he was married, but there is no mention of his wife on the gravestone. This often means that the couple were childless and, on the death of the second partner there would be no one left to record the wife's name on the stone. John Davies is described as a 'Pensioner' and that he had fought in a number of the battles of the Peninsular War of 1808 to 1814. The Census return describes him as a 'Pensioner' residing in Llanllwch, in fact, Chelsea Pensioner, who was married to a Mary Davies. He was originally from the parish of Newchurch and his wife from the parish of Trelech. There is an entry in the Baptism Register recording his baptism on February 2nd 1776. It is extremely difficult to come to any definite conclusion as to when or where the marriage of John and Mary took place. It may have been his wife's home parish of Trelech, or in Newchurch, in Llanllwch, or some other parish for that matter. However, there is the following entry in the Marriage Register of Llanllwch Church: 'John Davies, widower, married Mary Roberts, spinster, on November 6th 1817.' Is he the Chelsea Pensioner, I wonder? This is pure speculation on my part. It is interesting to note that if the entry referred to them, his wife would have been twenty-one years younger than he was; he would have been forty-six years of age and his wife twenty-five at the time of their marriage. Another entry records the marriage of 'John Davies of Merthyr Parish to Mary Lewis on May 22nd 1832.' Because of insufficient data the puzzle remains.

Looking through the Marriage Register of Llanllwch brought to light some other interesting facts. On November 19th 1822 a certain Albymus – a strange Christian name – Sydney married Jane Williams. Two years later, on December 28th 1824, this same Albymus, now a widower, married another woman of the same name as his first wife – Jane Williams.

In 1816 there are three entries that refer to the Battle of Waterloo. The three entries mention the 55th. Regiment, a regiment that could well have taken part in the battle. The full title reads: 'His Royal Majesty's 55th. Regiment of Foot, Capt. James Taylor Trevor's Co'y' or 'The Westmorland Regiment of Foot'. The Regiment was raised in 1785 at Stirling, Scotland when the Seven Year War broke out. By 1816, it had returned to this country and was stationed in Carmarthen, or it could be the case that the regiment was about to go overseas. The entries read:

June 16th 1816, David Davies, militiaman, the 55th Regiment, married Anne Jones. (He could write his name, she could only 'make a mark'.)

June 17th 1816, John Cambel (sic), militiaman, 55th Regiment, Married Mary Griffiths. (Again he could write his name but she could not.)

June 26th 1816, Jeremiah Fisk, militiaman, 55th Regiment, married Anne Walters. (Both unable to write.)

Returning to the churchyard there is another grave with the inscription: 'Er cof am Mary Evans, yr hon wedi gwasanaethu swydd 'clochyddes' yn Eglwys y Plwyf hon (sic) am 20 mlynedd, a hunodd mewn hedd Mawrth 29ain 1899, yn 59 mlwydd oed.' Translated, it recounts the death of Mary Evans, aged 59 years, 'bellringer' for 20 years.

Back in Carmarthen, we visit Christchurch which stands a mere stone's throw from St David's Church, Carmarthen. Whereas St David's is the Welsh language church, Christchurch is for English speakers. Building work commenced following the laying of the foundation stone on September 2nd 1867. The church was consecrated by Bishop Thirlwall on September 21st 1869. During the last few years the interior of the church has been divided in two, the northern half becoming the actual church in which services are held, while the southern half is used as a church hall.

In the apse-shaped east wall there are five stained glass windows. Beginning with the window nearest the north wall of the chancel they depict, a) The Adoration of the Magi, b) The Crucifixion, c) The Women at the Tomb, d) Jesus and Mary Magdalene, and e) Ave Maria – The Angel Gabriel and Mary.

Inscribed on the front of the choir stalls on the north side of the chancel is: 'The first marriage was solemnised on 2nd November of John Frederick, born 22nd October 1845, died 3rd November 1923, later Colonel R.E., son of the Rev. John Garwood, MA, Secretary London Mission, who came to Pembroke to build the Stack Forts, and Margaret, born 27th December 1850, died 3rd November 1931, whose father, Lt. Col. R.A. Scott, of 15 Picton Terrace, was sent to quell the Rebecca Riots, and remained as Chief Constable of Carmarthen for many years. These choir stalls were erected in 1935 by their three sons and seven grandchildren to commemorate over fifty years of happy married life in Quetta and other Indian stations, and after retirement at 1 Camden Hill, Kensington.'

From Christchurch we traverse Lammas Street, Hall Street and King Street before reaching the oldest building in Carmarthen still in use – St Peter's Church. In the twelfth century Chronicle of Battle Abbey, East Sussex, we find the first written evidence regarding St Peter's Church. The relevant entry in the Chronicle states: 'In the time of Abbot Ralph, (1107-1124), the King, cherishing a great affection for the Abbey, freely and of his own proper gift, conferred upon it a certain church dedicated to St Peter the Apostle in the city of Chaermedi in Wales with its appendages for ever.' The Chaermedi mentioned in the document is non-other than Carmarthen.

On the walls inside the church are a number of very interesting memorials. In the south aisle is the tomb and effigy of Sir Rhys ap Thomas and his wife. Sir Rhys ap Thomas was born in 1449, the son of Thomas ap Gruffith ap Nicholas. It was Sir Rhys's grandfather who founded the House of Dinefwr near Llandeilo. The family home was Newton House, the house recently renovated and refurbished by the National Trust. Trained as a soldier, Sir Rhys was very much involved in ensuring that Henry Tudor became King of England. On August 22nd 1485, Sir Rhys, along with thousands of Welsh soldiers, took part in the Battle of Bosworth and, during the battle, King Richard III was killed and Henry was established as king of the land.

Sir Rhys and his wife were originally buried in the Franciscan Priory in the town of Carmarthen but, following the Dissolution of the monasteries and abbeys, the bodies of both he and his wife were moved to St Peter's Church. Inscribed on the box-shaped tomb are the words: 'Here rest the remains of Sir Rhys ap Thomas, KG, who fought at Bosworth Field, and dame Eva, his wife; they were originally buried at the Monastery of the White Friars in this town, removed into this church when the Monastery was suppressed, and placed within the altar rails. Finally they were re-interred in this place when their monument was restored by the care of their descendant George Rice, 4th Baronet Dynevor, 1866.'

On the south wall of the chancel there is a carved effigy of Lady Anne, second wife of Sir William Vaughan of Torcoed, Llangendeyrn. It is said that the effigy, depicting Lady Anne kneeling at the side of her bed, shows how she was found when she died on August 15th 1672, aged 84 years. On the memorial this tribute:

Kind reader, underneath this Tombe doth Lye
Choice Elixar of Mortalite.
By careful providence Great wealth did store
For her relations and the poore.
In Essex born But spent her Gainful Dayes
In Terra Coed, to her Eternal Prayse,
Where by her Loanes in spite of adverse fates
She did preserve Mens persons and Estates.
A Great Exampler to our Nation,
Her intimate in Life and action.
Would you then know who was this good Woman,
Twas virtuous Anne, the Lady Vaughan.

On the north wall of the chancel is a memorial and effigy on which is inscribed:

Gradatin per ardua ad Astra.
The Reverend Mr Pritchard
Novbr ye 25th Anno Dom . . .

Richd. Pritchard, born at Llangadock, ye first and baptised ye 4th of August 1671; entered Js. Coll. Oxon, March ye 30th 1677. Master of Arts in June 1683, Fellow and Preacher of Dulwich College in Surrey for five years. Chaplain to ye Newcastle at ye bombardment of Calais, April ye 3rd 1696, Chaplain to ye Dreadnought 1697. On a dangerous Newfoundland voyage 1699, became minister fo Carmarthen 8br (sic), instituted Vicar of Llangan in 1709 which he quitted, and was instituted Vicar of Llanegwad 8br ye 25th 1712. Chaplain to ye Fate of Northampton . . . '

Also commemorated on the walls of the church are numerous other worthies, among them Sir Richard Steele, a famous essayist, politician and a friend and co-worker of Joseph Addison on a number of periodicals – The Tatler, The Spectator and The Guardian. His second wife, whom he met at his first wife's funeral, was Mary Scurlock, heiress of Tŷ Gwyn Farm in Llangunnor. She is buried not far from Poets Corner in Westminster Abbey. Sir Richard is buried in the Scurlock vault within the church.

A Latin inscription is to be found on a monument commemorating one Jonathan Oakley who died on September 19th 1677, age 39 years. Originally from Warwickshire, he went to Jesus College, Oxford and became an Advocate in Carmarthen.

Another memorial is in memory of Bishop Robert Ferrar, Bishop of St David's, who was burnt at the stake in Nott Square for his Protestant beliefs on March 30th 1555.

Buried in a box tomb near the path that runs alongside the north side of the church is General Sir William Nott and, inside the church, he is commemorated on a tablet on the south wall. He became famous as a result of his distinguished service in the Afghan wars. His monument can be seen in Nott Square, towards which Queen Victoria contributed 200 guineas.

Remembered on the north wall is John Johnes of Ystrad, MP for the County of Carmarthen. He became an MP in 1821 and remained a member until 1832. In the church vestry there is a memorial to Walter Devereux, KG, Earl of Essex, the first to carry the title, and father of

Queen Elizabeth I's much esteemed courtier. His son however, was subsequently charged with treason and beheaded on February 25th 1601. The first Earl is buried somewhere within the chancel of the church.

In the Carmarthen Journal dated January 31st 1873, there is a report of a stained glass window being placed in the east wall of the church. It reads: 'During the present week Mrs Horton of Ystrad and Clapham has caused to be erected a magnificent memorial window to her late husband in the east of the sacred edifice immediately above the communion table. It may not be known to all that Mr Horton, by acquiring the Ystrad estate, attained the position of lay vicar, and only a few years ago since he, at great expense, restored the chancel wherein the tomb of Sir Rhys ap Thomas, the tablets of memory of the Cawdor family, and last, though not least, that of the late lamented Mr Jones of Ystrad, the late lay vicar, not very long since erected as a mark of respect by his younger friend Thomas Brigstocke, the celebrated artist.'

The only drawback to the 'mizzen scene' we have observed is the suspension of the flags of the 23rd Fusiliers, hanging just over the screen, which shut out, to a great measure, the beauty of the window, especially from the west. Without prejudice we would suggest to the vicar and churchwardens that these should be moved to the summit of the arch over the Dynevor mausoleum which would be a graceful and appropriate addition to the already lasting acknowledgement of the late lord's liberty in restoring the same.

The tracery consists of the four beautiful figures commencing with 'The Good Samaritan', 'The Good Shepherd', 'The Sower', and the 'Knock on the Door' or 'The Light of the World'. The five large compartments below are descriptive of 'The Agony in the Garden', over which are the inscriptions 'Thy Will Be Done', 'The Betrayal by Judas', 'The Crucifixion of Our Saviour'; in the centre, we see Pilate's title INRI, on the right of which is Christ bearing the cross and the scourge, over which are the words 'For Thine Is The Kingdom'. At the summit is an adoring angel holding a scroll with the inscription 'I am the Way, the Truth and the Life'. There are two small pieces each side representing 'Alpha' and 'Omega', while the five lower compartments are based by angels holding scrolls, along which runs the text 'The Lord gave, and the Lord hath taken away. Blessed be the Lord'.

This exquisite window was executed by Mr Alec Gibbs, 38 Bedford Square, London, which was entrusted to his assistant William Taylor for firing, and which has been done with much satisfaction. In everyone's opinion the window is a perfect gem of glass painting, and is a worthy memorial to the gentleman to whom it is dedicated. At the extreme base runs the inscription: 'To the glory of God and in memory of Isaac Horton of Ystrad, near this town, Esquire, JP, died June 23rd 1872, aged 63 years.'

Much more could be written about the memorials in St Peter's Church and the people commemorated on them. For anyone interested in learning more about the memorials in the church, a book entitled *Carmarthen and Its Neighbourhood* by William Spurrell, first published in 1879, and republished by Dyfed County Council Cultural Services Department in 1995, lists all the memorials as well as details of 'Pious Benefactors to the town and Corporation of Carmarthen'.

Along the Tywi Valley

Leaving Carmarthen, we cross the river by the bridge below Jail Hill, or as some call it, Castle Hill, and head for the A48 through Llangunnor to join the B4300 towards Capel Dewi and Llanarthne. About half a mile from the junction of the two roads there is a sign for Llangunnor Church which is up a steep, narrow lane. We pass the Vicarage on the right, (built in 1833 for just under £1,000), and arrive at the lych gate, the entrance to the path leading down into the church. From the lych gate, not much of the church is visible; it is curtained by ten large, ancient yew trees. One of the trees has been certified to be at least 1,000 years old. Typically Celtic in design, the church stands a few feet below the brow of the hill and, from the churchyard, the visitor looks down on the village of Abergwili and along the Tywi Valley to the more distant Black Mountains and the Brecon Beacons. The church, dedicated to St Cynnwr, has two naves and two aisles. The north nave and aisle were added to the original south nave and aisle sometime during the 15th or 16th centuries.

There are a number of interesting memorials both within the church and churchyard and, buried in the churchyard are some well known people. Firstly, the church.

On the south wall of the Lady Chapel is a brass plaque in memory of Lieut. Robert Hugh Harries of Bryn Towy who was killed in the Battle of the Somme, one of the bloodiest battles of the 1914-18 War. The number of casualties suffered by the British, French and German armies totalled over one million men. A rather interesting memorial on the south wall of the nave commemorates a

Charles Diggle Williams, who died in 1853 from what was described in the Carmarthen Journal in the following terms: 'He suffered from a carbuncle in the neck, a peculiar disease which invariably carries off its victim in a comparatively short time. It limited Mr Williams's suffering to the brief period of about ten days.'

Remembered on the north side of the main door into the church is Sir Richard Steele. I have already mentioned that he was buried in St Peter's Church in Carmarthen and commemorated there by a tablet on the south wall. But one should not be surprised that he is also remembered in Llangunnor Church. His second wife was Mary Scurlock, heiress to Tŷ Gwyn Farm which stands a few hundred yards from the church. The memorial was placed in the church by a friend named William Williams of Ivy Tower.

The memorial records the fact that Steele represented several constituencies in parliament, that he wrote several plays, and that he was 'an incomparable writer on morality and Christianity'. Also on the memorial this verse:

Behold Llangunnor leering over the Vale
Portrays a scene to adorn romantic tale.
But, more than all the beauties of the site,
Its former owner gives the mind delight.
Is there a heart that can affection feel
For lands so Rich to boast a Steele
Who warm for freedom and with virtue fraught,
His country dearly loved and greatly taught,
Whose words the pure Stile conveys
T'instruct his Britain to the last of days.

Also inscribed on the stone is the fact that it was a William Williams of Ivy Tower who was responsible for erecting the memorial. On reading Major Francis Jones's book *Treasury of Historic Pembrokeshire and Historic Houses of Pembrokeshire* I discovered that Ivy Tower is a house a mile outside St Florence, near Tenby. Not only did he own Ivy Tower but, as can be seen on the memorial, he also owned Penddaulwyn Fawr in the parish of Llangunnor, a property once owned by Sir Richard Steele.

In the churchyard is the grave of the famous hymnwriter David Charles. He wrote some twenty hymns, the best known being 'O fryniau Caersalem', 'O! Iesu Mawr rho d'anian bur' and 'Rhagluniaeth fawr y nef'. Also in the churchyard is buried the granddaughter of David Charles's brother, the famous 'Thomas Charles o'r Bala'. Inscribed on her gravestone: is 'Sacred to the memory of Sarah, wife of David Charles of Carmarthen, granddaughter of the Rev. Thomas Charles, Bala, who departed this life January 13th 1833 in the 20th year of her age.'

Not far from the west wall is the grave of the Victorian poet Sir Lewis Morris. His wish, written in verse, was fulfilled in 1907:

Let me at last be laid
On that hillside I know which scans the Vale
Beneath the thick yew shade
For shelter, when rains and wind prevail.

Sir Lewis, a close friend of the poet Tennyson, also wrote a verse extolling the beauty of the scenery from the churchyard:

How fair and fresh from this gray churchyard shows
The rich green vale beneath. Upon the deep
Lush meadows, where the black herds grazing seem.

Like rooks upon the grass, a silver gleam,
Now lost and now discovered, marks the place
Where winds the brimming river. Here thick
Woods of oak and beech upon the sloping banks
Bends to the shadowy stream which glides beneath,
There, through the emerald meads, shallow or deep,
It hastes, or loiters, till the dark elms,
Grouped by the distance, hides it. And above,
On either hands the mountain rise,
Pine-clad below, upon whose upper heights
The unfenced heather purples. All the sky
Is flecked with soft, white fleecy clouds which cast
Bewildering charms of shadow, and beyond
A shining sapphire drawn 'twixt earth and sky,
Glitters the summer sea.

Outside the north wall is the grave of Sir Ewen John Maclean. Born in 1866, he qualified as a doctor in 1889. He died in Cardiff on October 13th 1953. During a distinguished career he was honoured with doctorates from the Universities of Edinburgh, Manchester, Wales and Melbourne, Australia. In the Great War of 1914-18 he commanded the Welsh Division of the 3rd West General Hospital and, in 1928, he was elected President of the British Medical Association. He was Professor of Obstetrics and Gynaecology in the Welsh School of Medicine, 1921-31, and in 1923 he was knighted. A brother of his, Donald, also a knight, was Member of Parliament for Cornwall, and a friend of Lloyd George. A nephew of Sir Ewen's was the infamous spy, Donald Maclean, who died in Moscow a few years ago. A window in the north wall of the church depicting the Ascension of Christ commemorates Sir Ewen's parents.

On the night of January 1st 1822 a boy of fifteen,

William Thomas, was murdered in King Street, Carmarthen. His grave can be seen on the right hand side of the path leading to the church porch, about five yards from the porch wall. The inscription reads: 'William Thomas (the murdered boy's father) died September 7th 1816, aged 63 years. William Thomas, his son, died January 1st 1822, aged 15 years.'

> Nid nychlyd, nid clefyd a'm clos,
> Nid ing, nid angau dihir lo's,
> Nid henaint aeth a'm heinios,
> Ond dynion fi yn dwyn fy o's.

> Nos trallod, nos hynod bu hyn,
> Nos gyntaf neu flaenaf o'r flwyddyn.
> Heb ochain na lle i'm achwyn,
> Y gwnelai'r ddau fi'n gelain ddyn.

The two verses recall that it was not disease, nor feebleness, nor pain caused his death but that it was a case of being killed by two men.

From inscriptions on various gravestones it becomes obvious that life during the years leading up to the second half of the twentieth century was fraught with danger from diseases that today have either disappeared from our land or are soon cured by modern medicines. Inscriptions such as these that follow make it abundantly clear that death was forever prevalent within households. I believe that the two following inscriptions prove this sad fact:

In memory of the dearly loved children of Aaron and Jane Roberts. (Aaron Roberts, MA, was Vicar of Newchurch and later Llangadog) Anne, born March

5th 1860, died March 30th 1860. Jane Caroline, born January 7th 159, died April 15th 1862. Charles Denston, born July 26th 1863, died November 4th 1863. Roberta Annie, born June 3rd 1861, died December 14th 1864. Aaron, born September 17th 1857, died January 7th 1865 – For such is the Kingdom of Heaven.

The other inscription reads:

Er cof am blant John a Margaret Evans, Blaengwastad o'r plwyf hwn. Henry, yr hwn bu farw Ionawr 23ain 1891 yn1 mlwydd a deg mis oed. Hefyd Margaret bu farw Mawrth 19eg 1891 yn 10 mis oed. Hefyd James bu farw Hydref 20fed 1892 yn 5 mis oed. Hefyd am Annie bu farw Mai 20fed 1911 yn 19eg oed.

The inscription records the death of four children in the early years of the 1890s and a daughter who died in 1911, and only 19 years old.

Also inscribed on numerous stones are verses that are typically Victorian as can be seen on gravestones in churchyards and cemeteries throughout the land. Their content often makes one wonder whether they reflect a strong Christian faith or a fatalistic attitude towards life. Some inscriptions lead one to conclude that the person commemorated was far too saintly for life in this imperfect world of ours. In Llangunnor it is possible to read examples of verses reflecting faith, saintliness and fatalism. On the gravestone of a 35 year old:

A sudden change in a short time I felt,
I had no time to bid my friends farewell.
Think it not strange, death happens to all,
My lot today, tomorrow thine may fall.

Another inscription, again of a 35 year old:

Ffarwel frodyr, ffarwel ffrindiau,
Fe ddaeth angau i fy hôl.
Rodia'i lwybrau'r o'r dieithrau,
Ni ddychwela byth yn ôl.

Roughly translated it reads:

Farewell brothers, farewell friends,
Death came to take me.
It travels paths from places strange
And I shall never return.

And a verse on a gravestone commemorating a three-year old child that will surely touch the heart-strings of the most hard-hearted:

Mourn not for me, parents dear,
I am not dead, but placed here.
My debts are paid, my grave you see,
Therefore prepare to follow me.

A doctor's wife who died in 1825, aged 31, is remembered as a saintly woman in both prose and verse:

Amiable and sincere, she was best loved, best known, she evinced a sensible approach of death in the triumph of those vital principles inculcated in the

Gospel of Christ and implanted only by the Spirit of God.

> No anxious wish, no fond attempt could save
> A much-loved wife from the silent grave.
> A loved companion and a friend sincere
> Still claims the silent tribute of a tear
> Whichever taught in heartfelt drops to shine
> Will flow forever o'er grave like thine.
> Reader pass gently on, respect her shade,
> Nor harm the tomb wherein her dust is laid.

I have already stated that much information can be gleaned about the social conditions and occupations of yesteryears and in Llangunnor we find listed the following occupations, many of them no longer followed in the area. John Burnhill who died in 1901 was keeper of the County Jail in Carmarthen. Thomas Thomas, who died in 1882, was a coach-builder, while George Moses, who died in 1881, was a fitter in the Old Foundry in the town. Thomas Owen, died 1914, was Assistant Overseer and Collector 1885-1914 and also Collector for Carmarthen Gas Company, 1891-1914, and a John Evans who died in 1903 lived and worked in the Caxton Printing Office in King Street, Carmarthen. Richard Hughes, died in 1829 aged only 27 was an ironmonger in the town. The fact that Carmarthen was at one time a busy port is made clear by the inscription on the gravestone of David Hughes Jenkins who is described as a shipping agent. The Lead and Silver Mine that was worked in the parish is also brought to light in the inscription on another stone:

In memory of T. Williams, Esq., of Gwennap in the

county of Cornwall who died January 8th 1859, aged 41 years. Lamented by a son and sorrowing widow and a large circle of friends. He opened and was in fact the first adventurer in the effectual working of the old Vale of Towy Silver and Lead Mine. The first steam engine for working lead and other metallic ores in the county was set for the said mine under his supervision, and the foundation stone being laid by the proprietor of the land, W. Bonville Esq., on the 29th of April 1832.

I have already mentioned William Williams of Ivy Tower, the person responsible for erecting the memorial to Sir Richard Steele. Before leaving Llangunnor Church, let me quote from the book *The History of Little England Beyond Wales* by a west Wales historian of the 1800s – Edward Laws. He states: 'But in Tenby at this period (the first half of the 1800s) it was fortunate in that it found many friends. Among the earliest was William Williams of Ivy Tower in the parish of St Florence, a wealthy man, notorious for eccentricity of conduct, but for all that benevolent and very highly educated for the time and place in which he lived. Four times he served as mayor, and to the end of his long life was always ready to spend money in the service of his native town.' His largesse obviously extended some distance from his native town; proof of this can be seen within Llangunnor Church. Laws notes that Williams was highly educated; I wonder, therefore if he might have been responsible for the verse on the memorial to Sir Richard Steele?

Although much more could be written about the memorials both inside and outside the church, it is time to make a move and travel about five miles to the village of Llanddarog. In order to do this we leave Llangunnor Church, rejoin the B4300 at the bottom of the hill, take a left turn, travel through the hamlet of Capel Dewi and, in a mile orso, reach another junction. We take the road to the right, pass The Polyn, now a public house, but so called because at one time it was a toll house, and 'polyn' is the Welsh word for a pole. In the days when there were toll charges on our roads a pole or gate would have been placed across the road, and only lifted or opened by the guardian of the gate and collector of tolls, who lived in the toll house, after payment. By taking this road we are in fact veering away from the actual river and its valley while we head for the picturesque village of Llanddarog and its church.

The church stands out in the surrounding countryside because of its 155ft. high spire which is topped with a weathercock. It is said that the present edifice dates from around 1854 and that it replaced a much older wooden building that was destroyed by fire. Some people claim that all the parish records were lost in the fire but this cannot be true as it is still possible to read the registers of baptism, marriages and deaths dating back to 1736 at the County Record Office.

Dedicated to a St Twrog, the church has a double aisle and at the east end, running parallel with the chancel, is the Puxley Chapel, named after a family who lived at Llethr Lluesty, known locally as Llethr Llestri.

Llethr Lluesty is a double-pile house of two storeys plus an attic storey. It stands on high ground, some three-quarters of a mile south of the village. Overlooking the Gwendraeth Fach valley, it dates from the seventeenth century, replacing an earlier house built in the sixteenth century, that house standing about fifty yards from the present one. The earliest known family living at Llethr Lluesty was the Penry family; they occupied it during the Elizabethan period. William Penry (1518-1613) married the daughter of the then Bishop of St David's. Their eldest daughter, Anne, married Walter Vaughan of Golden Grove. Their son, Penry, succeeded to the property following the death of his mother in 1622. It remained in the hands of the male descendants of the family until the death of Edward Vaughan in 1736. It then passed on to his aunt who had married Edward Horton, a Monmouthshire stationer. The next owner was their son Henry, and then Henry's son Walter Horton, attorney-at-law and Town Clerk of Carmarthen. It was following his death in 1825 that Llethr Lluesty was subsequently bought by John Lavallin Puxley of Dunboy Castle, Co. Cork, Ireland.

The members of the Puxley family are commemorated in stained glass windows in the Chapel of that name. The window near the entrance to the Chapel is in memory of Katherine Puxley and was designed from a portrait of her as a young girl of eighteen. She is seen holding a Catherine Wheel in her hand. This fact reminds us that St Catherine was tied to a wheel (later called a Catherine Wheel), which broke down, injuring bystanders; Catherine was beheaded. Katherine Puxley presented a pedal organ to the church which she herself played in the dedication service. The east window of the Chapel is: 'In ever loving memory of the Rev. Herbert Boyne Puxley, for 25 years rector of Patten with Stamford Bridge, who died January 20th 1908, aged 71 years. This window is dedicated by his wife.' One of the rector's names is a reminder of the battle of the Boyne in 1690 when the Catholic King, James II, was defeated by the Protestant, William III. It was the decisive battle in the War of English Succession and a battle that has been one of the root causes for the troubles in Northern Ireland over the years. The window in the north wall, adjacent to the east wall is: 'In memory of Edward Lavallyn Puxley who died at

Steep Vicarage, Hampshire, November 30th 1903, aged 35 years.' The middle window in the north wall of the Chapel is: 'In memory of Herbert Hardress Puxley who died at Goring on September 3rd 1931, aged 63 years.' The east window above the altar is: 'To the glory of God, and in ever loving memory of Lieut. Robert B.L. Puxley, Royal Artillery, who died after three months sojourn at Bombay, December 23rd 1894 on board the 'Dilwara' on his way home, aged 23 years.' On the north wall of the Chapel a white, marble memorial inscribed with: 'Sacred to the memory of Henry Lavallyn Puxley, Esq., son of John Lavallyn Puxley, Esq., of this parish who died at Sans in France, June 13th 1828, aged 28 years, on his return from Italy where he had gone for the benefit of his health – In the midst of life we are in death. I am the resurrection and the life, says the Lord.'

Immediately outside the north wall of the chancel there are two slabs lying on two graves surrounded by iron railings. Inscribed on them: 'In this vault lie Herbert B. Lavallyn Puxley of Llethr Llestry, July 1st 1836 – January 20th 1908, Catherine Lavallyn Puxley, his wife, August 30th 1852 – November 21st 1931. Also their son Othwell Lavallyn Puxley, born October 10th 1874, died February 24th 1916, also their daughter Zoe Hilda Lavallyn Puxley, born March 25th 1882, died March 26th 1970.' Another stone in the churchyard is inscribed: 'In memory of Edward Lavallyn Puxley, born at Clifton House, June 2nd 1835, died at Norton, Surrey, June 30th 1909, aged 74 years. Also Harry Othwell Lavallyn Puxley, their son and beloved husband of Winifred Lavallyn Puxley. Maria Winifred, wife of Edward Lavallyn Puxley, died April 10th 1885, aged 40 years, Herbert Horatio Lavallyn Puxley, son of the above, died November 30th 1903, aged 33 years.'

In 1994 a new west window was installed, commissioned by Mrs V. Hodges and, her husband Vincent Hodge, now deceased. The left lancet window depicts the agricultural nature of the district, while the right lancet shows the importance of coal mining to the village at one time. The two middle lancets show the living church and its spiritual influence as well as facets of its work in the world. The brass lectern is in the form of an eagle and bears the inscription: 'To the glory of God, and in loving memory of John Harries, Sexton, 1864 – 1926. Given by the Church.'

In the south wall there are two stained glass windows, one given by the Harries family of Pantypwll in memory of the parents, and the other given by the Harries family of the Old Post Office in memory of their parents. One of the windows is the work of the renowned artist John Petts who at one time had a studio in Llanstephan.

Buried in the churchyard is a woman with a rather strange Christian name. On her gravestone: 'Sacred to the memory of Choice, wife of John George, tailor, of Groes Wen in this parish, who died August 10th 1865, aged 84 years.' The question that arises regarding her name is whether her name was in reality Choice, or is it a case of the name Joyce incorrectly spelt by the person responsible for writing the inscription?

Also in the churchyard is a gravestone with details of a very tragic event that occurred in 1992 at Kidwelly. 'In loving memory of Susan McArthur, 1964-1992, and her dear children Christine, 1982-1992, Adelle, 1984-1992, Robert, 1987-1992. All died tragically on May 17th 1992 at Ger-y-Castell, Kidwelly.' This tragedy was the result of a faulty chimney in their home, resulting in death by carbon monoxide poisoning.

I mentioned that some parishioners, thought that at

one time, a wooden church had been destroyed by fire and that the church records were also destroyed. The fact is that all the Parish Registers are stored in the County Record Office and recorded in them is the existence of a silver communion cup made by a Carmarthen silversmith, and part of the church plate, proof that the story is incorrect. The cup was a gift to the church by Queen Elizabeth I, in 1574, and it is one of many given by the queen to several churches as a token of thanks to those parishes that had given assistance by sending soldiers to fight for her grandfather, Henry VII, at the Battle of Bosworth. At the time Sir Rhys ap Thomas who, it is claimed, had placed the crown that had fallen off the head of King Richard on to Henry's head, was probably overlord of the parish and the surrounding areas.

The visitor can also see that the churchyard is circular in shape, this giving rise to the word 'Llan' and confirming its antiquity. Incorporated in the southwest corner of the churchyard is the Parish Pound where in former times stray animals were kept.

We return to the Tywi Valley and proceed to the village of Llanarthne which nestles under a hill crowned by the famous Paxton Tower. Standing alongside the road running through the village is the church that is, again, dedicated to St David.

Like most churches in Wales that have the word Llan in their names, the origin of Llanarthne Church goes back to the Age of the Saints – 500 to 800 AD. Its large west tower is of the fifteenth century and, around the sixteenth century, a south aisle was added to what then became the north aisle. At this time, this addition seems to have happened in other churches as well in the diocese, e.g. at Llangunnor. It was in 1826 that the two naves and aisles were joined to form one large open building. Alongside the chancel is the vestry.

On entering the church porch the visitor cannot fail to notice the large stone cross that leans against the north wall. The stone was the subject of a special study by the Cambrian Archaeological Society in 1914. Among those present at that time were Canon Fisher of St Asaph, Mr Harold Hughes of Bangor, Mr W.D. Caroe, a well-known and nationally respected leading church architect (a close relative of his visited Llangunnor Church in 1962-63 to advise the vicar before restoration work took place). Also present was George Eyre Evans, Honorary Secretary of the Carmarthenshire Antiquarian Society and Field Club from 1906 until his death in 1939; he was one of the prime movers in establishing the County Museum, now in the former, bishops palace in Abergwili but originally in Quay Street in Carmarthen.

As a result of their study of the stone they issued a report on the history of the cross, which reads: Number 188, Cae'r Castell Cross. This famous memorial stone is said in Lewis's Topographical Dictionary of Wales (SB Llanarthne) to have formed in 1833 the step of a stile which led into the churchyard. It is said by Mr Williams, Dyffryn Arael, to have previously stood just west of the north end of the bank of Cae'r Castell from which his father, when a youth, helped to move into the churchyard, when it was probably broken across. The two portions have now been fixed, the one on top of the other and now stand within the church porch where the stone is safe from casual damage, and is excellently placed for study. The head of the stone has been worked into a rounded shape and on the side, confined within a border, surrounding the circular head is carved an equal-armed cross, the long limb of which has been carried from the edge of the circle down the length of the maenhir. The monolith was broken across almost at mid-height and the edges of the fracture are chipped away. There is however; no reason to think that any part of the bulk of the stone is missing. The total height of the pillar was about seven feet, the length of the cross stem about two feet, the fracture coming almost exactly mid-way in the length of the stem. Below the line forming the base of the cross is a space of one foot, cut off from the bottom of the block by two narrow incised lines which were probably intended to denote the depth beneath the soil of one foot seven inches. It is an easy matter to confine ourselves to facts and to copy what others have written but to read the inscription on this cross is not as easy. Are we sure of the Words? What do they mean? And what are they intended to convey? It is possible we have a mixture of Latin and Norman French for, according to some the reading would be: "Dierci et grace mare dic elmon fecit ho crucem." If this reading is correct we might believe it refers to Meredic who is none other than the great chieftain who appears in early Welsh genealogies as Moreuddig Warwidd whose descendants are said to have lived around Talgarth in Breconshire. This chieftain's burial took place at Llanarthne during a raid of the followers of Bernard Newbarch from Brecon around the end of the eleventh century. However, according to Professor Brown of Cambridge, there is another reading of the inscription as follows: Elmat fecit hank crusom pro anima sua. 'Elmat erected this cross for his own soul.' We cannot say who this Elmat was; he may have been the Abbot of the old abbey in the parish. It may be of interest to note that the so called wheel cross is unknown in Scotland, Ireland and England, although there are some examples in Wales, in Llantwit Major, Llangan, Margam, in Glamorganshire, Llanarthne in Carmarthen and also in the Isle of Man.

43

The suggestion by the people that examined the stone that there was once an abbey within the parish is interesting since, between Llanarthne and Llanddarog, and not far from Nantgaredig, there is a farm called Cefn Abbey (Abbey Rise). Unfortunately no one has been able to discover any trace of such a building in the vicinity of the farm

On the south wall inside the church is a memorial on which is inscribed' 'Memorial to the memory of William Paxton, Knight, of Middleton Hall in this parish, born in Edinburgh in 1745, died in London February 10th 1834. He served the office of High Sheriff of this county in 1790 and represented in Parliament both county and borough of the county of Carmarthen. Also of Dame Anne, his wife, who died 3rd December 1846, aged 81. Both are buried in the church of St Martin's in the Field, London. He left at his decease by his said wife eleven children, viz. Archibold Frederick HB, 11th Light Dragoons. Henry, late Captain 3rd Foot Guards, Charles Frederick, R.N., died August 2nd 1842, Stuart, EICCS died October 20th 1830, James William Llewelyn, Captain 69th Regiment, George Augustus, 6th Bengal NC, drowned in the Ganges March 15th 1825, Anna, died July 30th 1845, Sophia Matilda Laura, married Lieutenant Colonel Lewis Augustus Northey, died March 14th 1846, Caroline, married Daniel Chambers Macreight, MD, Anne, married M.G. Arthur Goodall Wavell, KFKCS, late Mexican service. This tablet was erected by their surviving issue, 1847.'

Sir William Paxton had made his fortune in Calcutta, India. He had been mayor of Carmarthen in 1802 as well as High Sheriff in 1790. In 1776 he bought Middleton Hall and, in 1785, built a new mansion on the same site, described as 'the most splendid mansion in south Wales.'

He was elected Member of Parliament for Carmarthen Borough in 1803. To win this election must have been very satisfying for him in view of the fact he had failed to win the county seat in a bitterly contested election that became known as 'Y Lecsiwn Fawr' (The Big Election) the previous year. Sir William was a Whig and his opponent was Sir James Hamlyn Williams, a Tory, of Edwinsford. Williams, with the backing of the Dynevor family, won by 117 votes.

During the election Sir William spent the incredible sum for those days of £15,000. He paid for 11,070 breakfasts, 36,901 dinners, 684 suppers, 25,275 gallons of ale, 11,086 bottles of whisky, 8,879 bottles of cider, and election ribbons costing £786. As if his election expenses were not enough he, some time later, built Paxton Tower on a hill overlooking the village of Llanarthne and the Tywi Valley, in honour of Lord Nelson. When mayor of Carmarthen, he prepared plans for bringing piped water to the town and offered to build a new bridge over the river Tywi. Furthermore, he did much to popularise Tenby as a seaside resort. In 1805 he built a bathing house in the town, replacing the amenity that had previously occupied the Chapel of St Julian on the quayside. It is obvious that bathing was important to visitors to Tenby many years before Sir William Paxton built the bathhouse because a memorial in the north-west corner of St Mary's Church in the town records the following: 'This tablet was raised by a few ladies and gentlemen to preserve from oblivion the memory of Peggy Davies, bathing woman for 42 years to the ladies who visited Tenby. Her good humour, her attention and gratitude made her employers friends. On the 29th of September 1809, in the water, she was seized with apoplexy and expired, aged 82 years.'

In Edward Laws' book *The History of Little England Beyond Wales*, first published in 1888, we read: 'Perhaps, however, the honour of refounding Tenby should be ascribed to Sir William Paxton, Knight, of Middleton Hall, Carmarthenshire, who seems to have taken up his residence in 1805. He purchased two properties . . . ' and also: 'It is ordered that the Freedom of this Corporation be presented to him as a token of respect and gratitude, and he is hereby ordered by the Mayor and Common Council to be admitted a Burgess of this Borough, this 17th day of October 1805.' Furthermore: 'No sooner were the new baths built at the foot of Castle Hill than they were burnt. Sir William, nothing daunted, rebuilt them, and until his death in 1824 continued to heap benefits on the town . . . He was instrumental in establishing a theatre, and when this failed (as it naturally did) purchased the building lest his associates suffer in pocket. The death of Sir William proved a heavy blow to Tenby, for that wealthy and public spirited gentleman had for a period of twenty years been in constant habit of improving the town, very greatly to the advantage of his fellow burgesses.' It cannot be denied that, according to Laws, Sir William Paxton was a philanthropist par excellence.

On the south wall of the church at Llanarthne there is a memorial commemorating another person who owned Middleton Hall. The rather complex inscription reads: 'Sacred to the memory of Edward Hamlyn Adams of Mioddleton Hall in the parish of Llanarthney in the county of Carmarthen, Esq., who died at Middelton Hall at twenty minutes before two in the morning of Thursday, 2nd of June 1832, aged 65 years, and was buried on Friday, the 10th of June in a vault built by the direction of his eldest son under the large yew tree on the north side of the church. He was second son of William

Adams, Esq., by his second marriage with Elizabeth Coxeter, both of Barbados, and was born at Kingston, Jamaica, on the 30th of April 1777. On the 5th of January 1796, at Philadelphia, U.S.A, he married Amelia Sophia, eldest daughter of Captain John Macpherson by his second marriage with Mary Anne McNeil, who was born at her father's seat, Mount Pleasant, on the banks of the Schuylkill, near Philadelphia, 25th of October 1776, died at Schneider's Hotel, Florence, and was interred in the Swiss burial ground there on Sunday, 3rd of April. On the 4th of October 1825 he settled with his family in this county, and in December 1832 was elected one of its representatives in Parliament, having the previous year filled the office of High Sheriff. He had issue by his said marriage, Mary Anne, born 25th of September 1807, (married to Thomas Cuff, Esq.) who died in Madeira 10th of January 1832 leaving three sons, Edward born 28th of April 1800, now living and has issue, Sophia born 31st of January 1811, died 11th of November following, Caroline, born 11th of April 1812, now living and married to Captain Charles Augustus Brook, 6th Royal Regiment, William, born 15th of September 1814, now living and married, Matilda, born 20th of December 1815, now living.

Oh! that the tears oe'r his grave are shed
Commemorates the virtues of the dead.
And yet beyond our hopes and feeble powers ye be,
Enshrined in the hearts of his posterity.

From vice and luxury he lived apart,
No baneful passion occupies his heart
Which rave, yet gentle, generous, just and true.
The noblest and tenderest emotions knew.

Not superstition's trembling slave was he
But the bright champion of morality.
Unawed by fear, by hope not blindly led,
He still the moral not the fable read.

Pope's purest words repeated with delight,
'He can't be wrong whose life is in the right.'
And to his children still would strive to show
Virtue alone in happiness below.

So may his words by you be understood
That still productive our future good.
His children's children will by them be led
To pay the noblest tribute to the dead.

Who most inspires in good to persevere
Indulges not in follies brief career.
Who proves most virtue past from him to you,
With sweetest roses that his grave be strew.

Thus shall it seem his guardian spirit flown
Returns from regions brighter than our own.
On earth to guide our steps with heavenly light
To peace and happiness in the path of right.

EA

This tablet is raised by his affectionate and grateful children to the memory of their lamented father as a token of love and memorial of grief for the loss of him, the sweet memory of whose virtues yet lives in their hearts though the bright sun may be set.'

The memorial was made by E. Gaffin, Regent Street, London. I am left wondering if this memorial is possibly one of the lengthiest in the churches of our Principality. The eulogy in sharp contrast to an inscription on a gravestone in the now disused church of Castell Dwyran, not far from Clunderwen on the Carmarthenshire-Pembrokeshire border. From the initials at the foot of the poem it is safe to assume that the writer of the seven verses to William Paxton was his son. It is a poem full of admiration for a father. The verse in Castell Dwyran churchyard was also written or sanctioned by the deceased's sons and reads: 'Richard Bowen Jones, Born 1811, Transferred 1887.

Here lie the remains of a "Classical Ass",
The accursed by his sons by the name of "Jabrass".
In the earth he is ammonia and triphosphate of calcium,
On earth a 'House Demon' and a ferocious old ruffian.'

Parliament passed The Reform Act in 1832 and, as a result, Carmarthenshire was able to send two county members to represent the county in Parliament. One of those was Edward Hamlyn Adams, the other a fellow Tory, Rice-Trevor, whose original name was George Rice Rice, the only son of Lord Dynevor.

Adams' eldest son, also named Edward and who, in writing the seven verses on the memorial, immortalised his father, adopted the surname Abadam, the 'ab' or 'ap' meaning "son of" in Welsh. The son has been immortalised, not in verse, but in having a public house named after him, situated in the village of Porthyrhyd which is within a mile or two of where Middleton Hall stood until it was completely destroyed by fire in November 1931. Although the mansion itself has disappeared the grounds and garden of the estate is now the location of The National Botanic Garden of Wales.

In the chancel of Llanarthne Church a memorial on which is inscribed: 'Erected in memory of Thomas Williams, Dyffryn – Arael, who died January 16th 1918, for 54 years Sexton of this church. He was the third generation of his family who acted as such, covering a period of 109 years.' On another memorial 'Sacred to the memory of William Rees of Capel Dewi who died December 3rd 1759, aged 77. As also his wife, Elizabeth, who died February 14th 1762, aged 85 years. – Universally loved and respected whilst living, they were equally lamented when dead.'

Before leaving the church we take a look at the vault on the north side of the church, under the yew tree, in which Edward Hamlyn Adams lies buried. The top of the raised vault is approached by a number of steps, and is surrounded by iron railings. And finally, as we take our leave, we look at one other grave. It is that of a David Jones, who is immortalised on the strength of a single verse of a hymn that is to be found in hymn books; it was he who wrote:

> Bydd myrdd o ryfeddodau
> Ar doriad bore wawr
> Pan ddelo plant y tonnau
> Yn iach o'r cystudd mawr.
> Oll yn eu gynau gwynion,
> Ac ar eu newydd wedd,
> Yn debyg idd eu Harglwydd
> Yn dod i lan o'r bedd.

In the verse David Jones takes us to the Book of Revelation with its description of the final day when the dead, in the words of St Paul, shall be raised incorruptible, and amongst those raised, if everything that Edward Adams Jnr. had to say about his father is true, will undoubtedly be the late Edward Hamlyn Adams of Middleton Hall.

And now to continue the journey up the valley. After a few miles take a left turn, cross the river and, after a mile or so, we arrive at Llangathen Church. The church is in the Deanery of Llangadog and Llandeilo. If the reader wonders why we are not visiting the churches of Llanegwad, Holy Trinity, Pontargothi, St Mary Cwrt Henry and the church of St Michael at Golden Grove before going to Llangathen, I can assure you that those churches will be visited on our return journey down the valley towards Llanstephan

The church at Llangathen stands on rising ground overlooking the valley and only a short distance from Grongar Hill made well known by the poet John Dyer in his poem of that name. The church is dedicated to a St Cathen, and between the church and Grongar Hill stands Aberglasney, its ancient gardens recently restored and now open to the public.

The church, like the other churches we have already visited, has its beginnings in the Age of the Saints. The Parish Registers go back as far as 1747 and The Bishops' Transcripts, to be seen in the National Library of Wales at Aberystwyth, cover the years 1680 to 1865.

Built into the outside of the east wall of the church is a rectangular stone on which is inscribed: 'Underneath lyeth the body of Robert Dyer, Esq., Barrister-at-Law. Married in 1720 Francis, the younger daughter of Sir James Herbert, Crosscroft Castle, in the County of Hereford, Baronet, by whom he had issue of several sons. Departed this life April 1748, aged 48 years. Robert Dyer was originally from Cydweli, and was the father of John Dyer, the poet and painter.

John Dyer was born in 1699 and died, aged 58, in 1757. He was a pupil at Westminster School, but ran away to become an apprentice to the artist Jonathan Richardson. At twenty-five he travelled to Italy. He lived for a time in Herefordshire, and then moved to Higham-on-the-Hill in Leicestershire. In 1742 he was inducted rector of Cathorpe in the same county. He is best known for his poem entitled Grongar Hill.

Grongar Hill invites my song,
Draw the landskip bright and strong;
Grongar, in whose mossy cells
Sweetly musing quiet dwells;
Grongar, in whose silent shade,
For the modest Muses made,
So oft I have, the evening still,
At the fountain of a rill,
Sate upon a flowery bed,
With my hands beneath my head;
And strayed my eyes o'er Towy's flood,
Over mead and over wood,
From house to house, from hill to hill,
Till Contemplation had her fill.
About his chequered sides I wind,
And leave his brooks and meads behind,
And groves and grottos where I lay,
And vistas shooting beams of day;
Wide and wider spreads the vale,
As circles on a smooth canal:
The mountains round, unhappy fate,
Sooner or later, of all height,
Withdraw their summits from the skies,
And lessen as the others rise;
Still the prospect wider spreads,

> Adds a thousand woods and meads,
> Still it widens, widens still,
> And sinks the newly risen hill.

Under a tree on the left hand side of the path leading to the church door there is a small grey stone and, written on it in Welsh, the verse:

> Nid nychlyd, nid clefyd a'm clo's,
> Nid ing, nid angau dihir lo's,
> Nid henaint aeth a'm heinioes
> Ond dynion fi yn dwyn fy o's.

The inscription tells us that a Mary Evans, a 17 year old girl, was murdered on September 1st 1844 near a place called Rhydygwydd (Gooseford) parish of Llandeilo, and the verse an exact copy of one to be seen on a gravestone of a William Thomas, a boy of 15 in Llangunnor churchyard who was also murdered.

In the Carmarthen Journal dated September 6th 1844 there appeared the following report:

Murder: A shocking murder was committed on Sunday last in the neighbourhood of Taliaris in the county to a young woman, a servant to a farmer. She went out in the evening to bring the cows home for the purpose of milking, and not returning at the usual time a person went in search of her and found the body lying by the side of the hedge in a field close to one of the lodges of Taliaris House. The body presented a dreadful appearance; the throat was cut and several other gashes were about the region of the neck and throat. The knife with which it is supposed the evil deed was effected was found some distance from the corpse. The coroner's inquest resolved and returned a verdict of 'wilful murder'.

Incidentally, in the same edition is this item of news:

Case Of Stabbing: On Tuesday evening last at about eight o'clock two lads of the ages of 14 to 15, William Jones and Benjamin Lewis had a dispute in Priory Street about some old grudge, and Jones, being afraid, ran off and was pursued by Lewis who overtook him and stabbed him on the left shoulder and under the left arm with a knife. We are happy to learn that he is out of danger. The prisoner absconded and is still at large. What more proof do we need that human nature has remained unchanged since the days of Cain and Abel.

Back inside the church of Llangathen, on the north wall, is a memorial with the following details: 'In memory of the Rev. George Wade Green, MA, of Court Henry in this parish, died 12th March 1868, aged 82 years. Also of Mary Anne, his wife, who died 2nd October 1864, aged 68 years. Also of Charles Bethel Green, midshipman in the Indian Navy, and fourth son of the above, who died on the 11th of July 1847, aged 20 years, and was buried in the Cathedral Yard, Bombay. Also of Theophilus Green, Major in the 48th Bengal Native Infantry, and second son of the above, who died 8th of April 1865, aged 42 years, and was buried in the cemetery at Norwood. Also Elizabeth Key, sister of the above Mary Anne Green who died 26th of April 1867, aged 64 years. Also of the Rev. Alfred J.M. Green, MA, Rector of Halkyn, Flintshire, youngest and last surviving son of George Wade and Mary Anne Green, died December 10th, aged 78 years at

Glencoe, Cleveden, Somerset.'

Standing against the inside of the south wall of the chancel is the elaborate tomb of Bishop Rudd and his wife. He was Bishop of St David's in the early 1600s. The recumbent figures of the bishop and his wife lie side by side, and there are two children kneeling at their head and similarly two children kneeling at their feet. The effigies of the bishop and his wife and the carvings of the children are surrounded by four pillars, one at each corner, and roofed with a triangular canopy. Above the canopy are the coats of arms of both the diocese of St David's and those of the bishop. On the wall at the back of the tomb is a Latin inscription: 'Hic Iacet Anthonvs Rudd Natione Anglvs Patria Eboracensis, I n Sacra Theologia, Doctor Glocestrensis Ecclesiae Qvondam Decanvs, Et Mae Nevensis Ecclesiae Episcopvs Vigilantissimvs, Qvi Plvs Minvs Viginty Anis Svma Cvm Prvdentia Moderabatvr Qvi E Lectissima Famina Anna Daltona Eqvestri Daltonorvm Famila Orivnd Dvos Svsepit Optimae Spei Filios Vixit Aternvmcv Ictvrvs marth Nono Ano Domini 1614 Aetatis Verosvae 66.' The inscription informs the reader that the tomb was erected by the bishop's wife following his death in 1614, that he was a native of York, had served as a priest in Gloucester for nearly ten years, and that he was Bishop of St David's for nearly twenty years.

The Bishop bought the nearby mansion of Aberglasney in 1610, hence his connection with Llangathen. He was responsible for the erection of the south nave and chancel of the church. There is a very interesting and extremely old communion table in the church. On it is exquisite Tudor carving, and it is believed that the table has been in the church since the days when the Bishop lived in the parish.

Before leaving Llangathen church, take a quick look at the war memorial in the churchyard; it has inscribed on it many surnames that are definitely of English origin. Many of the men who had these surnames were, before joining the army, servants at Aberglasney and originally from orphanages in England. Finally, as we walk out of the churchyard in a northerly direction we pass five graves in a line, each unmarked. It is traditionally believed that they are the graves of five young maids who were employed at Aberglasney, and who died under mysterious and totally unknown circumstances.

As promised, we now visit the churches of Golden Grove, Cwrt Henri, Llanegwad and Pontargothi.

Across the road from Golden Grove mansion is the church of Llanfihangel Aberbythych, better known to all in the area as Golden Grove Church. From the churchyard there is a pleasant view as one looks down the valley. In the churchyard there are a few yew trees dotted here and there and some gravestones on which there are quite interesting inscriptions. Although most of the present building dates from the nineteenth century the Parish Registers date from 1674, and are kept in the Carmarthen Record Office. In the National Library at Aberystwyth the Bishops' Transcripts are available for scrutiny.

One of the gravestones has on it: 'Laura Gemmen, born Paris 1837, died at Penparc 1924. Lived 71 years in England as governess and friend of the Turner, Smith and Freemantle families. "There remaineth, therefore, rest for the people of God."' On another memorial, details about a husband and son, with two verses. 'Sacred to the memory of David Rees of Penybont in this parish who died May 9th 1850, aged 47 years.

My wife and dear parents all,
Prepare to come when Christ doth call,
And think of this that you must die,
And lie in dust as well as I.

In this tomb while sleeping here,
A faithful husband, a friend so dear.
The loss is great that I sustained,
I hope in heaven to meet again.'

A box-shaped tomb near the south wall has inscribed on the south face, details in Latin of a David Lloyd. 'Memorae Sacrum David Lloyd De Hac Parochia Eilii Praedicti Davidis Et Margarettae Lloyd Oui Mortis Est 24 April is Anno Domini 1858 Atque Ejus itatis 90 Et Jane Uxoris Suae Obit 2 Mai AD 1853 Aet 95.' Despite a limited understanding of Latin I have been able to work out that a David, the son of David and Margaret Lloyd, and his wife Jane Lloyd are interred in the grave below; that one of them died May 2nd 1853, aged 90 and that the other occupant of the grave died aged 95. A problem arises in that, on looking carefully through the Burial Register of Llanfihangel Aberbythych for the 1850s, there is no mention of either a David or Margaret Lloyd in it. The only conclusion to be made is that their funeral services most probably took place in another church and then their bodies brought to the churchyard at Golden Grove for burial. What their connection was with the parish and the district remains a mystery. I hope that one day an answer to the puzzle will be found.

While looking through the Burial Register I discovered details that could have a bearing on the mystery outlined above. An entry for May 6th 1853 relates to a Jane who had originally been entered as Lloyd but the Lloyd had been deleted and replaced with Rees, and that this person had died aged 95, the exact age of one of the two in the tomb with the Latin inscription. This person is thought to have died on May 3rd 1853. Incidentally, it is generally believed that people overall did not live as long in the 1800s as people generally do today. In the Golden Grove area there were quite a few exceptions to the rule. For the year 1853 three had died aged 95 years, one at 80 years. In 1854 one died aged 97, one aged 85 and one aged 81. On December 11th 1829 a Mary, widow of John Thomas Hopkin of Llwynfedwen, died aged 103. In 1845, on the 16th of September, Jeremiah Morgan Warren died aged 100 years while on March 20th 1850 and May 7th 1850 a husband and wife, William and Mary Lloyd reached the ages of 90 and 76 respectively. But obviously not everyone in the parish lived as long as those mentioned above. In 1832 eight died with ages ranging from 13 days to 30 years, the 30 year old the mother of the 13-day old baby; it is safe to assume that the mother died as a result of giving birth to the baby, a rather common occurrence even up to the middle of the 1900s. Another point of interest is the rather odd name given to the home in which 19 year old Anne Thomas who was buried on October 27th 1858, lived. Her home was called Menagerie, a name also entered in an entry for 1815.

On another gravestone is a rather strange four-line verse in Welsh relating to a Johanna Williams who died August 22nd 1896, aged 70 years.

Iôr a bia rhoi bywyd –
Ac anadl cu einioes, ac iechyd;
Hawl a fedd i alw o fyd
Man a mynno mewn munud.

[It is God's prerogative to give life – / And breath of life, and health. / He has a right to call from earth / Any time He likes, anyone He wants in a minute.]

I think that it would be right to think that the deceased named on the stone must have died suddenly.

From Golden Grove we cross the river Tywi and visit the church of St Mary, Cwrt Henri. The fact that there is a church there at all is entirely due to the Rev. George Wade Green, who was vicar of Tytherington, Gloucester. In the west wall of the church is a stone tablet on which are the words: 'This church was built in the year of Our Lord, 1852, at the expense of the Rev. George Wade Green, MA, Cambridge.'

In 1830 the Rev. Green bought the house and estate of Cwrt Henri from a member of the Lloyd family of Laques, Llanstephan. Two years later he built on a field called Cae'r Odyn (Kiln Field) a Chapel-of-ease dedicated to St Mary. This chapel was smaller than the present edifice, only reaching as far as the present chancel, although it had a tower at the west end. During the latter part of his life the Rev. Green, assisted by a Rev. John Nicholls, conducted services in the building. By 1892 two of the Rev. Green's granddaughters, Mary and Ellen Saunders, had raised enough money to enlarge the chapel, and a chancel, two transepts and a porch were added, thus changing it from a chapel to a proper church.

The reverend gentleman had intended that on his death he would be buried in the aisle of the chapel. When the vault was dug it very soon filled with water from the springs under the building. The result was that he and his wife were buried in the churchyard at Llangathen, where there is a memorial to them on the wall of that church. No burials have taken place at Cwrt Henri because of the problems posed by the springs in the immediate vicinity of the church

Centenary celebrations were held at the church in 1932, and attending the celebrations were the Bishop of St David's, the Rt. Rev. D.L. Prosser, and the founder's grandson, the Rt. Rev. Charles Wade Green, Bishop of Bangor.

Six years later, in 1938, the church became a part of the Church in Wales. Up until 1964 the church had had a curate for many years, but in 1964 the vicar of neighbouring Llangathen Church became responsible for the church.

Inside the church there are some interesting memorials. The east window commemorates the Rev. George Wade Green and his wife and sister-in-law. It was this sister-in-law, Miss Elizabeth Key, who opened a school at Cwrt Henri, where she was schoolmistress for a number of years. The window in the south transept is in memory of the Rev. Green's daughter, Mary Anne Saunders, who had been the wife of Captain Francis David Saunders of Tŷ Mawr, Ceredigion.

The font came from the ancient church of St Cynllo in Ceredigion. The St David's Diocesan Year Book shows three present day churches dedicated to St Cynllo; one at Llangynllo, not far from Bangor Teifi and Henllan, the church at Llangoedmor and the church at Nantcwnlle. One can assume that it came from a church that had been closed before to the church at Cwrt Henri was built. Another stained glass window in the church is in memory of fourteen men from the district killed in the Great War of 1914-18, and three who were killed in the Second World War of 1939-45. Below the window is recorded the names of these men. In the 1914-18 War, Col. C.B. Moreland, Welch Regiment, Cmdr. S. W. Green, RN,

DSO, Arthur Birch, John Knight, Tom Davies, John T. Davies, Ernest Davies, Benjamin Griffiths, David Harries, David Jones, Tom Lewis, Matthew Mansell, Harry Shuter, William Watts. In the 1939-45 War, Sqdr. Ldr. Rhys Martin Lloyd, DFC, RAF, William Samuel Northwood, L/Aircraftsman, RAF, Thomas John Davies, Gunner, R.A.

Not far from the window and plaques is another bronze plaque. Inscribed on it, "In memory of Lieutenant Henry Ernest Green, Royal Engineers, son of the Rev. Alfred John Morgan Green, MA, born on the 5th day of March 1871 at St David's. Pembrokeshire. Killed at Shadkadar by a fanatic on 25th March 1900. 'Those that seek me early shall find me.' A white marble cross with the above inscription has been placed by his brothers and sisters over his grave at Pesawar where he was laid to rest with military honours by the officers and men of No. 1 Co. The Bengal Sappers and Miners. He served in the Tochi campaign, and received a medal and cross. A brass plaque has also been put up to his memory in the church at Rurki by his brother officers of the RE, and a tablet in the Cathedral in Calcutta by Dr Welldon, Bishop of Calcutta, his former Headmaster at Harrow School, where he gained a mathematical scholarship. He was the grandson of the late George Wade Green, MA, of Court Henry, being the fourth son of the Rev. Alfred John Morgan and Elizabeth Bond Green of Halkyn Rectory. This brass was put up by his loving parents in memory of 'a most dutiful son, beloved the like by Europeans and natives.' "

When we later visit St Anne's Church, Cwmffrwd, we shall once again come into contact with another member of the Green family – a Francis Green, solicitor, and son of the Rev. George Wade Green.

Travelling down the valley we come to the village of

Pontargothi. Turning right into a narrow lane we soon reach Holy Trinity Church that stands in a picturesque and secluded location alongside the river Cothi. The church with its narrow, sharply pointed spire would not look out of place in one of the eastern seaboard states of the United States of America.

The church was built by the Bath family who bought Alltyferin mansion in the 1860s. Incidentally, I believe that the correct name of the mansion would make far more sense if it was Alltyfyrddin – Merlin's Wood – the second part of the name, 'ferin' is the mutated form of the English word 'sea', and there is no sea within many miles of the mansion. It should be remembered that not far from the church is Merlin's Hill and the town of Carmarthen – Caerfyrddin – both according to tradition having very close associations with the wizard Merlin. I stand to be corrected if my reasoning is faulty regarding the name of the mansion.

A member of the Bath family, Henry James Bath, was a very successful businessman who built a completely new mansion in 1869 not far from Alltyferin farm. The family occupied Alltyferin until 1923, and not only did he replace the original house but he also built the church.

On stepping inside the church the visitor comes face to face with interesting and unusual murals depicting scenes from the life of Jesus as recounted in the Gospels. They cover a large part of the four walls. In the east wall, above the altar, is a stained glass window which depicts Henry James Bath and, between the altar and the window there are five tablets on which five members of the family are commemorated.

Starting with the tablet nearest the north wall we see [1]the name of Henry Bath who died in 1864, then Susan Bath,[2] died in Swansea January 7th 1861. Next, Charles

Lambert,[3] died in London January 10th 1859, and finally, Richard[4] Spears Lambert, died in Swansea August 1st 1858. Above each name on the tablets are quotations from the Bible.

Sadly, the mansion was demolished soon after the end of the 1939-45 War.

Let us now go to the nearby hamlet of Llanegwad, now by-passed by the busy A40. The church at Llanegwad is dedicated to a St Egwad, again one of the many saints associated with the period in our country's history known as The Age of Saints, fifth to eighth century.

Alongside the narrow road that winds through the hamlet and only a few yards from the lych gate leading into the churchyard, is a large, ancient oak tree. At the base of the tree there are stone steps that, in the days when the mode of transport was either by one's own two feet, or on horseback or by carriage, enabled the rider to mount or dismount with comparative ease.

The large church, with its double nave and twin chancels, is surrounded by an extensive churchyard which at one time was probably circular, thus denoting a true 'llan'. At the west end of the church there is a large square tower, and at the time of writing this is fenced off due to its rather dangerous condition.

On walking around the churchyard one cannot fail to notice the number of graves that are surrounded by iron railings, all by now red with rust. Although most iron railings throughout the land were taken away during the Second World War for melting down by the arms industry these seem to have been missed.

In the southwest corner of the churchyard, seen with some difficulty because of nature endeavouring to eliminate any trace of man's effort and activity, are the graves of the family of a Colonel Hughes of Tregyb, near Llandeilo. The inscriptions read' 'To the memory of William Garnon Hughes, Captain, Royal Staff Corps, son of Col. Hughes of Tregyb in this county who died May 1878, also of Emily, his wife, who died August 1859. Also of Emily Garnon, Maria Maud, Mary Elizabeth, and John William Hughes, Captain, 1st Royal Scots, children of the aforesaid William Garnon Hughes and Fanny Hughes.' On the second stone: 'In loving memory of Col. W. Gwyn Hughes, DL, JP of Glancothi, born 28th March 1841, died 9th January 1920. Also of his dearly loved wife, Anne Adelaide, born 23rd August 1852, died 29th November 1921.'

Near the two graves stand another four graves, surrounded by metal posts and chain. On one of the gravestones: we read 'Charles Lambert, born at Bruchsal, died at Alltyferin August 4th 1876.' Moving to the west end of the church there is a grave covering quite a large area, and in the middle of it is an imitation Celtic cross, inscribed, 'In loving memory of Edward ----- Bath, Alltyferin, died May 8th 1908, aged 57 years. Also of his daughter Katharine Edith, wife of Rowland H. Barclay, who died July 24th 1908, aged 26 years. "Weeping may endure for a night, but joy cometh in the morning." – Psalm 30, verse 5.' On the north face of the stone: 'Also of his wife Esther who died 23rd March 1924, aged 72 years, and buried at Buckland Brewer, North Devon.' On the south face of the stone: 'Also of his only son, Henry, who died April 19th 1921, aged 45 years, buried at Oare, Somersetshire.' In front of the Celtic cross memorial is a small, rectangular granite stone. Inscribed are the words, "In loving memory of John Fairchild Taylor, Craig y Rap (sic), who died September 7th 1939, aged 87 years. Also the wife of the above, who died November 27th 1929, aged 79 years. 'The Lord is my shepherd.' Also Kate, their daughter, who died May 1st 1949, aged 60 years. Also Hannah, their daughter, who died November 28th 1954, aged 76 years."

Yet another grave that has at its west end a short, rectangular pillar; inscribed on its east face, "In loving remembrance of William Lewis Jones, LRCP, LFP, SLM, Glyncothi House, Llanegwad, who died June 16th 1884, aged 31 years. 'Be ye therefore ready also, the Son of Man cometh at an hour when you think not.' Also Elizabeth, wife of the above, who died May 7th 1886, aged 33 years. 'I know that my Redeemer liveth.' On the south side, "Also in loving memory of Thomas Jones, BA, Priest, Curate of Hannington, who died August 2nd 1908. Also John Lewis Jones, Pembroke College, 2nd Lieutenant. 3rd Battalion Welch Regiment, died August 17th 1917, aged 32 years. Also of William Z. Jones, BA (Hons.) CF, Vicar of Baldesbury, Yorkshire, who died December 26th 1919, aged 41 years. Buried at Baldesbury. The sons of the late Dr and Mrs Lewis Jones, Cothi House. 'Greater love hath no man than this, that he lay down his life for his friends.' (I believe that this verse refers to 2nd Lieut. John Lewis Jones who was probably killed during the 1914-18 Great War.) On the north face of the stone, "Also in memory of Sarah Jane Jones, Glan Cothi House, born December 23rd 1880, died February 2nd 1881." From the above details it can be clearly seen that the family must have endured much sadness, with death a regular visitor.

In the northwest corner of the churchyard is another replica of a Celtic cross. On it: 'To the beloved memory of Thomas Mayberry Williams of Pontypridd, born April 14th 1863, died February 7th 1928, "Thy will be done." Also of Jane, beloved wife of Thomas Mayberry Williams, died June 4th 1944 at Glan Cothi in her 81st year.' On the north face: 'Also Eleanor Owen Williams, died July 6th 1895, aged 3 years.' Resting in the centre of the grave there is a bronze plaque backed by red granite, inscribed on it: 'Also Herbert Llewellyn Williams, QC, DC, JP, MA, (Oxon), Emeritus Bencher of the Middle Temple, Recorder of Carmarthen, 1941-1950, Chairman of Glamorgan Quarter Sessions, 1949-1961, Stipendiary Magistrate of Swansea, 1950-1960, son of the above and loved husband of Hilda, born 15th May 1890, died 11th May 1964.'

On the outside of the north wall of the chancel, there are three large, rectangular memorials. Iron railings surround the large family grave. The stone on the left has on it: 'The Lord gaveth and the Lord hath taken away, blessed be the name of the Lord.' Under the above verse: 'In affectionate remembrance of Adlai, the beloved wife of T.J.L. Richards of Broadway House, in the township of Laugharne and relict of the late Captain J.I.B. Jones of Gelliglyd in this parish, who departed this life on the 20th day of February 1876, aged 48 years. "Thy will be done." Also of T.L.J. Richards, Esq., of Broadway House, born 23rd May 1831, died 15th August 1887. "He that hath pity on the poor leadeth unto the Lord. 'Prov. 19v7."' Unfortunately it is not possible to read the inscription on the middle stone, but on the third memorial, a verse from the Bible: 'Prepare to meet thy God.' Underneath: 'Sacred to the memory of John Jones, Esq., Surgeon, 3rd Regiment, Light Cavalry of the Honourable East India Company, eldest son of John Jones and Elizabeth his wife of Gelliglyd in this parish, who died at Kamptee in Nagpoor, Madras, May 16th 1829, aged 46 years, and was buried in the same place. Near this spot lieth the body of Mary Samuel Richards, wife of Samuel Richards, Gent., of Llwyn-y-Fran in the parish of Meidrim in this county, second daughter of the said John and Elizabeth Jones, who died in childbirth May 23rd 1831, aged 43 years. Also the body of the above named John Jones who after being a zealous member of the Church for upwards of 33 years died in the faith of Christ July 5th 1832, aged 79 years. Also the body of John Jones Richards, son of the said Samuel and Mary Richards, who died September 4th 1832, aged 3 years. Also the remains of the above named Elizabeth, relict of the said John Jones who departed this life the 13 day of November 1838 in the 82nd year of her age. "Dust thou art, and unto dust shalt return." Genesis 3v19.' There are another two entries on the stone but, except for the fact that they refer to John Jones and his wife, the words cannot be read.

Standing against the north wall of the churchyard are two memorials next to each other. Inscribed on them are the following details: 'Sacred. Near this place are deposited the remains of John Griffiths of Aber Cothi in this parish, Gent., who died 19th day of July 1825, aged 67 years.

Ddyn deffro, dyro dro di,
Daw dirfawr derfyn dy deithie.
Dysg di dasg deisif trugaredd Duw Dad,
Dyn deall, daw dydd dy droi dan draed.'

The four lines tells Man to wake up and realize the inescapable fact that the day will come when his life will come to an end, and that he will, in the words of the last line: 'one day be turned aside.' It is a verse reflecting the Victorians' dour outlook on life. Also the following inscription: 'Near this place rest the remains of Elinor, wife of William Davies of Tirbica in this parish, Gent. and daughter of John Griffiths, late of Aber Cothi in the said parish, Gent., who died the 2nd day of February 1850, aged 57 years. Also of Sarah, wife of Thomas Jones of Coedsaithpren in this parish, and daughter of the above named William and Elinor Davies who died June 15th 1856, aged 29 years. Also of the above named William Davies, who died 21st day of November 1856, aged 72 years. Also to the memory of Anne the wife of John Evans of Lanlash in the parish of Llangathen, and daughter of the above named William and Elinor Davies, who died 22nd November 1859, aged 30 years. Also the above named Thomas Jones who died March 12th 1860, aged 40 years.'

Above the north porch arch is a stone on which is inscribed the fact that the present church was rebuilt in 1849. The Parish Registers dating from 1701 to 1905 and the Bishops Transcripts from 1679 to 1875 are in the National Library of Wales at Aberystwyth.

And finally, before leaving the church at Llanegwad, here is a quotation referring to a former Vicar taken from The Episcopal Register of St David's, 1397 to 1518: "Guy, Bishop of St David's, etc., to Rees ap Gressanol, perpetual vicar of the parish of Llanegwad of our diocese, greetings, etc. Trusting entirely in thy faithfulness, etc., we appoint thee to be Dean of the Deanery of Llandeilo of our said diocese with power of enquiring into, correcting and punishing according to the canons, the crimes and excesses of all subjects whatsoever of the said deanery elsewhere by custom punishable by deans; to do and further all and singular things which by law or custom are well known to belong to such office of dean, commanding all and singular of the subjects of the deanery aforesaid that they obey thee, with effect, in all things which belong to the said office. In witness whereof, etc., Dated in our Inn at London. 26th June 1407."

St Anne's, Cwmffrwd and
St Maelog, Llandyfaelog

Our next journey takes us south of the town of
Carmarthen, to visit the two churches named above.

Some two miles from Carmarthen, on the A484, stands
the village of Cwmffrwd and on the right hand side of the
road leading to Cydweli is the church, dedicated to St
Anne. At one time it was grouped with the church of
Llandyfaelog but a few years ago it was placed under the
charge of the vicar of Llangunnor.

The rather small, but very attractive church, was built
in 1878. It has a three sided east wall and there is no arch
separating the nave and chancel. It also has a small
transept on the north side of the nave. The stained glass
window in the east wall is: 'To the glory of God and in
loving memory of John Jenkin Lloyd, Physician and
Surgeon, Llanelli, born 5th June 1853, died April 19th
1905, and his wife Mary, born 12th June 1865, died 11th
January 1944.' One of the two windows in the south wall
is: 'To the glory of God and in loving memory of Mary
Ann Francis, 1893-1977, and Philip John Francis, 1890-
1970, Gore Terrace, Swansea.'

The other window in the south wall commemorates
the members of the family of Gelliceirios, and was placed
in the church by Mr & Mrs Dennis Davies, nephew and
niece-in-law of the departed members of the family. There
is one other stained glass window in the church; it is to be
seen in the north wall. At the bottom of the window is
written: 'To the glory of God and in memory of Joseph
Evans, Gelliddu, died 27th August 1925, and Eleanor
Evans, died 30 January 1931. Erected by their daughter
Mary Ann Francis.' This is the same Mary Ann Francis

commemorated in the window in the south wall. In the transept there is a rather squat, four sided marble pillar, about a yard high with sides about a foot and a half wide. Inscribed on it: 'In memory of Elizabeth, wife of Francis Green, Esq., Oaklands in this parish who died October 11th 1870 in her 50th year. Also the said Francis Green who died September 26th 1898 in his 83rd year.' Both Elizabeth and Francis Green are buried beneath the stone, and it is interesting to note that Francis Green was the son of the Rev. George Wade Green of Cwrt Henri who built the church at that place. He had expressed a wish that he be buried under the nave of Cwrt Henri church but owing to the fact, as I have already mentioned in the preceding chapter, that the church had inadvertently been constructed over a spring it became impossible for his wish to be carried out, and he was buried in Llangathen church. His son managed something that his father failed to achieve, that is, to be buried under the floor of a church.

On the south wall there are two memorials, one of bronze and the other of brass. On the bronze memorial the words: 'To the glory of God and in memory of Pte. Sydney Barnfield, PY, William Anthony Jones, RWF, and Pte. Tom Thomas, RWF, who fell during the Great War of 1914-18.' A family gravestone in the churchyard shows that Pte. William Anthony Jones was killed in the Battle of Ypres in 1916, a battle that resulted in heavy casualties. The brass memorial records the following sad details: 'In proud memory of Guardsman Eirwyn John Phillips, Pantyrodyn, died on active service at Bluff Cove, Falkland Islands, 8th June 1982, aged 20 years.' Guardsman Phillips was one of the unfortunate Welsh guardsmen trapped aboard the ship Sir Galahad when an Argentinian aircraft bombed and set fire to the ship. Sad to relate that the incident resulted in great loss of life and horrific injuries among the guardsmen.

In the churchyard are two gravestones worthy of note. A few yards from the west wall of the church is a white cross atop a white simulated rock on which is inscribed: 'In affectionate memory of I.C. Ibrahim of Ahamadabad, India, for 19 years faithful servant and friend of Col. W.C. Aslett, Bolahaul, died January 26th 1916, aged 35. "Intreat me not to leave thee, or return from following after thee, for whither thou goest, I will go, and where thou lodgest, I will lodge, thy people shall be my people, and thy God my God." Ruth 2v16.' The grave next to Ibrahim's grave is that of the colonel himself. He was a colonel in the Indian Army, and died August 2nd 1936, aged 80 years. Immediately outside the east wall of the church are two identical stones, and they commemorate members of the same family. Inscribed on one the words: ' . . . Also Captain J.M. Pentland, son of the late George Pentland, Esq., of Black Hall, County of Louth, Ireland, who died October 28th 1871, aged 71. This Officer sailed in the ship Northumberland with Napoleon Bonaparte to St Helena in 1815, and returned to England in 1818.' Also commemorated on the same stone his wife as well as his daughter. 'In memory of James Murphy son of Captain Pentland of Diegoed(sic) in this parish, died July 3rd 1870, aged 16, also Rhoda Sophia, daughter, died May 26th 1881, aged 32 years.' On a nearby stone another daughter of the captain: 'Emily Louisa, wife of William Jones of Diegoed who died November 22nd 1883, aged 32 years.' On a nineteenth century OS map the spelling for Diegoed is Dugoed, a name that makes sense – Black Trees.

The property known as Oaklands was built during the middle of the 1800s by Francis Green who was a solicitor, he having bought in January 1859 part of Llwynyreos farm plus a public house named The Foxhole for £800. The following year he bought the adjoining farm, Tynewydd, and ten fields for £467. It was on this land he built Oaklands. This Francis Green is, as already mentioned, buried in the north transept of the church.

Following the death of Col. Aslett of Bolahaul the property was put up for sale; the sale catalogue describes it as having a hall, staircase and landing, library, dining room, drawing room, seven bedrooms, back landing, storeroom and domestic offices.

It is obvious from a report in the Carmarthen Journal, dated January 24th 1873, that Francis Green was an energetic and faithful member of St Anne's Church:–

"Entertainment at St Anne's, Cwmffrwd

It would be difficult to name a locality where the friends of the established church are struggling with greater success under adverse circumstances than at Cwmffrwd to provide for the religious and educational needs of the people. A church has been built here, and through the energies of F. Green, Esq., Oaklands, and Captain Wilson of Cwmffrwd and others, a resident clergyman has also been secured. An organ has also been obtained, and a new transept is about to be built for its reception, so that services will be of a proper musical type. Not only so but a school has been erected and only needs to be furnished. This facts prove singular proof of the fallacy sometimes urged that the Church of England depends on endowments alone, and discards the voluntary principle, declining to utilise the energies and willing sacrifice of the people. The new school is a substantial structure, and on Sundays is tenanted almost to the full by teachers and scholars. Shortly we hope to be able to announce that a day school has been commenced. In order to provide funds for providing furniture for the school a musical and literary entertainment was given on Thursday evening in the schoolroom which was literally crammed by a highly respectable audience. F. Green, Esq., President."

There follows a detailed account of the programme for the evening and that the net proceeds amounted to £13.

We now leave St Anne's Church, Cwmffrwd and head for the village of Llandyfaelog, situated just off the A484 road, a journey of approximately three miles. In the village stands the ancient church, dedicated to St Maelog. The chancel and nave date from the thirteenth century and in the fourteenth century north and south transepts were added. The east window in the south transept is the original window. Other parts of the church date from the fifteenth century. The Parish Registers, 1695 to 1970, are in the National Library of Wales, as also are the Bishops' Transcripts of 1672 to 1862. Alongside the road, and forming part of the churchyard wall, there is a shelter in which stands a village pump that was placed there to commemorate the Jubilee of Queen Victoria in 1897. Inscribed on a tablet set into the wall of the structure are the words: 'This supply of water was given to the inhabitants of Llandyfaelog in commemoration of the long and glorious reign of Queen Victoria, 1837-1897.' I wonder who paid for the project?

Inside the church there are many interesting memorials and stained glass windows. On the south wall, near the door, there is a bronze plaque with a wooden surround bearing the following inscription: 'To the memory of David Daniel Davies, MD, 1777-1841, of Tredegar in this parish. In 1819 he was in attendance at the birth of Queen Victoria. He was the first appointed

73

Professor of Midwifery at the University of London in1829.' Further along the wall, towards the chancel, a white marble memorial with a rather long inscription: 'In affectionate remembrance of my beloved child, George Thomas Griffiths, third son of E.M. Davies, Esq., of Uplands in this parish, and Maria Thomas his wife, and grandson of the late John Jones of the above place and Dolwar, Meirionethshire, who departed this life the 27th of October 1862, aged 6 years and 8 months, at 15 Milner Street, London, whose mortal remains are interred in Highgate cemetery. "Of such is the Kingdom of Heaven."

Cease longer to detain me
Fondest mother drowned in awe.
Now thy kind caresses pains me,
Morn advances, let me go.
Weep not o'er these eyes that languish,
Upward turning toward their home;
Raptured, they'll forget all anguish
While they wait to see thee come.
Yet to leave thee sorrowing rends me,
Tho' again his voice I hear.
Rise! May ever grace attend thee,
Rise! And seek to meet me there.'

Uplands, the house mentioned in the memorial, stands on high ground above the river Tywi. It is a large house of three storeys with five windows on the front of the two upper floors. The pillared entrance probably dates from the sixteenth century and the house is marked in Kitchin's Map of 1754. In 1704 a John Morgan, who was High Sheriff, lived there. By 1768 it was occupied by a Edward Parry. The E.M. Davies mentioned in the memorial was living there in 1865.

In the south wall of the south transept there is a stained glass window, inscribed along the bottom: 'To the glory of God and in loving memory of Harper, Eric and Patrick Lowry, who laid down their lives in the Great War, 1914-1918.' The three named were brothers whose names are also on a Celtic-like cross in the churchyard.

In the north wall of the north transept is a stained glass window on which is written: 'To the glory of God and in memory of William B. Lowry, died February 2nd 1927.' William Lowry was the father of the three brothers killed in the 1914-18 War.

In the west wall of the south transept is another stained glass window, in memory of two brothers killed in Burma. They were the grandsons of William Lowry, and nephews of the three Lowry brothers killed in World War I. Inscribed on the window are the following details,' In memory of Stephen Charles Francis, DSO, Captain, West Yorkshire Regiment, killed in Burma 1942, aged 24 years, and James Lowry Francis, Major, The Royal Berkshire Regiment, killed in Burma 1945, aged 24 years.'

The Lowry family lived in a house (across the road from the church and the public house) named Tŷ Un Nos (One Night House). At one time the Lowry family owned three farms in the district. Two sisters of the three brothers killed in the 1914-18 War still own the house and, although they do not live in the village, it is known that they stayed there during Easter time in 1995. One of the two sisters lost two sons in Burma during the Second World War. The widow of William Lowry, mother of the three brothers and two sisters, died a few years ago at the advanced age of 97. Lowry family members have over the years been generous benefactors of Llandyfaelog Church.

On the north wall is a memorial to the Rev. Peter Williams, 1723-1796. 'To the honoured memory of the

Rev. Peter Williams, annotator and commentator of the Welsh Bible and author of a Concordance. This tablet erected by his descendants in admiration of his life and work on the occasion of the bi-centenary of his birth, January 7th 1923.'

As already referred to, in the church is commemorated a David Daniel Davies, the gynaecologist who attended at the birth of Queen Victoria. David Davies was born and brought up in a cottage that stood on the other side of the road to Rama Chapel, the road that goes from Carmarthen to Cydweli.

The window in the east wall is: 'In memory of Augustine Homie Bull, who died January 22nd 1872, "To the glory of God."'

And now let us go out to the churchyard itself where there are some interesting gravestones.

Near the south wall is a stone in the form of a Celtic cross and at the foot of the grave, a small rectangular stone. The small stone commemorates the parents of the three Lowry brothers killed in the war and the base of the cross provides full details about them. The inscription makes sad reading: on the east face: 'To the glory of God and in ever loving memory of three sons who gave their lives for king and country in the Great War, 1914-18. This cross is erected by their parents. "Dulce et decorum et pro patria Mori."' On the south face: 'William Augustine Harper Lowry, Temp. 2nd Lieut. IARO, attached 14th (KGO) Sikhs, born 21st February 1890, killed in action at Gully Ravine Ansac, Gallipoli, 4th June 1915.' On the west side: 'Auriol Ernest Eric Lowry, DSO, MC, Captain (acting Lieut. Col.) 2/PWO, West Yorkshire Regiment, Born 4th December 1892, killed in action at Arleux, France, 23rd. September 1918.' On the north side: 'Cyril John Patrick Lowry, Lieut. (acting Captain), 2/PWO, West

Yorkshire Regiment, born 23rd January 1898, killed in action near Villers Carbonnel, France, 25th March 1918.'

On the rectangular stone at the base of the cross: 'Sacred to the memory of William B. Lowry, my beloved husband who died at Bournemouth, February 2nd 1927. "They may rest from their labours, and their works follow them." – Rev.14v13, and of Anne, his wife, died March 20th 1942.'

The trauma and turmoil suffered by the parents of the Lowry brothers is impossible for us to comprehend. To lose three sons, one aged 20 years, another 25 years and yet another at 26 years of age must be something that only those unfortunate to have had the experience can understand. In addition two were killed within six months of one another, and this within only eight and two months respectively before the war came to an end. This was a tragedy of the highest order – the price of war!

Again, in the very same churchyard, is a gravestone recording the fact that two brothers were reported missing, presumed dead, during the Second World War of 1939-45. They never returned so both were probably killed in action. The inscription on the gravestone records: 'In loving memory of Anne Elizabeth, the dearly loved wife of Herbert Jones, Cillefwr, Carmarthen, died October 4th 1951. Also their dearly loved sons, Flt/Sgt. Mervyn Anthony, RAF, missing April 3rd 1942, Flying Officer William Howell Anthony, DFC, missing November 14th 1944. Also Herbert Jones, devoted husband and father, died March 3rd 1957.'

It was Benjamin Franklin who wrote: 'There never was a good war, or a bad peace.' If only mankind took these words to heart and acted upon them.

The following item of news appeared in the Carmarthen Journal of April 12th 1995. It is a copy of what was reported in The Welshman on April 12th 1940:

There was jubilation in Carmarthen on Friday last when a Carmarthen man, Sergeant Mervyn Anthony Jones, Royal Air Force, younger son of Mr and Mrs Herbert Jones, Cillefwr Farm, Johnstown, rode Bogskar to victory in the Grand National Steeplechase at Aintree, Liverpool.

Mervyn Jones comes from a racing stock. He is nephew of the brothers Anthony, the famous trainers, his mother being formerly Miss Anthony of Cilveithy, Llandyfaelog. His brother H.A. Jones rode National Flight in last Friday's great race, and the horse, which threw its rider at one of the fences after the first round, by a strange coincidence finished first at the winning post – riderless. Only two years later Sergeant Mervyn Jones was reported missing presumed killed.

The above named Mervyn and Anthony Jones are the two commemorated on the gravestone in Llandyfaelog churchyard.

They, and the members of the Lowry family, were not the only ones to pay the ultimate price while serving their king and country.

Another gravestone in the churchyard has this inscription on it: 'In loving memory of Ordinary Seaman Elwyn Evans, RN of this village, killed on HMS Glorious 8th June 1940, aged 18 years.'

HMS Glorious was an aircraft carrier, and what immediately followed its sinking has led to a great deal of controversy. Accounts of what actually took place differ greatly. The aircraft carrier, along with other Royal Navy ships, was sailing across the North Sea from Norway to Britain. The British Expeditionary Force was being evacuated from Norway and on one of the ships was King Haakon of Norway, escaping from the Germans.

A Cambridge undergraduate working at Bletchley Park at the time noticed signals coming from the two German battle-cruisers, Scharnhost and Gneisnau, that they were sailing from the German port of Kiel. When he asked for the messages he had intercepted from the two German ships to be passed on to the Admiralty, his request was turned down. The Glorious' captain refused to allow any flying of aircraft off the carrier, aircraft that could have spotted the two German ships heading towards them, and would have enabled HMS Glorious to take evasive action. A German camera team recorded what became a one-sided battle between the German cruisers and the aircraft carrier. HMS Glorious was out-gunned, and her guns out-ranged, and within two hours the battle was over. The Glorious' captain was killed when the third salvo fired by the enemy hit the ship which started to sink rapidly. The crew of around 1,600 men abandoned ship, and only 41 were rescued three days later.

Two British destroyers, the Ardent and Augusta, also sailing in the area, put up a brave fight, so brave that even the enemy admired it. The Admiralty learnt of the battle and heard of the sinking of HMS Glorious from a German radio broadcast.

The wireless operator on HMS Devonshire, the ship carrying the Norwegian royal family and members of the Norwegian government, heard radio signal giving details of what had taken place. He said that he had passed on the signal to the ship's bridge on which stood the ship's captain and Admiral Cunningham; it seems that the message was ignored.

What really happened that day remains a mystery, but

some believe that strict radio silence was kept on the part of the British ships so as not to endanger the very important people who were on board HMS Devonshire. Whatever the truth, the loss of life was horrendous and, sadly, a young man from Llandyfaelog, along with many other young men perished that day, never to return home. Was HMS Glorious and the crew sacrificed for the sake of a Norwegian king and his government?

Incidentally, the young Cambridge undergraduate at Bletchley Park at the time later became Sir Henry Hinsley, Vice Chancellor of Cambridge University.

Also in the churchyard is the grave of a famous Welshman whose name became very well known throughout Wales two centuries ago. On the face of the box-shaped tomb is inscribed: 'Underneath are deposited the remains of the Rev. Peter Williams, late of Gellilydnais in this parish. All his labours were invariably directed to promote the temporal and eternal welfare of his countrymen for whose benefit he published three editions of a 4o Welsh Bible with explanatory notes, one edition in 8vo, a Concordance, and a number of pamphlets in the same language for which, alas, he experienced nothing but persecution and ingratitude. He continued a faithful and laborious minister of the Gospel for 53 years, and died rejoicing in his God August 8th 1796, aged 74 years. "For it was not an enemy that reproached me; then I could have borne it; neither was it that hated me that did magnify itself against me; then I could have hid myself from him." – Psalm 55, verse 12. And also the remains of Mary the relict of the said Rev. Peter Williams, who died March 8th aged 98 years.' Also resting on, and towards the bottom of the stone slab on top of the tomb, a tablet on which is inscribed: 'This tablet is to commemorate the bi-centenary of the Rev. Peter

Williams' Bible, 1770-1970'.

There is undoubtedly a note of extreme bitterness emanating from the contents of the inscription on the tomb, and knowledge of what actually happened during his lifetime gives credence to this fact. Born at Llansadurnen, Carmarthenshire in 1733, he was converted to Christianity by the preaching of the famous George Whitefield in 1743. Later ordained, he served as curate in several parishes in south Wales. He was refused full priest's orders because of his Methodist inclinations, and in 1747 joined the Methodist movement. For the remainder of his life he was an itinerant preacher, although he was still a deacon of the Anglican Church. He built his own chapel, Water Street Chapel in Carmarthen, in 1771. By 1791 he was the subject of bitter controversy, and was suspected of believing the doctrine put forward by Sabellius who lived in the third century AD. In his doctrine Sabellius maintained that the Three Divine Persons of the Holy Trinity are merely aspects of One Divinity.

The suspicions of leading Methodists regarding Peter Williams' belief in the teachings of Sabellius led to his excommunication from the Methodist denomination. A sad end to a person who was undoubtedly a great Welshman.

Not far from Llandyfaelog is the church of St Ishmael, near Ferryside, and that is where we go next.

St Ishmael's, Ferryside, Llanfihangel Abercywyn, St Clears

Standing on a steep-sided slope above the narrow road that follows the east bank of the river Tywi estuary, and between Ferryside and Cydweli, is the ancient church of St Ishmael. It overlooks the estuary, the waters of Carmarthen Bay and, visible on the horizon, Caldey Island. Directly across the river stands Llanstephan Castle. The church is located in a delightful spot and, with its rather unique external architecture, well worth a visit.

It is believed that the nave and the font are of Norman origin, and that the north aisle and tower date from around the fourteenth century. The tower is topped with a simple saddle roof. The churchyard's very steep slope has resulted in the graves having to be set out in terraces, and the carrying of coffins to the graves by the bearers must be a hazardous task. Many of the gravestones stand at various angles from the perpendicular. Placed in the south wall, above the entrance porch to the church, is a slate sun dial, and inscribed on it the date, 1725. For students of history and all those researching their family tree, the Parish Registers, 1560 to 1920, can be studied in the Carmarthen Record Office, now located off Richmond Terrace in what was at one time The Boys' Grammar School, and after that Ysgol Bro Myrddin. The Bishops' Transcripts, 1671 to 1879, are housed in the National Library of Wales.

Among the inscriptions on the gravestones, one that caught my eye read: 'In memory of Rachel, wife of John Thomas, gardener of Iscoed, who died October 15th 1864, aged 71 years. 'My flesh and heart faileth, but God is the strength of my heart and my portion for ever.' – Psalm 73, verse 26.'

The Iscoed mentioned on the above gravestone is now a ruined, red brick mansion that stands overlooking the villages of Ferryside, Llanstephan and the river Tywi estuary. At the beginning of the 1800s it was bought by General Sir Thomas Picton for £30,000, equivalent today to about £2,000,000. The general only lived in the mansion for a very short time, having arrived home after serving with distinction in the Peninsular War. In 1815 he was recalled to serve in Europe against Napoleon. During the Battle of Waterloo he was killed, and his body now lies buried in the crypt of St Paul's Cathedral in London, within a few feet from the body of the Duke of Wellington who was Commander-in-Chief of the British troops at Waterloo. I wonder if Rachel Thomas' husband worked as a gardener at Iscoed when Sir Thomas Picton occupied the mansion? It is possible as Rachel Thomas would have been about twenty-one years of age at the time, and possibly her husband, John Thomas, about the same age.

On a narrow gravestone with the inscription crudely repainted in silver paint are the following details: 'Here lies Charles William Nevill of Ferryside, 1907-1973, Her Majesty's Lord Lieutenant for the county of Carmarthen from 1967 until his death in 1973. 'Recce et forticcer (or possibly, forcitter).' An account of the Nevill family can be found in Howard M. Jones' interesting book, *Llanelli Lives*, published in the year 2000.

Built into the south wall of the tower is a stone with this inscription written on it: 'Underneath are deposited the remains of Richard Bonnell, Esq., who departed this life May 6th 1776, aged 50 years, likewise his mother and four of his children. Here also lie the remains of Mary, wife of the above Richard Bonnell, who departed this life May 17th 1793, aged 60 years. To perpetuate the memory of George, the 4th son of the above Richard and Mary

Bonnell, who lost his life in defence of his country at St Lucia, West Indies. Likewise, John and Owen Bonnell, 2nd and 3rd sons who died at sea. Here also were deposited the remains of William Bonnell, Esq., their eldest son, aged 43 years. "He was a good Christian, sincere friend, and died lamented". Sacred also to Catherine Bonnell, widow and relict of the above William Bonnell, who departed this life 6th December in the year 1836, aged 72 years, and whose remains lie buried underneath. "Blessed are the dead which die in the Lord from henceforth, Yea, saith the Spirit, They may rest from their labours and their works follow them."'

The surname Bonnell can still be found in the Llanelli area.

An inscription on another gravestone tells of a tragic accident that happened at Ferryside to a nine year-old boy in 1962. The son of the local headmaster, while playing on the beach, dug a tunnel in the sand that collapsed on him with the result that he suffocated: 'Er serchus gof am Russel, annwyl fab Graham a Joyce Rees, Greenhirst, Ferryside, bu farw trwy ddamwain ar y traeth Ebrill 27ain 1962, yn naw mlwydd oed.'

Soon after this very sad occurrence the family emigrated to Canada.

Leaving St Ishmael's we travel back to Carmarthen and join the dual carriageway and head for St Clears but, before going there; visit the ruins of the very old church of Llanfihangel Abercywyn. To reach what remains of the church we turn off the dual carriageway at a point where stands what looks like a typical American church of the eastern states of that country. This church replaced the ruined church and carries the same name, and is dedicated to St Michael.

We now travel along a narrow road until we reach a

junction; we take the right lane and travel on until arriving at Trefenty Farm. This is as far as one can go by car, so we must cross two fields until we see on the right, hidden behind some trees, the few remaining walls of the old church. Not far from the old ruin is the river Cywyn that runs into the estuary of the river Taf.

Standing among the ruined church and churchyard gives one a strong sense of spirituality. One almost wishes that the silence could be broken by the few remaining stones speaking and recounting the history of the church and those long forgotten people who worshipped there over possibly hundreds of years.

Near Trefenty Farm are the remains of a twelfth century motte and bailey castle and it is probable that the church was founded by the lords of the castle. The church had a single nave, probably thirteenth century, a fifteenth century chancel and a western tower also of that period. The Norman font was removed to the other church built in 1848 at a more convenient position alongside the A40, about a mile from St Clears.

It is believed that the church was what is known as a 'Pilgrims Church' on the route to the cathedral at St David's in Pembrokeshire. In the churchyard there are six interesting, enigmatic, ancient graves marked by decorated slabs and small, rounded headstones and footstones. The belief is that they date from the twelfth to the thirteenth century. According to the book, *A Guide to Ancient and Historical Wales,* by Sian Rees: 'Two of the slabs are the so called "hog-backed" form, and are decorated with a cross, the long arm of which runs along the ridge of the stone. The other four are flat slabs. Two of these show female figures, one full length, the other occupying only half the stone, the remainder decorated with lattice pattern. This latter figure holds a rod in one hand and there is an animal on either side of the head. The figure on the third slab is too broken to allow identification, but had a knee-length tunic; the horseman with lance in one hand, depicted on both head and foot stones, suggests that the occupant was a male, perhaps a knight. The fourth figure is small, dressed in a long skirt, and appears to be standing at a barrier. Its small size suggest that it may mark the grave of a child.'

The occupants of the graves will never be revealed. Were they inhabitants of the castle or the farm, or were they pilgrims on their way to St David's Cathedral? Sir Walter Scott wrote this verse:

> If thou would'st fair Melrose aright,
> Go visit by the pale moonlight,
> For the gay beams of lightsome day
> Gild, but to flout, the ruins grey.

I cannot speak about Melrose because I have never been there, but I can state with certainty that a visit to this tranquil spot with its ruined church and ancient churchyard not far from St Clears is a really worthwhile, and also an unforgettable experience, whether it be by day, or as Scott wrote, 'by the pale moonlight'.

And now back to the car parked in the farmyard but, before we leave to go to St Clears, a few words about Trefenty Farm itself.

The farm is what Major Francis Jones in his book, *Historic Carmarthenshire Houses*, describes as a 'double-pile'. It stands about 140 feet above sea level, overlooking the river Taf and the land above the township of Laugharne. Again according to Major Jones Francis, toward the end of the sixteenth century it was owned by Sir John Perrot (1532-1620), politician and Lord Deputy of

Ireland from 1584 to 1588. (Incidentally, 1588 was the year the first Bible in the Welsh language was published.) It is believed that Perrot was the illegitimate son of Henry VIII, and that his mother was a Mary Berkeley who was later married off to Sir Thomas Perrot of Haroldstown, Pembroke.

In 1562 Sir John Perrot was appointed Vice-Admiral of the south Wales coast, and in 1563 he became a Member of Parliament for Pembrokeshire. He had many enemies and, as a convinced anti-Catholic, spent a period in Fleet prison during the reign of Queen Mary. During his time in Ireland he antagonised a number of people who later placed him in the Tower of London on a charge of treason. He was condemned to death but died before sentence could be carried out. Sir John fathered an illegitimate son, the mother a Sibyl Jones of Radnorshire. Their son, James, later became Sir James Perrot, Member of Parliament during the reigns of James I and Charles I, and like his father he was also an anti-Catholic. His granddaughter, Penelope, inherited Trefenty and married Sir William Lower of St Wynnows, Cornwall. Sir William was a scholar and astronomer. They had two children, Thomas, who died unmarried in 1661, and Dorothy, who married Sir Maurice Drummond, and set up a charity to help the poor in the parish. Her only child, another Penelope, married Edmund Plowden of Plowden Hall, Shropshire, and their descendants owned Trefenty until the 1870s, when it was bought by the Ecclesiastical Commissioners. On the Disestablishment of the Church in Wales from the Church of England in 1920 Trefenty was sold to the University of Wales.

In the book *The History of Little England Beyond Wales* by Edward Laws, published in 1888, the author wrote the following about the Perrot family: 'If the Devereux family of Lamphey assumed first place in South Pembrokeshire in society, the Perrots of Haroldston certainly ranked second. Thomas, son of Sir Owen Perrot, joined Sir Rhys ap Thomas in welcoming Henry VII when he disembarked at Dale in 1485, and so became "persona grata" at Court. Late in life he married Mary, daughter of James, the second son of Maurice, Lord Berkeley. She was a professional beauty whose charms fascinated King Henry VIII, and who, about the year 1527 bore him a son, subsequently Sir John Perrot, the Lord Deputy of Ireland. As a youth, John Perrot was brought up in the establishment of the Marquis of Winchester, and on one occasion yielding to the uncontrollable temper (which was the bane of his life) fell out with two yeomen of the Royal Guard. This fracas came to the king's ears, who forthwith sent for the culprit, inquired concerning his name and kindred and promised him protection. Possibly Henry recognised his son . . . He was one of the four bearers appointed to uphold the canopy of state over Queen Elizabeth at her coronation. Sir Thomas Naunton who married John Perrot's granddaughter in his book *Fragmenta Regalia* wrote, "If we compare his (Perrot's) picture, his qualities, his gesture and voyce (sic), with that of the king, whose memory still remains among us, they will plead strongly that he was a surreptitious child of the royal blood."'

George Owen's history, *Cambrian Register*, vol. II, page 164, wrote: 'Sir Thomas Perrot is remembered as the introducer of pheasants into Pembrokeshire. These he brought from Ireland and turned down at his house near Haroldston.'

On we go to St Mary Magdalene Church, St Clears. The church is approached by an impressive lych gate and stands at the end of a long path off the road that goes to Laugharne. It is a large church, and the nave and chancel, divided by a fine arch, are of Norman origin. It was founded in 1120 as a Cluniac priory. The tower was added in the thirteenth century. The walls of the church must be among the thickest walls of any church in the land; they are about four feet thick.

Lodged in the Carmarthen Record Office are the Parish Registers dating from 1681 to 1970, and the Bishops' Transcripts, now in the National Library of Wales, cover the years1672 to 1854. On the Episcopal Register of St David's, 1397 to 1518, there is this entry: 'Also on 11th August (1402), in the year and place above-said, the bishop admitted Sir John Lange priest of his diocese, to the vicarage of the parish of St Clears, vacant by the death of Sir David Brownyng, last vicar of the same, to which he is presented to him by our most excellent prince in Christ, Lord Henry, by the grace of God, king, etc., true patron of the same by reason of the alien priory of St Clears being in his hand on the account of the war between him and his adversary of France, and instituted him etc. And it was written to the Archdeacon of Carmarthen, etc., Guy (i.e. the bishop) etc., to our Dean of Carmarthen greeting etc. We have received a grave complaint of Sir John Lange, vicar of the parish of St Clears, containing that Sir David Brownyng, vicar of the above-said (died) leaving some evident and notorious defects in the chancel, books and other ornaments, of the said church, the property of the vicarage, as well as in the manse of the same vicarage and the glebe unfinished, the repair and replacement of which are well known to pertain to the said David while he lived, and to his executors after his death. We therefore commit to you our powers to make inquisition in due form of law by rectors, vicars and other craftsmen, having the best experience in the premises, touching such defects and that they consist and for how much they can be suitably repaired, and to what person or persons the repairs of such defects is known to pertain, and in whose times they occurred, summoning for all this all who of right should be summoned with full powers besides to sequestrated goods of the said deceased to the estimated value of the repairs found to be needed, with the power of every kind of canonical coercion whatsoever. And when the business has been set forward, certify us in legal manner of what you have done, with the tenour of these presents. Dated in our manor of Lantefey, 11th August 1402.'

The above must contain one of the longest convoluted sentences in the English language; a total of one hundred and forty words and fourteen lines. According to the Encyclopaedia Britannica the word tenour in the passage is the British variation of tenor; among its meaning (a) drift of something written or spoken, (b) an exact copy of a writing, (c) concept, object or person meant in a metaphor.

In the church, on the south wall of the chancel is a stone tablet. Inscribed on it: 'Here lyeth the body of Timothy Powell, Clerk, AM, late Vicar of St Clears and Rector of Robeston West, who in the year of trial, 1691, was derived of all that he could keep, with a safe conscience, died 29th July 1719, aged 66.' These words hold a mystery begging to be solved. On another memorial on the south wall: 'Here lyeth the body of John Rich, Gent., who departed this life 28th March, Anno Domini, 1717, aged 64.' On another memorial, this time on the south wall of the nave, this verse:

> I've weathered many a stormy sea,
> But now life's arduous service o'er.
> I yield my spirit, Lord, to Thee,
> And with a joy a happier shore.

One can assume the verse refers to a seafarer.

In the churchyard there are also some memorials worthy of note. A few yards from the south wall, lying in a hedge, a stone on which is inscribed: 'Sacred to the memory of David Harry and his son George, of this town, who were accidentally drowned near Laugharne 3rd May 1855.

> Ti a chwythaist wynt ar y môr
> A hwynt, suddasant fel plwm
> Yn y dyfroedd at dy fron.'

The words tell us that God caused a strong wind to blow at sea, the father and son sank like lead, but came to rest on God's breast.

Near the east wall a stone in memory of another father and son is placed. 'Sacred to the memory of Walter Nangreaves Williams, Esq., Captain 23rd Regiment RWF, late of Pencoed in this county, who died 15th May 1857, aged 60 years. Also to the memory of Arthur Nangreaves Henry, youngest son of the above who was lost at sea on the 14th of January 1873, aged 16 years and 3 months. Deeply regretted. RIP.'

Major Francis Jones, in another of his excellent books, *Historic Carmarthenshire Homes and their Families*, provides a wealth of information. He informs us that Pencoed is a large country house some two and a half miles north of St Clears, that the house dates back to the seventeenth century, and that the first known owners were members of the Bevan family. Griffith Bevan was Mayor of Carmarthen in 1575 and 1581. A Timothy Powell, JP, had also lived in Pencoed, and it is highly likely that he was a descendant of the Rev. Timothy Powell, vicar of St Clears at the end of the seventeenth century and the beginning of the eighteenth century.

To the left of the path leading into the church are two stones, next to each other, on which is inscribed: 'In memory of Elizabeth Posthuma, daughter of David and Anne Thomas, draper and chandler of this town, who departed this life the 17th of April 1864 in the 16th year of her age.

> O! Mother do not weep, Elizabeth's asleep.
> She'll wake again on the great Judgement Day,
> She'll quit this house of clay
> Clothed in immortal ray with Christ to reign.

Also in memory of William, third son of D. and A. Thomas, who died at sea after unparalleled privation, and suffering for 15 days on board the waterlogged ship 'Jane Lowden' of Padstow, on the 7th of January 1866 in the 21st year of his age.

> "The sun went down, it was yet day."'

On the stone next to it: 'To the memory of David Thomas of this town, draper and chandler, who departed this life May 21st 1848 in the ?? year of his age. "The clods of the valley shall be sweet unto him, and every man shall draw after him, as there are innumerable before him." Job 21:31, and "For his anger endureth but a moment; in his favour is life, weeping may endure for a night, but joy cometh in the morning." Psalm 30:5'

Taking the dates into account it seems that the daughter with a name like Posthuma must have been born soon after her father's death. A similar name and situation can be seen on a stone in Llanllwch churchyard. Finally, it is interesting to note from some of the inscriptions on memorials in St Clears churchyard that the sea must have played a prominent part in the lives of the inhabitants of St Clears at one time.

The Churches of Laugharne, Llandawke, Llanddowror and Llansteffan

The church at Laugharne, dedicated to St Martin, stands surrounded by trees on a steep slope to the left of the road leading into the town-ship of Laugharne. It is one of four churches in the Diocese of St David's dedicated to St Martin, the others being Clarbeston and Havefordwest in Pembrokeshire and Merthyr near Carmarthen.

There are three St Martins listed in the Oxford Dictionary of Saints; Martin of Tours, c.316-397, a monk, bishop; St Martin I, died 655, pope and martyr; Martin de Porres, 1579-1639, a Dominican lay brother. St Martin of Tours was one of the most popular saints of the Middle Ages. Born in Hungary, his father was a pagan officer in the Roman army. St Martin also served in the army but became convinced that his commitment to Christ prevented him from continuing to serve as a soldier. In effect he became an early example of a conscientious objector and was, as were many in this country during the Great War, 1914-18, imprisoned because of this. He is depicted by artists cutting his cloak in half in order to clothe a nearby beggar with one of the halves. In 372AD he was made Bishop of Tours but continued to live as a monk.

At that time Christianity was more or less confined to urban areas and he believed it was important to evangelise in the rural areas. His twenty-five years as a bishop was marked by the healing of lepers and it was also believed that he had raised a dead man back to life. His cult in France has resulted in 500 villages and 4,000 parish churches dedicated to him. By the year 1800 a total of 173 churches in Britain had been dedicated to him.

The other St Martin, known as St Martin I, was born in Umbria, a mountainous region of Italy in the central Apennines. Its capital is Perugia, and the river Tiber rises in the region.

Elected Pope in 649, he held a council that condemned Monothelitism, a belief that Christ had a human will. Martin was supported by the bishops of Africa, England and Spain, but was arrested by Constans II and taken to Constantinople. Jailed for three months, the food he was given making him sick, and not allowed to wash for forty-seven days, he was then charged with treason. Condemned unheard, public insults, flogging and imprisonment followed. The Patriarch of Constantinople interceded on his behalf, and his life was spared, but he was exiled to the Crimea, and there he died on April 13th 655AD.

St Martin's Church in Laugharne is quite a large fourteenth century church building. In the south transept there is a piscina (a perforated stone basin for carrying away water used for rinsing the chalice and paten), and a squint (opening in the wall making it possible for a person outside to view the altar, originally to enable lepers to watch the priest officiate at the service of Holy Communion). Church restoration during the 1800s saw the building of two porches and the installation of nearly all the stained glass windows which are Victorian. The Arms of Sir Guido de Brian are in the north window of the chancel and, at one time, his effigy also lay in the chancel. There are tenth and eleventh century cross-slabs and a late medieval cope as well as many memorial tablets inside the church.

Near the southeast corner of the churchyard there is a memorial in the shape of an obelisk; inscribed on it:

'Sacred to the memory of Captain William Laugharne, Royal Navy, who died in the city of Bath, November 6th 1856, aged 71 years. Of him it may be justly recorded that to his country, relatives, friends and the poor of this parish, he faithfully carried out his duty in that state of life to which it pleased God to call him. Also of Martha, widow of Major General George Prescott Wingrove, and sister of the above Captain, William Laugharne, who died in the city of Bath, October 31st 1861, aged 81.' The Laugharne family home was Gosport House, and it is reported that Cromwell stayed there when attacking the castle during the Civil War, 1642-1649. It is also said that two sons of the family saw the ghost of a woman outside their bedroom window.

Built into the west wall of the tower is a tablet on which is inscribed: 'Sacred to the memory of Thomas Skeel, of this town, who departed this life June 7th 1850, aged 69 years. Formerly a grenadier in the 40th Regiment of Foot under the command of the Duke of Wellington in the actions of Veniera, Roleia, Talavera, and was wounded by a musket shot in the breast, and it remained in his body until his death.'

It is possible to learn a great deal about Thomas Skeel because in the Carmarthen Record Office there is a book of one hundred pages that he wrote about his life. It seems from the title page that he had every intention of writing a second book that was to include an account of his service as a grenadier in the 40th Regiment of Foot in Ireland, Portugal, Spain and France.

In the book in the Record Office he gives an account of the years when he served in the Somerset Militia. Born in Laugharne, one of five children, he became a farm servant in a place called Twickenham, not far from Bristol. In July 1801 he joined the 2nd Somerset Militia and remained with his unit until 1807. At this time he joined the 1st Battalion, 40th Regiment of Foot. The regiment took part in the American War of Independence, and the wars against Napoleon, including the Battle of Waterloo. He begins his book with: 'The life of Thomas Skeel, Grenadier in the 40th Regiment of Foot, with an account of his travels through England and Wales, Ireland, Portugal, Spain and France.' He also wrote: 'I think I shall be abel(sic) to give the Reader a littel(sic) more intertainment(sic) in the next vollom wich(sic) will be the largest. Cpn(sic) Clark gave us Eight gines(sic) to drink at Portsmouth. The end of the manuscript.'

From his account in the book it is obvious that Thomas Skeel led a life that had its fair share of adventure, and a visit to the Record Office to read the 'vollom' will, I feel sure, prove worthwhile.

In the part of the churchyard reached by crossing a bridge built over a lane is the grave of Dylan Thomas. Most visitors to his grave are very surprised at the simplicity of his memorial – a simple wooden cross with the briefest of details. Dying in America in 1953 aged only 39, he is considered to be one of the most important poets in the English language that lived during the last century. Although born in Swansea, he had strong family connections with Carmarthenshire. Many books have been written about his life and work by more than one writer and books of his poetry, stories and plays are readily available in bookshops.

From Laugharne we proceed next to St Margaret's Church, Llandawke. I can imagine many on hearing the unusual name, Llandawke, looking rather puzzled. Where is it?' To get there we travel from Laugharne Church into the township and, on reaching the town square, turn sharp right into a narrow, winding lane.

After approximately a mile and a quarter we reach the little church that is tucked in behind what was once the Vicarage. There is not another house in sight, and the only other buildings are what seem to be the vicarage's out buildings on the other side of the road.

The church is now only used on rare occasions, and the visitor is able to walk into the church since the door is permanently open.

The nave and chancel date from the thirteenth century and the west tower has a pyramid-shaped roof, also belonging to the thirteenth century. In the chancel the two windows date from the fourteenth century and the one in the nave belongs to the same period. Two other windows in the nave are from the fifteenth century, and the low doorway could also be from that time. Surrounding the church is a churchyard that has an air of neglect, understandable when one considers that the church is hardly used. Many of the gravestones lean at various angles.

Of all the things to look at both inside and outside this ancient church most interesting is an effigy located near the north side of the altar. It is that of a woman, and the inscription on the side reads: 'This effigy is probably that of Margaret Marlos, daughter of Robert Marlos, Knight, and Margaret his wife, sister of Guy de Brian, KG, Lord Marcher of Laugharne, 1350-1391, who partly rebuilt this church and the neighbouring church of Eglwys Cymmin, and dedicated them to his ancestress and patroness, St Margaret of Scotland, in honour of his niece. This effigy, broken in three places, was found outside in the churchyard and placed here at the expense of the late Thomas Jones Harries, Esq. by the Rector Thomas Jenkins, AD 1902.'

St Margaret of Scotland mentioned on the inscription

was the wife of King Malcolm III of Scotland. Both she and her husband died, coincidentally, on the same day, November 13th 1093, Malcolm died with one of his sons while on a military expedition against William Rufus, third son of William the Conqueror and king of England from 1087 until his death in 1100. Rufus died whilst hunting in the New Forest. King Malcolm reigned for thirty-nine years. In 1072 St Margaret ordered the rebuilding of the famous abbey on the Isle of Iona. Through Margaret and her daughter, who became queen of England from 1141 to 1153, the present royal family can trace their descent from the pre-conquest kings of England.

In the floor, halfway down the aisle, is a stone slab on which is written: 'In memory of Thomas Evans, died June 29th 1763, aged 75 years, his wife Anne, died April 4th 1771, aged 84 years, his son John Evan, died December 6th 1785, aged 53 years, and Barbara, his wife, died April 6th 1790, aged 52 years.

Mourn not my friends, I'm only gone before,
In this vain world you ne'er shall see me more.
Prepare to follow, mind the Word, Prepare,
Let not this world too much your care.
Trust in the Lord, He will dispel your fears,
And guide you through this vale of tears.
To every faithful soul by Christ is given
A certain promise they shall meet in heaven
With Cherubs joined their noble Anthems raise
To Carol out the Great Jehovah's Praise.'

In the words of the verse there is quite a mixture of sentiments, a dire warning, great hope, and the certain promise of eternal life – sentiments found time and time again on gravestones and other memorials from the 1600s to the end of the Victorian era and the early years of the twentieth century. The kind of faith reflected in such verses must have been a great comfort to people when death of loved ones occurred with such suddenness and regularity from diseases that are now easily controlled.

In the churchyard there is a small gravestone, and inscribed on it: 'Sacred to the memory of Rebecca Uphill who departed this life September 3rd 1850, aged 25 years.

> O! Ponder well her sudden fall
> Ye thoughtless, blooming wenches all.
> Ye little think who read this stone
> How soon the case may be your own.

The verse, with its dire warning to 'thoughtless, blooming wenches all' refers to the fact that the unfortunate Rebecca Uphill had become pregnant outside wedlock and had, sadly, died on childbirth; death during childbirth was a common occurrence up until the middle of the last century.

Not very far from the church there is a large house also called Llandawke. It was built by Lord Kensington and it replaced a previous house on the same site. In his book *Historic Carmarthenshire Homes* the late Major Francis Jones recounts an interesting tale about the house, and I quote: 'There is a story that a quantity of gold was found buried at the back of the old mansion. And another story tells of a bride being murdered at Llandawke on her wedding day and her body thrown into the pool behind the church. On the same day her husband was also murdered, his body being found outside the church door without any marks of violence on him, the deaths said to be due to jealousy. In the twilight the ghost of the murdered lady, dressed in white with a broad lilac sash tied with a large bow, a large straw hat, and lilac ribbons can be seen leaning over the church gate.'

Are there any volunteers to go along to the churchyard and spend the night there in order to prove whether the ghosts of the unfortunate young couple do appear?

Leaving Llandawke with its unsolved mysteries we travel to Llanddowror. Little do many of the thousands who pass the church of Llanddowror in their cars and coaches on their way to the coast realise the important part the ancient church, standing alongside the main road, has played in the life of Wales.

Except for the tower, which probably dates from the sixteenth century, the church was rebuilt in 1865. It was to this church and parish in 1716, at the age of 33, that the Rev. Griffith Jones was appointed rector by one of his patrons, Sir John Phillips, despite the fact that Griffith Jones had displeased the bishop of St David's on more than one occasion.

Griffith Jones was born in the parish of Penboyr, like Llanddowror, in the county of Carmarthen. He started his working life as a shepherd, but as the result of a religious conversion he decided to enter the Christian ministry. He managed to attend the Grammar School at Carmarthen, and at the age of 25 was ordained as a priest. Following a period as curate at Llandeilo he took up the living of Llanddowror. He was a very active member of the Society for Promoting Christian Knowledge. He soon came to the conclusion that an ability to read The Bible was essential if the Society's aims were to be fulfilled. An attempt had been made to teach monoglot Welsh speakers literacy through the medium of English, and Griffith Jones soon came to the conclusion that the policy was doomed to failure.

In 1713 he started a school in the church porch, his one aim being to teach those who attended the mechanics of reading Welsh, using The Bible as textbook. The school was attended by both children and adults and he chose the best pupils to start similar schools in the neighbouring parishes. The venture was so successful that schools were set up throughout Wales and by the time he died in 1761 over 3,000 schools had been established and 158,000 pupils had attended them. He was greatly helped by Madam Bridget Bevan of Laugharne who provided about £30,000 towards the project.

Griffith Jones's great and very successful achievement was three-fold; firstly, the citizens of Wales became literate; secondly, their knowledge of the contents of The Bible was greatly increased, and thirdly, it helped to an immeasurable extent to keep the Welsh language alive at a time when many in authority were working towards its demise. There was a classic case of this in the 1840s when the government sent three monoglot English speakers to carry out a study of education in Wales. The result was a report that became known, and is still known as 'The Treason of the Blue Books' because it commented on the Welsh character in the most disparaging manner possible.

On the north wall of the church there is a memorial to Griffith Jones inscribed as follows: 'Sacred to the memory of the Rev. Griffith Jones, Rector of this parish and Llandeilo. He was presented to the latter July 3rd 1711, to the former July 27th 1716, and from his first admission to Holy Orders he devoted himself fully to the duties of his sacred function, which he continued faithfully and conscientiously throughout the course of his long life. Conscious of the vocation wherewith he was called he applied himself all his time and attention to that one great concern which came upon him daily, which he enforced upon the minds of his hearers with a truly Christian zeal, and in so interesting a manner that none could depart unaffected or unedified, nor was he an instructor from the pulpit only, his own example added weight to every precept. His whole life was a constant illustration of the religion which he taught. The Welsh Circulating Charity Schools owe their rise, life and progress and continuance to his humane and beneficent disposition; this undertaking was attended with such success of his management and conduct, as at the time of his decease the number of schools exceeded 3,000 and of scholars 158,000. He was indefatigable and successful likewise in procuring two large impressions of the Welsh Bible which were sold at a low price for the benefit of the poor. He composed and published several useful books in the Welsh and English languages. He sought out all opportunities of doing good. It was the business of his life to approve himself on all occasions the vigilant and faithful patron. A sincere and devout Christian, the good man though placed in an inferior position in the Church, performed the cause of religion which would have reflected lustre on the highest. A divine providence which had lent him long as a blessing to his country was pleased to remove him on the 8th day of April 1761 in the 78th year of his age, to an eternity of happiness in heaven where his conversation had always been. This monument was erected by a person desirous of paying every mark of regard to such distinguished merit.'

On the same wall is a memorial to Griffith Jones's supporter in his great work, Madam Bridget Bevan: 'Sacred to the memory of Mrs Bridget Bevan, formerly of Laugharne, who was interred in this church, AD 1779, aged 82 years. This pious and charitable lady was at the expense of educating several young men for the work of the ministry, and contributed largely to the publication and cheap distribution of at least two impressions of Welsh Scriptures. To her the Principality is also indebted, if not for the origin, certainly for the permanent endowment of the Welsh Circulating Charity Schools to which she bequeathed funds amounting together with accumulations which accrued during protracted suit at Chancery to more than £30,000.'

Madam Bridget Bevan was the daughter of John Vaughan of Derllys Court, a mansion not far from Merthyr, some three miles from Carmarthen. She became the wife of Arthur Bevan of Laugharne, one time member of parliament for Carmarthen. Following the death of her father in 1722, she, along with her sisters Arabella and Elizabeth, inherited the Derllys estate. Her inheritance consisted of ninety-two properties and when she died in 1779 she left most of her property to enable the Circulating Schools to continue their good work. However, her will was contested, and the dispute went on in Chancery for thirty years. As a result the schools ran out of money, and had to close.

In the churchyard are several gravestones with inscriptions that may be of interest to the visitor. 'Er cof am Willie Jones, mab John a Mary Jones o'r pentref hwn, yr hwn fu farw Chwefror 7fed 1897 yn 20 oed. Pregethwyd yn ei angladd gan y Parch W.E. Prydderch, Abertawe, ar yr adnod, "Gwell yw enw da nag ennaint gwerthfawr, a dydd marwolaeth na dydd genedigaeth."'

The inscription tells us that 20 year old Willie Jones died on February 7th 1897, and that a Rev. W.E. Prydderch from Swansea preached a sermon at the funeral, his text from Ecclesiastes chapter 7, verse 1: 'A good name is better than precious ointment, and the day of death than the day of one's birth.'

Four graves lie in a row belonging to one family with only one body recorded in each of the three graves and two in the fourth. This is rather similar to a situation I came across in the churchyard at St Florence near Tenby where there a total of ten graves in a row with only one body recorded for each one, and again, all of the same family. Details on the graves in Llanddowror read: 'In memory of Thomas, son of Thomas and Elizabeth Evans of Graigydilo, who died November 22nd 1873, aged 22.

My neighbours all behold and see
How quickly death has conquered me.
You see that I was cut down soon;
My morning sun went down at noon.'

'In memory of Henry, son of Thomas and Elizabeth Evans, Graigydilo, who died December 17th 1875, aged 16.

Days and moments quickly flying,
Blend the living with the dead.
Soon will you and I be lying
Each within a narrow bed.'

'In memory of Daniel, son of Thomas and Elizabeth Evans, who died March 7th 1877, aged 23 years.

Farewell my wife and parents dear,
For me no sorrow take.
Bring up the child in the fear of the Lord,
And love him for my sake.'

A similar sentiment regarding a young son, husband

and father can be seen expressed on a gravestone in Llanllwch churchyard.

The fourth grave in Llanddowror has the following written on the gravestone: 'In memory of Elizabeth, daughter of Thomas and Elizabeth Evans, Graigydilo, who died December 14th 1878, aged 17 years.

> Short was my life,
> Great was my pain,
> Great was your loss,
> But greater my gain.'

In the second of the four graves is buried the mother, Elizabeth Evans, who died June 23rd 1886, aged 67 years, and the verse: 'The Lord gave and the Lord hath taken away, blessed be the Lord.' Job 1:21.

Yes, that last verse was certainly true of this family, losing four children and all so young. This was common place up until the twentieth century, and is still true in so many under-developed countries today. It is also interesting to note that the father's death is not recorded; this often happened to the last member of the family to die, as noted previously.

Before going to Llasteffan we will pay brief visits to the churches of Eglwys Cymyn, Pendine and Llansadurnen. So it is on to the A477 from Llanddowror to Red Roses, there to turn left and soon we reach Eglwys Cymyn.

The church's name is derived from the Latin word Cunegni and the word is inscribed on a fifth century stone in the church. The churchyard is circular, denoting a 'llan', that is, a defensive enclosure that dates from the Age of the Saints. The present building dates from the fourteenth century; it has a vaulted roof, traces of murals and the Ten Commandments in both Welsh and English. These again are possibly from the thirteenth to fifteenth century, and are still visible on the north wall. To the west of the present entrance can be seen the outline of what was once another doorway, now blocked up. There is a memorial stone in the church with an inscription in Latin as well as Irish Ogam. Commemorated on it is Avitoria, daughter of St Cynin, a fifth sixth century saint. The Latin inscription reads: 'AVITORIA FILIA CUNIGINI'. In the windows, parts of which are very old, are depicted St George, St Michael, St Nicholas, St Brychan and St Teilo. Near the font is a window depicting St Cynin.

Near the lych gate is a memorial in the form of a Celtic cross; it commemorates a G.G.T. Treherne who died June 10th 1926. The stone was erected on the orders of his widow and daughters. In a copy of the Carmarthenshire Historian, Vol. XIII, 1976, there is a chapter from Treherne's autobiography. In it he writes that he was born at midnight, December 30th 1837, at Tooting Lodge, Surrey. His father, Rees Goring Thomas – second of the name (his grandfather had changed the surname from Treherne to Thomas) – was Lord of the Manor of Tooting Graveney, and Tooting Lodge was the manor House. At four years of age his family moved to Llannon, four miles from Llanelli where his grandfather's estates were situated. After a few years at Llannon they moved again, this time to Llys Newydd, a mansion on the banks of the river Teifi, near Henllan Bridge.

He was living at Llys Newydd when the Rebecca Riots broke out and a troop from the 4th Light Dragoons, commanded by a Captain Low, was quartered in his house.

He continues by stating that he was sent to school at Stevenage, Hertfordshire, and that it took four days to get there, sleeping one night at the Ivy Bush Hotel, Carmarthen. From Carmarthen to Gloucester he travelled by coach and from Gloucester to London by train. In 1850 he left the school at Stevenage and went to Eton.

In 1847 the family left Llys Newydd and moved to live at Iscoed, Ferryside, the mansion General Sir Thomas Picton had purchased at the beginning of the 1800s for the princely sum of £30,000.

George Treherne went on to study at Oxford University and became a solicitor in 1865. He developed a keen interest in history and was one of the founder members of the Carmarthenshire Antiquarian Society. He became closely associated with Eglwys Cymyn and in the south wall of the chancel there is a window that shows St Nicholas holding in his right hand a model of a yacht. George Treherne was a keen yachtsman and, while sailing in Harwich in 1905, his yacht sank but he was rescued from drowning. This incident led him to design and donate the window to the church. (St Nicholas is reputed to have saved three sailors from Turkey from drowning.)

George Treherne found, according to a report in the Western Mail at the time: 'a stone forming a step on the right of the path leading through the churchyard' that aroused much interest among archaeologists. The article continues: 'Notice of the discovery of an Ogam Stone at Eglwys Cymuun Church, Carmarthenshire by G.G. Treherne and Professor Rees, MA . . . It bears the inscription "AVITORIA FILL CONIGNI", which the able professor interprets with the cunning of the expert learned in the ancient lore of these islands. . . . By means of this inscribed stone, and "mutely eloquent" witnesses of the past, the Celtic scholar is able to draw inferences of great pith and moment. With respect to the Picts and Scots of St David's he writes, "They probably came from

Ireland because the stone had an Ogam inscription as well as a Latin one."'

Commemorated inside the church, on a wooden board, is a reverend gentleman we have come across already when visiting Llandyfaelog Church; he was the Rev. Peter Williams, who published a Welsh Bible. He was curate at Eglwys Cymyn in1744. A first edition of The Bible that he published is to be seen in a wooden display case standing alongside the north wall of the nave. The Bible bears an inscription written by Madam Bevan, the ardent supporter of the Rev. Griffith Jones and his Welsh Circulating Charity Schools.

Also of interest inside the church there can be seen a 'Lists of the Lords of the Manor' from the time of Henry III, and a panel on which are written the names of all the rectors who have served the parish since 1329. There are also copies of paintings of St Margaret on the wall of the church.

To the right of the path leading into the church a memorial on which is written: 'Sacred to the memory of David Lloyd who lived at Middlepool in this parish who died October 11th 1837, aged 80 years.

Death snatched an anxious father first away,
The best of mothers next became his prey.
May he who knows events of future years,
Protect their offspring thro' this vale of tears.'

Also to the memory of Jennet Lloyd, relict of the above David Lloyd. She died May 20th 1840, aged 80 years. Likewise to the memory of Jennet Lloyd, daughter of the above David and Jennet Lloyd; she died July 14th 1840, aged 39 years.

Go home dear friends and shed not a tear,
We must lie here 'till Christ appear.
When He comes we hope to have
A joyful rising from the grave.'

Not far from the church there are earthworks and underneath them, the remains of houses, gardens and fields. They are all that is left of what was at one time a village which, for some unknown reason, has completely disappeared.

Our next stop is the church of St Margaret, Pendine. It stands on a hill in the centre of the old village, or in Welsh, Llandeilo Pentywyn. Most of the church, except for the fifteenth century saddle-back tower, was rebuilt in 1869. The church was described in a document of 1672 as 'out of repair'. The Parish Registers, now in the County Record Office, cover the years 1783 to 1977, and the Bishops' Transcripts in the National Library start in 1716 and end in 1875.

There is a most unusual memorial in the churchyard, which cannot be called a gravestone, although from a distance it looks like one; it is made of cast-iron, red with rust, and on it: 'In memory of Bridget Hodge, Wiseman's Bridge in Amroth Parish, who died October 22nd 1888, aged 87.' Also a gravestone set into the wall that takes us back over three hundred years; Philip Price, died in December 1683, and his son Zecharius (sic), died November 1693.

We continue our journey and travel to Llansadurnen. I believe every visitor would agree with me that it is worthwhile visiting the church if it is only to enjoy the panoramic view from the churchyard. Stretching under and before the visitor is Carmarthen Bay, with the Gower Peninsula on the horizon to the east and Caldey Island to the west. Directly below is the famous Pendine beach, with its golden sand stretching for many miles, the venue over the years of attempts by various people to break the land speed record. Alongside the path into the church there is a sun-dial dated 1805, very similar to one in the churchyard at Llangunnor that dates from the 1700s.

The church is dedicated to St Sadyrnin, a Bishop of St David's, who died in 832 AD. In the Record Office are kept the Parish Registers, baptisms and burials, 1663-1812, marriages, 1677-1969. The Bishops' Transcripts in the National Library are from 1677 to 1888. The present building dates from 1859 but there is a medieval niche in the east wall.

Before returning to Carmarthen let us visit the ancient church at Llansteffan. The church, a cruciform structure with a tall, square tower, nestles among the houses in the centre of the village with the castle, first mentioned in 1146 when it was captured by the English, standing guard over both village and church.

William Spurrell in his book, *Carmarthen and its Neighbourhood*, published in 1879, wrote: 'The castle is said to have been built by Uchtred, Prince of Meirioneth about 1138, soon after which the Normans and Flemings gained possession of it, but it was rescued in 1143 by Meredydd, Rhys and Cadell, sons of Gruffydd ap Rhys, Prince of South Wales. In 1215 Llewelyn ab Iorwerth successively besieged, took and demolished the castles of Carmarthen Llanstephan, St Clears and Laugharne, and in 1257 Llanstephan Castle was again destroyed by Llewelyn ab Gruffydd, following his defeat of the English at Dynevor.'

The church, dedicated to St Stephen, in Welsh, St Ystaffan; he was the founder of the church at this Llanstephan and also the Llanstephan in Radnor. The church was for a time the property of the Knights Hospitallers or Brethren of St John, an Order founded during the Crusades, a series of wars from 1096 to 1291 undertaken by European rulers to recover Palestine from the Muslims. Motivated by religious zeal, the desire for land and the traditional ambitions of the major Italian cities, the Crusades were varied in their aims and effects.

The Parish Registers for Llanstephan and the Bishops' Transcripts are in the National Library at Aberystwyth, the registers from 1697 to 1971 and the transcripts from 1671 to 1884.

The chancel and transepts probably date from the fourteenth century while the nave wagon roof, the east window, the Laques Chapel and the porch date from the sixteenth century. In the chapel there is a monument to David Lloyd, who died in 1670. In the porch there is a holy water stoup, the water used by Catholic worshippers to cross themselves before entering the church. In the tower there is a peal of eight bells that were hung during restoration work carried out in the 1870s, the cost of which was met by a local benefactor, Henry Parnall who had made his money as a draper in London. The gratitude of the parishioners for his undoubted generosity is recorded on a panel in the porch. The font is a Victorian copy of a much older one and paid for by Miss Lloyd of Laques at a cost of £3.15.

John Petts the artist, his wife, son and daughter have left their mark on the church. John Petts designed the oak door and the east window that is entitled The Thanksgiving Window. It depicts the Holy Trinity and it was made in 1980. He also designed frontals for the altar, lectern and pulpit, which were embroidered by his wife, Michael, his son, designed and made the Baptistry Cross and Candlesticks, and Catrin, his daughter, the letters on the Incumbents Board in the porch. Besides the Petts window, there are another six stained glass windows in the church. Among the many memorials on the walls there is one of polished red granite, rather unusual as nearly all wall memorials in our churches are white or black marble, bronze or brass.

In the churchyard there are quite a few gravestones on which are commemorated men who drowned in the nearby Carmarthen Bay and the treacherous river Tywi estuary. Two gravestones testify to the longevity of the Rogers family of Parknook. 'Sacred to the memory of Jane Rogers of Parknook in this parish who died October 23rd 1798, aged 90, Also Jane Rogers of the same place who died May 31st 1828, aged 80. Also George Rogers, Mariner, of the above place of Parknook, who died May 22nd 1832, aged 82, Also Elizabeth Rogers of Parknook who died August 10th 1867, aged 88 years.' And: 'Sacred to the memory of Captain Thomas Rogers of Llanstephan who departed this life December 29th 1858.

> Time was, 'tis past, thou cans't recall,
> Time is, thou hast, the portion small,
> Time future is not, and may never be,
> Time present is the only time for thee.'

The path above the cliff, between the castle and the beach, leads to St Anthony's Well, the waters of which were believed in days gone by to have miraculous properties. When Spurrel wrote his book in 1879 he stated: 'The niche where the image of the saint was placed still remains above the well.' I can remember as a child going to the well and, like others who visited it, dropping a pin into the water and making a wish; this was supposed to bring good fortune to all who did so. This practice was very popular with young girls whose wish was usually that they would meet and marry a handsome man.

And so we leave Llanstephan and head back towards Carmarthen, not that our wandering has come to an end; there are many more churches for us to visit in Carmarthenshire and in other neighbouring counties.

Churches to the north of Carmarthen

Six miles north of Carmarthen is the church of Llanpumsaint, 'the church of the five saints'. They were Gwyn, Gwynno, Gwynoro, Ceitho and Celynin. Tradition has it that they were five brothers, in fact, quintuplets. More than one legend surrounds their lives. It is said that they were the sons of Cynyr Farwyn of Cynwyl Gaio, and that in that parish there is a stone on which there are five hollows where the five are said to have laid their heads to sleep. In the river Gwili at Llanpumsaint there are five pools, whose waters, it is claimed, alleviate arthritic pain. In the church there is a squint, a small window through which lepers would be able to watch the incumbent celebrating Holy Communion at the altar. Beneath the altar there is a stone on which are inscribed five crosses, but although some people attribute them to the saints the reality is that they represent the five wounds of Christ on the cross. The visitor, on standing at the west end of the church, will notice that the nave and chancel are not in line, the church at Llangunnor having the same feature. Such churches are called 'weeping churches', and are reminders of the winding road to the cross on Calvary, the Via Dolorosa in Jerusalem.

Legend has it that when the five brothers reached the hills surrounding Llanpumsaint they had made up their minds to build a church in the area but were undecided as to where exactly it should be built. In order to ascertain the exact spot where it should be constructed they decided that one of them was to twirl a hammer around his head, in the manner of throwing a discus, let it go, and wherever it landed was where the church would stand.

On a table under the pulpit is a statuette of the

Madonna and Child and inscribed around its base is: 'Er cof am Sarah Anne Thomas, Brynmeillion, 1906-1992.' On the sill of the window of the south wall, near to where the chancel begins, there is a statuette of St David. Inscribed on it: 'Er gogoniant i Dduw, ac i gofio'n dyner am Canon John Byron Davies, BA, Ficer y Plwyf hwn, 1967-1974.' In the Madonna and Child a parishioner is commemorated; the St David statuette commemorates a vicar who served the parish. There are also stained glass windows in the church.

Under an ancient yew tree that stands to the north of the church is a simple, plain, slate gravestone. On it are inscribed details of a person the vast majority might not have heard of but her life is full of interest to the historian. The casual visitor's interest might not possibly be aroused by reading the inscription, and he or she would leave the churchyard none the wiser. It reads: 'Er cof am David Lloyd, Glanrafon, o'r pentref hwn, bu farw Gorffennaf 28ain 1844 yn 84 mlwydd oed. Hefyd am Martha, ei wraig, bu farw Hydref 16eg 1845 yn 79 oed. "Coffadwriaeth y cyfiawn sydd fendigedig."' Also on the same memorial: 'Hefyd am Mary Lloyd, Lleine, orwyres yr uchod, bu farw Gorffennaf 21ain 1931 yn 82 mlwydd oed.' The words on the stone tell us that buried in the grave are husband and wife David and Martha Lloyd, and their great-granddaughter, Mary Lloyd. Glanrafon; their home a semi-detached cottage across the road from the church, and facing School House.

Of the three mentioned, the person that is of interest is Martha Lloyd. Among many other events, the eighteenth century is remembered in Wales for 'The Methodist Revival' that took place during those years. It spread throughout the country, and three names associated with it stand out – Howell Harries, Daniel Rowlands and

William Williams Pantycelyn. It is reported that Howell Harries preached at Llanpumsaint, before the disagreement in 1749 that soured the relationship between him and Daniel Rowlands. Some of Rowlands's followers moved to live in the Llanpumsaint district, among them a David Lloyd. He married Martha in 1785 when she was nineteen years of age. Daniel Rowlands officiated at the wedding. Martha was born on a farm called Nantbendigaid in 1766, in the parish of Cynwyl Elfed, a parish next to the parish of Llanpumsaint.

Martha had very little education, if at all when a child, and it can be seen that she could not write because, in the Marriage Register, she put a cross where her name should have been written. Her husband, David, was a counsellor in the Methodist Fellowship, and according to a short biography of Martha's life written by a person who called himself Rhuddfawr, the couple were pillars of the Methodist movement in the area.

They had nine children, and it is very surprising to learn that she is described as 'feeble and frail'. However, for much of her life she was severely disabled, unable to walk, and was carried to chapel in a kind of sedan chair by two men.

During the time she lived in Llanpumsaint, a Carmarthenshire man by birth, Thomas Charles, or to give the name he is usually called, Thomas Charles o'r Bala', started the Sunday Schools in Wales, and Martha became a faithful member of the school that was established in the village. At the school she must have learnt to read and write because according to the biography, she wrote some two hundred verses, one of the verses describing her own ill-health.

Wel bellach, frodyr, dewch,
Pwy wyr na chewch eich gwrando.
Gweddiwch ar Jehofa'r berth
Am ychydig nerth i'm eto,
Fel gallwyf ddod oddiyma'n rhwydd
I dŷ yr Arglwydd weithiau,
Rhyfeddod fraint i mi fan hyn
Gael dyfod ar ffyn baglau.

A rough translation of the verse reads: Come now, brothers dear,/Who knows your plea may be heard./ Pray to God on my behalf/To give me a little strength once more,/Enabling me to move with ease from here/ Occasionally to visit God's house./A wondrous privilege to me,/To do so on my crutches.

It is also said that the 'Prince' of Welsh hymn-writers, William Williams, Pantycelyn, visited Martha on numerous occasions; one can easily believe this because he used to travel roughly three thousand miles a year on horseback, preaching throughout Wales and also selling tea. His influence can be seen in some of her hymns:

Mae fy nghalon yn hiraethu
Am gael gweld eto'r wawr,
Rhwygo teyrnas y tywyllwch,
A gweld caerau'n dod i lawr.
Gweled Iesu a'i ogoniant
Yn ben moliant yn y byd,
A gweled miloedd di-rifedu'n
Dod i garu'r Iesu 'nghyd.

Roughly translated it reads: My heart yearns/To see once more the dawn/Of tearing down the kingdom of darkness,/And its fortresses falling/To see Jesus in all

His glory,/Praised above all else on earth,/And to see untold thousands/Turning to Jesus with all their love.

Some of her poems are reminiscent of the work of the famous vicar of Llandovery, Rhys Pritchard, 1579-1644.

> Y bachgen a aned, Mab rhoddwyd yn rhad,
> Ar fore Nadolig, mae'n debyg fe'i cad.
> Mab tragwyddoldeb mewn undeb a dyn,
> Ym Mhethlem gan Mari yn cymryd Ei drin.

[The boy that was born, a Son freely given,/On Christmas morn, it seems He came forth./The Father eternal in union with man./In Bethlehem see Mary attending the One.]

I became acquainted with the life story of Martha Llwyd during the time I lived in Llanpumsaint, 1956-64. The members of the Womens' Institute of the county arranged a pageant in the grounds of Cydweli Castle. The local branch of the movement performed as part of the pageant, the story of Martha Llwyd. The local carpenter, the late Jim Evans, was asked to make the, 'sedan chair', and one of the members of the W.I. played the part of Martha and was carried in the chair by four other members. The performance was much appreciated by all those who saw the pageant.

Before leaving this peaceful location let us read a few inscriptions on other stones in the churchyard. 'Er cof am Thomas, mab Evan ac Anne Thomas, Gwndwngwyn, plwyf Cynwyl, bu farw Gorffennaf 22ain 1880 yn 18 oed.

> Blodeuyn hardd a theg ei wawr
> Yn fore iawn a dorrwyd lawr.
> O blith y byw i byrth y bedd,
> Gan angau glas a'i finiog gledd.'

Translated, it tells us that an 18 year old son named Thomas had died, and the verse reads: A beautiful and pleasant flower,/Early one morning was cut down,/From the living to grave's door/By death's sharp, steel sword.

Another inscription on another gravestone reads: 'Sacred to the memory of the wife of the Rev. William Henry Powell, Pantycelyn, in this parish, who departed this life the 3rd day of May in the year 1858, aged 64 years. "Blessed are the dead which die in the Lord from henceforth. Yea, saith the Spirit that they may rest from their labours, and their works do follow them also." In loving memory of the above named Rev. William Henry Powell who died September 28th 1879, aged 82 years. He served the churches of Llanpumsaint and Llanllawddog for the long period of 53 years, first as Curate and afterwards as Incumbent, and was distinguished as an able preacher and an impressive reader of Divine Services, as well as for his extensive knowledge of Holy Scriptures.'

Another gravestone records the death of six children in infancy of the Rev. Evan Davies and his wife Mary, and as if that was not enough of a tragedy, the passing of another three, aged 2, 4 and 17 years. 'Er coffadwriaeth am chwech o blant y Parch Evan Davies a Mary, ei wraig, a fuont farw yn eu babandod. Thomas a fu farw Mawrth 13eg 1870 yn 2 flwydd oed, Mary Ann, fu farw Mai 9fed 1878 yn 4 mlwydd oed, David Llawddog a fu farw Gorffennaf 1af 1878 yn 17 oed.'

And now permit me to digress. I have already stated that I lived in Llanpumsaint during the 1950s and 1960s. It was in School House that I and my family spent eight years, from 1956 to 1964. I digress not in order that I could make that fact known but because the history of the school and School House are worth recalling.

A boy was born in the year 1788 in a farm called Tredarren, the farm situated between Llanpumsaint and Cynwyl Elfed. The boy's name was William Williams, not to be confused with William Williams, Pantycelyn. The education this boy from Tredarren received was minimal; he attended a school held in Llanpumsaint Church for a short time but the lack of education did not deter him from becoming, in later life, an industrialist and a politician. Having made his money in the cotton trade, in 1835, at 47 years of age, he was elected Member of Parliament for Coventry, and served that city until 1847. Three years later he was made a Member of Parliament for the borough of Lambeth, representing that part of London until his death in 1865, aged 77 years.

Surprising as it may seem to most Welsh men and women today, William Williams was convinced that the Welsh language was a hindrance to the people of Wales if they wanted to 'get on in the world'. In 1846 he stood up in the House of Commons to ask a question about the state of education in Wales, and 'praying Her Majesty to direct an inquiry to be made in the Principality of Wales, especially into the means afforded to the labouring classes of acquiring knowledge of the English language.' The Secretary of State for the Home Department decided that such an inquiry should be instituted and three Englishmen were appointed – R.R.W. Lingen, MA, Fellow of Balliol College, Oxford, J.C. Symons and Henry Vaughan Johnson, the last person's name was at least a corruption of a Welsh word and surname, Fychan. Lingen covered the three counties of Glamorgan, Carmarthen and Pembroke. Symons looked into the situation in the counties of Brecon, Cardigan, Radnor and Monmouth. Johnson covered North Wales. In 1847 they published the report and, as I have previously stated, condemned the people of Wales out of hand (see The Treason of the Blue Books).

However, one good thing resulted from the inquiry; William Williams had the school and School House built in Llanpumsaint and the school opened in 1862. Not surprisingly, the first headteacher appointed by Mr Williams was a monoglot English speaker who had been trained at Borough Road Teachers' Training College, London. Nevertheless it must be said that William Williams was very concerned with the state of education in the country, and he played a prominent part in the movement to establish the University of Wales.

Before leaving Llanpumsaint let us look at one other gravestone, the inscription in Welsh containing a number of errors: 'Yma y gorwedd Marwol ran Deiiana Willia(ms), Calcyt, ymhlwyf Co(n)wil. Rhon a fy farw y Dydd 1 o Fai 1831, Oediog 35 O flwyddau.' It should have read: 'Yma gorwedd marwol rhan Diana Williams, Calcut, ym mhlwyf Cynwyl, yr hon a fu farw y dydd 1af o Fai 1831, yn 35 mlwydd oed.' The letters in brackets had originally been left out of the inscription and scratched into the stone at a later date. The writing tells us that a Diana Williams of Calcut, in the parish of Cynwyl died May 1st 1831, aged 35 years.

In 1955 Aneirin Talfan Davies's excellent book, *Crwydro Sir Gâr*, was published. Among the places he visited was the isolated chapel of Ffynnonhenry, located off the beaten track between Llanpumsaint and the village of Cynwyl Elfed. The author tells us that the road leading to the chapel was extremely narrow with many twists and turns. But, on arriving at his destination, he found the chapel standing at the bottom of an idyllic, steep-sided valley. Running alongside the chapel was a bubbling stream of clear water. He goes on to inform the reader that there was not a house in sight, nor a living soul to be seen.

Aneirin Talfan Davies had gone to Ffynnonhenry in order to see the chapel in which, for a time during the 1800s, a certain Dafydd Evans was the minister in charge. Dafydd Evans, a Baptist, was a gifted preacher, and his sermons were full of natural humour, something the stalwarts of nonconformity failed to appreciate.

Some years after reading Talfan Davies's account, I decided to follow in his footsteps. One summer afternoon in the late 90s of the last century, nearly half a century after his visit, I set out to the chapel. Aneirin Talfan Davies had approached the chapel from Cynwyl Elfed; I journeyed to it from Llanpumsaint. Taking the wrong turning, I found myself at the dead end of a very narrow lane, and had to reverse the car about two hundred yards. Fortunately, I did eventually reach a spot where I could turn the car around, receiving assistance from a farmer driving a four-wheel vehicle. Not only did he give me such assistance but he also directed me to the chapel. It was a matter of going back along the road I had already journeyed for a matter of half a mile, turn right at a junction, and sure enough, after about another half a mile the chapel came into view.

Talfan Davies description of the chapel and its location could not be bettered. The typically box-shaped chapel stood a few yards from a bubbling stream and on each side, the land rose steeply skywards. The peace, isolation and silence of the location could be felt. A question some may ask is, 'Why build a chapel in such an isolated spot and so far from human habitation?' The answer is simple; it has not always been the case that the religious freedom we enjoy in this country today was previously enjoyed by the people at the time when the chapel, along with many other chapels in equally isolated places, was built.

Whoever decided upon where it was to be erected must have been prepared for some hard work since it stands where the solid rock has been hacked out of one side of the valley. One thing that can be said about the chapel is that it was most definitely 'built on the rock'. Set high up, and built into the front wall, are two stone tablets. On the top of one are the initials of four people, possibly the founding fathers – DE, JD, RW, EE, and the date 1714. On the other tablet: 'This chapel was rebuilt in the year 1828 by James Davies and David Evans – Ministers, and John Williams and Evan Evans- Deacons.'

The graveyard is divided into three parts by both the stream and also the narrow road that passes alongside. On the other side of the road the graveyard is on an extremely steep slope, and taking a heavy oak coffin up to a grave must have been, and possibly still is, both difficult and dangerous for the bearers, especially during frosty weather.

On one side of the stream, away from the chapel, inscriptions on three slate memorials are worth recalling. The middle stone records the death of 'John, the son of Thomas and Rachel Griffiths of Bedw, in the parish, who died May 21st 1850, aged 21 years.

> Ni chawn dreulio'r dydd i ben,
> Cyn un o'r gloch ces ergyd marwol,
> Cwympodd daear ar fy mhen.'

[In the morning I never thought/I would not see the end of day./The earth above fell on my head.]

It goes without saying that this young man must have

been killed when the ground above him smothered him. It makes one wonder what exactly happened; if it was in a mining area it would be understandable, but in such a rural environment it is difficult to really understand what exactly happened. The next stone, on the left of that recording John Griffiths's death, tells us of the death of his brother, David, who died five years later, age 18 years, but the verse, unlike that for John Griffiths, does not give a clue as to what caused his death.

> 'Blodau ieuenctid syrthio wnaeth
> Trwy angau caeth i'r beddrod.
> Rwy nawr yn llechu yn y llwch,
> A'm tegwch wedi darfod.'

[The flower of youth fell,/Imprisoned by death and the grave./I now am lying in the dust,/My beauty disappeared.]

The third family memorial stone records the death of the two young men's parents: 'Er cof am eu rhieini, Thomas Griffiths o'r Bedw yn y plwyf hwn a fu farw Ionawr 31ain 1871 yn 68 oed. Hefyd am Rachel, ei wraig, yr hon fu farw Ionawr 21ain 1870 yn 69 oed.'

It is strange to see three graves and three stones for just four bodies; no scarcity of land in those days. It is also interesting to note that in this particular graveyard four line verses on the stones was very prevalent, and here is another example. The inscription records the death of David Davies, Closybugail (what a beautiful Welsh name for a farm, The Shepherd's Farmyard), a farm within the parish, who died October 14th 1809, aged 60, and this verse:

Oddiwrth ei lafur gorffwys mae,
Gadawodd wae a gwasgfa.
Fe gwyd i'r lan yn llon ryw bryd
Gan floedd yr utgorn ola.

Translated it tells us that From his labours now he rests/ All pressures and troubles left behind/ One day he will joyfully rise/ To the sound of the last trumpet/

Before leaving this haven of peace and tranquillity I must mention Dafydd Efans, a gifted minister. He served the chapel and its members for a number of years. He was noted for his humour, wit and dramatic presentations from the pulpit. He also spent some time in Carmarthen Jail, serving a sentence for an offence that he never committed.

A staunch Baptist, he was anything but a puritan in his outlook and philosophy of life. Benjamin Thomas, bardic name Myfyr Emlyn, wrote a biography entitled *Cofiant Dafydd Evans*, 'A Biography of Dafydd Evans', first published in 1870 and reprinted and republished on a number of occasions since then. One of his gifts was that he could tell stories from the Bible in a way and idiom that would be familiar to his listeners. He turned the account in the book of Genesis of Noah building the Ark into a drama that must have brought a smile to the faces of many in his congregation. His account would also have brought home to them a very important Christian concept – the true extent of the Salvation offered to mankind through Jesus Christ.

His dramatic sermon opens with Noah's son, Sem, asking his father, 'What size should the door of the ark be?'

'Look at the plan,' Noah replied.

'I have looked, but it isn't down on it,' said Sem, 'you have a look.'

'Well, it isn't, too,' said Noah, 'Go and find an elephant, and when he walks between two trees mark on the trees its height and width. As long as we make a door big enough for him, every other creature will manage to get in.'

Shortly afterwards Sem returned with a very long face and told his father that he had seen a giraffe.

'Wel, that old gentleman will have to bend down, or remain outside,' said Noah, 'Salvation's extent? The same extent as the greatest sinner. The door is both high and wide enough. The biggest of all the elephants has managed to get in. Even old elephants like Saul the persecutor and Manasseh the murderer; they both got in. And then the Corinthian elephants and the she elephant Mary Magdalene, and the old elephant standing before you – all will or eventually get inside! As for the Pharisees, the giraffes that they are, they will have to bend their heads in order to be able to enter the ark.'

And that is the kind of sermon that the members of Ffynnonhenry chapel, and all the other chapels he preached in listened to. It could not possibly have been described as – Boring!

And now we must leave this remote, little known, but idyllic spot, and move on of a couple of miles, to visit the church at Cynwyl Elfed. Dedicated to a sixth century saint, the church is one of three bearing his name, the other two Cynwyl Gaio in north Carmarthenshire and Aberporth in Ceredigion. The church at Cynwyl Elfed is tucked in between two houses and back from the A484 road between Carmarthen and Cardigan via Newcastle Emlyn.

St Cynwyl was a brother of St Deiniol who became Bishop of Bangor; its cathedral dedicated to him. It is said that Deiniol is one of the 20,000 saints buried on Bardsey

Island, off the Llŷn Peninsula.

Cynwyl is mentioned in The Mabinogion; in 'Culhwch and Olwen' he is the third man that escaped from the battle of Camlan, and he was the last who parted from Arthur on Hengroen his horse. In Emlyn Jenkins' book *Cofiant Elfed* he wrote the following about Cynwyl Elfed: In the 1860s Christmas did not mean much to its inhabitants: 'It was half Sunday and half work-day, a colourless day. People were afraid to work and avoided amusing themselves at all costs. Its chief importance was that it was within a week of New Year's Day, the biggest day of the year for us children.'

The little church, with its simple bell-cote, has twin naves, the original dating from the fourteenth century while a new chancel and nave were added in the sixteenth century; this is something that happened to many of the churches in the Diocese at that time. The font and stoup at the west end of the church are also thought to date from the fourteenth century.

The Church was at one time a Chapel of Ease to the Parish church of Abernant and during the Norman period was dedicated to St Michael. When the Norman influence waned the dedication reverted to its original – St Cynwyl, and it has remained so over the centuries to this day. During the twelve hundreds a Mardydd ap Richard attacked the town of Carmarthen and its Priory. In 1290 Mardydd, as an atonement for perpetrating what was considered a crime, endowed land to the Priory Church at Carmarthen and the names of the Church of Abernant and the Chapel of Ease at Cynwyl Elfed are mentioned in a document drawn up at the time. On the 30th of December 1401 an episcopal injunction stated that the obventions and oblations (1. act of making a religious offering – the act of offering the Eucharistic elements to

God, 2. Something offered in worship or devotion: a holy gift offered usually at an altar or shrine) of the Chapel of Abernant were assigned to the office of cellarer of the Priory to minister to its necessities.

The Parish Registers, dating from 1743, are now in the National Library of Wales at Aberystwyth. Facsimile copies are kept in the church itself. The Registers, like all Parish Registers, are a rich source of information about the social life of parishioners down through the years. One entry records that the Rev. Peter Williams, who became a household name in Wales through the Welsh Bible he produced, was ordained and licensed by the then Bishop of St David's to read Prayers in the Parish of Abernant with the Chapel of Ease at Cynwyl Elfed.

Some two feet from the south wall of the Chancel there is a large stone slab lying on top of supporting brickwork. The inscription on it is difficult to read, but some words can be recognised. Buried in the grave under the slab is a Thomas Howell who was born in 1661 and died in 1720. This Thomas Howell claimed that he was descended from 'The ancient Princes of Caernarvon'. He was undoubtedly a cousin of the author and Royalist James Howell and of Thomas Howell who became Bishop of Bristol. His uncle, another Thomas Howell, was his cousins' father, and was Vicar of Abernant and Cynwyl Elfed from 1589 to 1631. The Howells' family home was Pen-y-Caerau which stood about two miles south-east of the village of Cynwyl. The last in the male line of the family was a Benjamin Howell, who drowned in the river Gwili around the year 1715.

The Royalist James Howell was born in 1593 and died aged 69 in 1666, having lived an eventful life. He was educated at Jesus College, Oxford, and had a flair for languages. Returning home in 1623 after much travelling in Europe, he was sent to Madrid by merchants of the Turkey Company to try and obtain compensation for a ship that had been captured by Sardinians who were at the time subject to Spain. He was a secret agent to the Earl of Stratford, who was beheaded in the Tower of London. James Howell went on several diplomatic missions and was well known in the Royal Courts of Denmark and Spain. His literary achievements led him to become well acquainted with Ben Johnson. Being a gifted linguist, he compiled a Dictionary in four languages – English, French, Italian and Spanish, with an appendix of Welsh proverbs added. Not only a linguist, he also wrote many books and pamphlets, his chief writings being Epistolae Ho Elinae, Dodona's Grove, and Familiar Letters; the books were translated into French, Dutch and Latin, resulting in their distribution in a number of European countries. In addition to all this he was a Member of Parliament for Richmond and, following the Restoration of Charles II, he was appointed by the king as Historiographer Royal. On his death in 1666 he was buried in the Temple Church, London.

Thomas Howell, James' brother, and cousin to the Thomas Howell who lies in Cynwyl Elfed churchyard, also attended Oxford University. There he was very successful and distinguished himself in the academic field. Ordained in the Church of England he was appointed Vicar of St Stephen's Church, Walbrook, London, a Canon of Windsor and Chaplain to King Charles I. Described as a man 'of great candour, solid judgement, sweet temper and good repute' he became Bishop of Bristol. During the Civil War of 1642 to 1649 he suffered greatly as a result of Thomas Fairfax, a General and Commander-in-Chief of the Parliamentary Army's forces attack on Bristol in September 1645. His palace was pillaged, the lead was stripped off the roof under which his wife lay in childbirth, and this resulted in her death. He was also violently ejected from his high office, and the rough treatment he received at the hands of the Cromwellians undoubtedly hastened his demise in 1646. He was buried in the Cathedral, his grave marked by the Latin word 'Expergiscar' – 'awake; bestir oneself'. The citizens of Bristol undertook the care and education of his orphaned children 'in grateful memory of their most worthy father'. He was considered to be an excellent preacher, described by Fuller as follows: 'His sermons were like the waters of Siloah softly gliding on with a smooth stream; and his matter did steal secretly the hearts of his hearers'. He has also been described as 'a person of great clearness, candour, solidness, sweetness and eloquence with an insight into state affairs as well as those of his own office as Bishop'.

The names of all the Vicars who have served the Parish since 1552 are known, one, named David Lewis, having held the office for an incredible sixty-four years, from 1787 to 1851. Of other clerics who have served the parish, their incumbency exceeded forty years each.

The east window depicts the five wounds of the crucified Jesus. There are sixteenth century windows in the church and an early English holy water stoup with a trifoliated head, symbolising the Holy Trinity, built into the wall behind the font. It is reported that the church had at one time an Elizabethan chalice bearing the inscription 'Poculum Eclesie De Kinwill, 1574'. It was kept in the Churchwarden's house, but unfortunately the chalice was destroyed in a fire in Lleine farm in 1915.

Leaving the church at Cynwyl Elfed, we head along the A484 towards Llangeler, passing through the hamlet of Cwmduad with its small church standing on rising ground to the left of the road. The church is dedicated to St Alban who was the first martyr in Britain. He was, according to St Gildas, beheaded at Verulamium, today known by the martyr's name, St Albans in Hertfordshire.

The church in Llangeler stands alongside a narrow bend, the churchyard wall forming one side of the road. The church is dedicated to a St Celer and the water from a well (Ffynnon Geler) named after him and located not far from the church, is said to contain medicinal properties. Ffynnon Geler was, until the eighteenth century, a well that was visited by pilgrims in order to bathe in its water. Edward Llwyd wrote in *Parochalia:* Not far from the church at the bottom of a steep hill issueth forth a fountain. Over the fall thereof a little chapel is erected. Hither every summer infirm people make a frequent resort, but particularly from the 21st of June to the feast of St Peter (June 29th) there will be such a concourse of people that no fair in Wales can equal in multitude, out of an opinion that the saint imbued it with such virtue as will cure infirmities. The tradition obtains that about two years since, some infirm persons left their crutches behind in the church in memory of their being cured by bathing in this well."

On the south wall of the vestry there is a memorial, its inscription difficult to decipher. However, it is possible to make out that it commemorates a Thomas James of Henfryn who died April 3rd 1795, aged 35 years, also Thomas James, son of the aforesaid, who died November 1st. 1812, aged 27 years, also Rebecca, wife of Thomas James senior, who died January 9th 1819, aged 60 years.

It is reported that Thomas James senior took part in a horse race against a John Beynon of Newcastle Emlyn through Llandysul. On approaching the bridge over the river Teifi, James' horse failed to negotiate the very sharp bend leading to the bridge, and both horse and rider fell into the river, resulting in the death of both Thomas James and his horse.

This memorial may be linked to one in Llangunnor Church. Low down in the north wall of the Sanctuary in the church is a black, rectangular stone on which is recorded: 'Sacred to the memory of Harriet Elen James the wife of Tudor James of Henfryn in the parish of Llangeler in this county who died June 20th 1720, aged 20 years.' I am left with the unanswered question as to why Elen James is commemorated in a very important position within the church despite there being no record of her having been buried either inside the building or out in the churchyard at Llangunnor.

To return to the church at Llangeler; on the south wall there are twelve memorials, all in memory of members of the Lewes family of Llys Newydd, and also a memorial on the north wall which recalls a Lieut. Col William Lewes, DL, JP, who died August 18th 1952. He is buried in the churchyard.

Llys Newydd has been in the hands of the Lewes family since 1610, when it was bought by a John Lewes, third son of David Lewes of Gernos, Ceredigion. Towards the end of the eighteenth century the original house was pulled down and around the years 1790 to 1800 a new house was built, the architect being none other than John Nash. He was the person that designed the prison at Carmarthen; a ceiling for St Peter's Church, that subsequently collapsed; Regent Street in London and also Clarence House as well as the Pavilion in Brighton. By August 1971 however Nash's work in the county had disappeared and it is now only visible in photographs or paintings and in the memory of some local inhabitants. The imposing house which stood on the west side of the road between the village of Drefach and Henllan bridge was demolished on the orders of the last owner, J.P. Ponsonby Lewis of Llanaeron, Ceredigion. The house had been owned and lived in by the Lewes family for over three hundred and fifty years and I am left wondering why a house with so much history attached to it had to be destroyed.

In the churchyard there is a gravestone on which is inscribed a couplet written in Latin and a most unusual name to the house of the person commemorated on it: 'To the memory of David Parry, Parcswadog, in this parish who died 25th June 1854, aged 73.

Malum, mali, malo, mala,
Conulit omnia mundo.
Time runs on, we daily see,
Into that eternity.
Make good use of time today
Every moment seems to say.'

A David Oliver of Llwynderw who died January 1st 1852, aged 38 years is commemorated with this verse:

The poor, the rich, the conqueror, the slave,
Must all become tenants of the grave;
And all must rise – but to a different lot,
As they who have served the Lord, or served Him not.

On leaving Llangeler we make our way to another church near the river Teifi – the church at Llanllwni. The traveller will have to look hard for the church because it stands on rising ground a mile or two to the west of the Carmarthen to Lampeter road. The church, according to the St David's Diocesan Year Book, boasts two dedications, to St Luke and to St Llonio. St Luke should not be difficult to identify but St Llonio is another matter. In his book *The Book of Welsh Saints* T.D. Breverton calls the saint Llwni of whom, he admits, nothing as yet is known.

To reach the church one must turn off the A485 and travel along a narrow road for approximately a mile to a mile and a half. The church's solid square tower, nave and chancel all have thirteenth century walls, and the edifice is surrounded by a large churchyard, the east end of which rises steeply. It is in a delightful location above the river Teifi, with rolling farmland to the south and east and Llanllwni Mountain on the horizon. The views to the west and south are blotted out by trees. In the churchyard there are some interesting gravestones, tombs and inscriptions.

To the left of the path leading into the church there is a small, white marble 'angel', and buried in the grave beneath, two children who died in 1911 and 1913. The rather charming inscription reads: 'October 23rd 1911, Death's angel came for Harriet Mary Eva (Eva Fach), the beloved child of D. Channing and Harriet E. Thomas, aged eight months. Likewise January 29th 1913, Thomas Theodore (Theo Bach) of the same parents, aged one month.' Adjacent to the children's grave is that of the parents – Harriet (Meck), 1873-1956, and D. Channing Thomas, The Ton, Llandysul, 1879-1960. Underneath the wife's name: 'She lived for those she loved, and those she loved remember.' On the plinth below a vase: 'In the garden of memories it is always summer.'

Not far from the church door is a grey, slate stone with, an inscription in Welsh: 'Er coffadwriaeth am blant Thomas a Mary Parry, Brynmartin, plwyf Llandysul, y rhai a fu farw fel y canlyn, John, a fu farw Mawrth 15fed 1851 yn 2 oed, Thomas, a fu farw Medi 9fed 1858 yn 5 oed.

Gyda Crist a chyda'u gilydd,
Iddynt gwn yn llawer gwell.
Wedi cwrdd mae John a Thomas
Yn y tragwyddoldeb pell.'

Commemorated are two brothers who died ages two and five years. The verse maintains that both are together with Christ; that they are better off than while living on earth, and that the brothers have met in far off eternity.

The visitor, while exploring the churchyard, will, I feel sure, be very surprised on coming across two most unusual tombs; each one unique in its own way. I venture to use the word unique to describe them. A few feet from the east wall of the church there is a mausoleum-like construction of dressed stone with a flat stone across its top. There is on its west-end a heavy, padlocked iron door, the door reminding me of the oven door in the kitchen of my home when I was a child. On the west-end there is a white marble tablet on which is inscribed: 'In memory of Charles Edward Bowen, infant son of Charles and Margaret Lloyd of Waunifor, born March 24th, died May 14th 1877. "And Jesus called a little child unto Him."'

On the south wall another tablet on which is written: 'In memory of the Rev. Charles Lloyd, MA of Waunifor in the county of Cardigan, for 31 years Rector of the parishes of Betws Bledrws and Cellan in the same county, died 9th June 1867, aged 61 years. "All things work together for good to them that love God." Also of Frances Elizabeth Lloyd, wife of the above, died May 15th 1888, aged 73.'

Waunifor stands on the bank of the river Teifi, not far from the hamlets of Maesycrugiau and Capel Dewi. Waunifor is mentioned in a will that was proved in 1655.

The Bowen family were descendants of a David ap

Rhydderch whose son Owen was an Attorney in Sessions. As a result of hearing a sermon preached by Daniel Rowland, a Thomas Bowen, who lived between 1727 and 1805, paid for the erection of a Methodist Chapel, Capel Waunifor.

The estate was later inherited by a John Lloyd, son of John Lloyd of Gilfachwen. It was from his brother John that the Rev. Charles Lloyd commemorated on this tomb inherited Waunifor.

The other 'unique' tomb in the churchyard, that stands a few feet to the east of the Waunifor grave, is in the form of a Caernarvon-slated, saddle-roofed, dressed stone, one-roomed cottage. On the arched recessed west wall there is a white marble tablet surmounted by a cross. Inscribed on it: 'Also to the treasured memory of Sir Courtney Cecil Mansel, 11th Baronet, of Maesycrugiau Manor in this parish, born 25th February 1880, died 4th January 1933.' On the east wall another inscription: 'In memory of Elisa Rosa, second daughter of John and Elisa Jones, Maesycrugiau Manor, and wife of Henry Harries Davies, Surgeon, Llandysul, born March 17th 1850, died September 9th 1894. This tablet was erected by the son of the above – John Bowen Davies.'

On the north wall: 'In loving memory of Henry Jones who died at Maesycrugiau, 18th June 1848, aged 21 years. "Heb Dduw, heb ddim; Duw, a digon" (Without God, without anything; God, and plenty). Also M.S.M.B. Mansel, wife of Sir Richard Mansel, Bart, and beloved daughter of Elisa Jones of Maesycrugiau, Carms., born June 1861, died 12th September 1885. "The Lord gave and the Lord takes away. Blessed be the name of the Lord"' And finally, on the south wall: 'In affectionate remembrance of John Jones of Maesycrugiau, who died June 28th 1877, aged 63 years. "Have faith in God. Be ready for ye know not what a day may bring forth." And of Elisa, wife of the above, who died January ?? 1897, aged 6? Years. "For the Lord is a great God."'

Maesycrugiau Manor is mentioned in the year 1609 when Dwnn stayed there in order to record the family history of the then owner, a John Lloyd. By the first half of the 1700s the house was in the possession of a Thomas Thomas and his daughter Margaret's first husband was a John Bowen of Waunifor. By the end of the 1700s the estate comprised of some sixty properties in Carmarthenshire and Ceredigion. By 1862 the Manor was owned by a John Jones whose daughter Maud Margaretta married Sir Richard Mansel, Baronet, and descendants of theirs occupied the house until well into the 1900s.

Not far from the church at Llanllwni are two other churches that are worth a visit – St David, Capel Dewi, near Llandysul, and St Michael, Troed-yr-Aur, near Newcastle Emlyn.

In the churchyard at Capel Dewi, on the north side of the church, stands a gravestone of blue-grey slate with an inscription that tells the reader of a tragic event that happened on a farm in the parish of Llanwennog in March 1875. The inscription reads as follows:

Er coffadwriaeth am blant
John a Margaret Davies,
Brynllwyd, Plwyf Llanwenog,
Pa rai bu farw fel y canlyn.

William Davies a fu farw yn ei fabandod
Tachwedd 1af 1874.

Evan a fu farw Mawrth 2 1875 yn 5 oed,
Hannah a fu farw Mawrth 3ydd 1875 yn 11 oed,

Johnny a fu farw Mawrth 4ydd 1875 yn 3 oed,
David a fu farw Mawrth 5ed 1875 yn 14 oed,
Tom a fu farw Mawrth 5ed 1875 yn 8 oed.

Hefyd eu tad, John Davies, yr hwn a fu farw
Mehefin 13eg 1894 yn 63 oed.

Hefyd am chwech o'u plant a fuont farw yn eu
Babandod ac a gladdwyd ym mynwent
Eglwys Llandysul.

Translated, the inscription tells us that five, yes, five children from one family, died within four days, two dying on the same day – David, aged 14, and Tom, aged 8. The final entry on the stone records that another six children of the family had died in infancy, and are buried in the churchyard at Llandysul. And in 1874 William had also died in infancy.

The question that immediately springs to mind is: 'What did the five children who died in March 1875 die of?' The answer that most people living in the area will give you is that they had died after drinking milk that had been poisoned by rats. The correct answer, and this, according to the Death Certificates, is that they died from Scarletina Maligna, a virulent form of scarlet fever that was responsible for more deaths among children in this country in the 1800s than any other disease.

I feel sure that the reader, like me, finds it impossible to comprehend the feelings of John and Margaret Davies at the time, and the event must have coloured the remainder of their lives.

Now to the Church at Troed-yr-Aur. But firstly, let me take you to Bath. Yes, dear reader, Bath. I believe it is right to say that there are as many, if not more, memorials on the walls of Bath Abbey as any other ecclesiastical building in Britain. The north, west and south walls, up to a height of approximately eight feet, are covered with literally hundreds of memorials reflecting the fact that, at one time, Bath was the place for the aristocracy and landed gentry to spend what was termed 'the season' every year. It was while visiting the Abbey that I first came across and noticed with surprise, the name Troed-yr-Aur. Now, Troed-yr-Aur lies mid-way between the A475 – the road from Newcastle Emlyn to Lampeter, and the A487 – the road that can take the traveller from Haverfordwest to Dolgellau, passing through St David's, Fishguard, Cardigan, Aberystwyth and Machynlleth. It would be correct to say that Troed-yr-Aur lies off the beaten track, and the traveller could easily pass through it without realising having done so. I would maintain that the two most important buildings in Troed-yr-Aur are the church, and Troed-yr-Aur Mansion; Gwernant, now a ruin, was another important house in the area. Commemorated on the south wall of Bath Abbey is, indeed, a Dr William Bowen of Troed-yr-Aur, Cardiganshire, who died in 1815, aged 54 years.

Coincidentally while reading David Noakes's biography of Jane Austen I came across this account on page 267: originally written by Jane Austen. 'Throughout their years at Sydney Place, Mr Austen, (Jane's father) was subject to intermittent bouts of a feverish complaint which even the most assiduous efforts of Dr Bowen – who had supplanted Mapleton as the physician of choice – were ineffectual to cure . . . Then early in 1804, Mrs Austen was very ill, and Bowen was frequently at her bedside.' In Claire Tomalin's biography of Jane Austen she also quote's Austen's words: 'Mrs Austen felt such grateful relief at her recovery that she was inspired to record in some humorous verses entitled

Dialogue between Death and Mrs Austen.

Says Death, 'I've been trying these three weeks and more
To seize an old madam here at Number Four,
Yet I still try in vain, tho' she's turned of three score;
To what is my ill success owing?

I'll tell you, Old Fellow, if you cannot guess,
To what your'e indebted for your ill success-
To the prayers of my husband, whose love I possess,
To the care of my daughter, whom heaven will bless,
To the skill and attention of BOWEN.'

So it was said that two unrelated incidents – seeing the memorial to a Dr Bowen on the wall of Bath Abbey, and the reading of two biographies of the life of Jane Austen – aroused my curiosity and led me to try and discover some facts about the Bowen family of Troed-yr-Aur.

Was the Dr Bowen mentioned on the memorial the same person as the Dr Bowen mentioned by Jane Austen in her writings, and where exactly is the Dr Bowen of Bath buried?

Troed-yr-Aur was a large house, the home of the Bowen family. Incidentally, there is no doubt that the area derives its name from the house. The Bowen family played an important part in the life of the district and the church during the eighteenth and nineteenth centuries.

The church, dedicated to St Michael, is rectorial, and was, at the beginning of the last century, in the gift of the Lord Chancellor. It consists of a nave, chancel and south aisle and it was rebuilt towards the end of the nineteenth century.

141

On the inside walls of the church there are a number of memorials, many of them to members of the Bowen family. In the churchyard and adjacent to the south wall of the chancel there are a number of graves of family members.

The first memorial the visitor will notice on the south wall is inscribed, 'In memory of Rebecca Bowen, relict of William Bowen, Troed-yr-Aur, Esq., who lived in Pious Observance of every Religious and Moral Duty. An affectionate wife, a tender Mother and a faithful friend. Having long sustained her painful Infirmities with Christian Fortitude, she resigned her immortal Spirit into the hands of her Creator October 30th 1791, aged 80 years. This humble Tribute of Gratitude was erected by her much afflicted daughters Rebecca and Hester Bowen.'

After reading the inscription I am left wondering whether Rebecca Bowen was Dr William Bowen's mother. If she was, then she would have been 43 years of age when giving birth to her son.

Underneath the memorial to Rebecca Bowen is a brass plaque on which is inscribed, 'Revered and honoured memory of Lieut. Col. Henry Griffith Bowen, late 88th Connaught Rangers, third son of James Bowen, Esq., Troed-yr-Aur. Born August 8th 1841, died at Colchester August 16th 1909. "Until the day break the shadows flee away."'

The next memorial, like the first, of white marble, reads: 'In remembrance of Frances, second wife of the Rev. Thomas Bowen, AM, Rector of this Parish, who died lamented and beloved after a few days illness on 29th April 1834, aged 66 years. By her death an affectionate husband and numerous relatives have experienced an irreparable loss, and the poor a generous benefactor. Her memory will be long cherished by those who knew her many virtues, and she has left an example worthy to be followed by the present and future generations. "A woman that feareth the Lord shall be praised." – Proverbs 31, part of the 30th verse. Also in memory of the Rev. Thomas Bowen, MA, 50 years Rector of this Parish. He was a magistrate, Deputy Lieutenant for the County, who died May 3rd 1842 at the advanced age of 84. Universally beloved and regretted by all who knew him. To the poor he was an unwearied benefactor. The bulk of his property he bequeathed to James Bowen, Esq., second son of Llwyngwair in the county of Pembrokeshire.' Again a question arises, 'Was the Rev. Thomas Bowen the doctor's father?' He could very well have been because he would have been 33 years old when Dr William was born. According to Major Francis Jones in his book, *Historic Cardiganshire Homes And Their Families,* Thomas Bowen's first wife was a Sarah Malvina Vaulker of Hampton, Middlesex; they were married in 1792. In 1802 he married his second wife, a Francis Norton, also of Hampton. And when we come to look closely at the life of the long serving Rector of Troed-yr-Aur, many aspects of his life were left out of the 'Universally beloved and regretted by all who knew him.' Dr Baker-Jones in his excellent book, *Princelings, Privilege and Power* explains that the 'beloved Reverend' had another side to his character, 'His grave moral lapses, especially in a priest, were totally ignored by those who erected his memorial . . . his adultery, fornication and inconsistency, neglect of his ministerial duties and other enormous Crimes . . . had absconded and hid himself from the mandatory, concerning his soul's health and the Lawful Reformation and Correction of his vices and excesses." He had in fact run away from the person carrying out the consistory court order. Reverend Thomas Bowen was obviously quite a lad in his day!

Another white marble memorial has the inscription, 'In memory of Ellen Easter who died July 23rd 1869, age 32 years, also Elizabeth Alicia who died at Cheltenham August 22nd 1861, age 31 years, and was buried there. The above were the daughters of James Bowen, Esq., Troed-yr-Aur, and Dorothea his wife. "Those who sleep in Jesus will God bring with Him."'

At first I found the Christian name Easter interesting because in the churchyard at Nevern, where members of the Bowen family of Llwyngwair are buried, there is, among the names of those interred in the churchyard, a person named Easter. I soon discovered that the James Bowen of Troed-yr-Aur was originally from Llwyngwair, near Nevern. He inherited Troed-yr-Aur on the death of the Rev. Thomas Bowen.

On the south wall of the chancel in Troed-yr-Aur Church is a memorial on which is inscribed: 'Sacred to the memory of John Bowen of Clunllebyng, in this Parish, Esq., who died 6th December 1756 in the 74th year of his age. Also of William Bowen only son of the same place, Esq., who died 7th April 1780 in the 55th year of his age. Also of Mary Ann Bowen, eldest daughter of the said William Bowen, who died 23rd June 1781 in the 29th year of her age. Also Elizabeth Bowen, youngest daughter of the said William Bowen, who died 17th September 1787, aged 27 years.' It is rather surprising that there is no mention of William Bowen's wife, the mother of Mary Ann and Elizabeth Bowen. This is possibly another example of the wife and mother being the last to die, and with no remaining close relatives, had no one to insert details about her.

On the north side of the altar, on the east wall, is a white marble memorial on which is inscribed: 'Within these rails are deposited the remains of Mrs Sarah

Malvina Bowen, wife of the Rev. Thomas Bowen, Rector of this Parish, died in the 36th year of her age. This tablet is placed by her husband as a token of his affectionate regard to the memory of a beloved wife, whose domestic virtue endeared her to those who knew her, and whose many and able and excellent qualities made her loss almost insupportable.

Why heaves the sigh, why falls the selfish tear
Of soft Affliction o'er the untimely bier?
Oh! rather Gratitude the Spirit freed
From mortal pain to reap a glorious Meed
Which at an Instant burst incumbring Clay,
And with her Infant Cherub wing'd her Way
To offer humbly at the eternal Throne
A spotless soul scarce purer than her own.'

The line, 'And with her infant cherub wing'd her way.' makes it abundantly clear that Sarah Malvina died on the birth of her child. Sarah Malvina was the first wife of the Rev. Thomas Bowen, the philandering rector. (Possibly the reason for philandering, of course.)

On the north wall, and starting in the chancel, is a memorial that tells us: 'To the cherished memory of James Bowen, Esq., of Troed-yr-Aur, JP, DL to the counties of Cardigan, Carmarthen and Pembrokeshire. The best of husbands, the best of fathers, a humble and consistent follower of Jesus. "He was not, for God took him", died October 28th 1872, aged 66 years. Also in loving memory of Dorothea, widow of the above, who died August 4th 1880 in the 80th year of her age. Her last words were, "I will dwell in the house of the Lord for ever."' Next on the north wall a memorial on which is inscribed, 'In memory of William Rice Bowen of Troedyraur, Esq., late of the

Royal Artillery, and JP for the counties of Cardigan and Carmarthen. The beloved eldest son of the late James Bowen and Dorothea, his wife, who died deeply mourned 3rd February 1874, age 36 years. "The Lord is at hand." – Phil. 4v5, "Every eye shall see Him." – Rev. 1v7, "Prepare to meet thy God." – Amos 4v12.'

Two other local families are commemorated on the inside of the north wall of the church: 'In memory of John Lloyd Williams, Esq., of Gwernant Park in this parish who departed this life 23rd January 1838 in the 93rd year of his age. He was a Senior Fellow of the Royal Society, a Fellow of the Society of Antiquaries, and for upwards of thirty years, discharged the active duties of magistrate, and for some portion of that period, officiated as Chairman of the Quarter Sessions and Deputy Lieutenant of this county. He was of considerable attainments and conferred great benefits on the poor of this neighbourhood.' John Lloyd Williams had been a surgeon in India, and had married a Martha Louisa Saunders of County Wicklow in Ireland. He farmed 440 acres and was very interested in fostering modern farming methods. He owned six different breeds of cattle and, when planting trees in Gwernant park, had them arranged in such a way that they represented battle positions of soldiers during the Indian campaign!

The memorial tells us that he was a Senior Fellow of the Royal Society; the Society's full title was Royal Society of London For The Promotion Of Natural Knowledge; the oldest scientific society in Great Britain and one of the oldest in Europe, founded in 1660. In 1671 Sir Isaac Newton was elected to the society and, seven years later, in 1678, Edmund Halley, the astronomer, joined its ranks. In 1768 the society sponsored the first scientific expedition to the Pacific, under James Cook. Candidates for membership in the Royal Society must be recommended by several fellows and, in the late twentieth century, membership numbered over 1,000 fellows, 90 of whom were from foreign countries. As the title tells us, the Society of Antiquaries, was set up for people who were interested in all things ancient. One of the founders of the society was a Sir John Davies, born in 1569, died in 1626, a poet and a lawyer. On the death of Queen Elizabeth I in 1603, Davies was one of the messengers who carried the news to James VI of Scotland. In 1626 Davies was appointed Lord Chief Justice, but died before he took office.

It is obvious that John Lloyd Williams must have moved in a high and intellectual circle in order to become a Fellow of two such important and illustrious societies.

The last memorial on the north wall records: 'In memory of John Enoch, Esq., Captain and Paymaster of the Cardigan Militia, who died February 10th 1833, age 74 years.' There follow words extolling his virtues so typical of memorials of the Victorian era: 'In perfect charity to all men, he was a gentleman universally respected for his kind and sociable disposition and the unblemished purity of his private character, and for his honourable bearing in his profession. Few men ever descended into the tomb who when alive was more sincerely esteemed, and the loss of whom when gathered to his Father was deplored with more general and genuine sorrow.' There is more, 'Also Anne, his wife, who died October 16th 1825, aged 61 years. Much lamented for her many estimable qualities. Joshua, son of the said John and Anne Enoch, who died 22nd June 1824. To the regret of all his relatives, friends and acquaintances who he attached to him when alive by the goodness of heart and frankness of disposition. Charlotte, daughter of the forenamed John and Anne Enoch, who died 30th May 1818, age 23 years. She was much beloved by her relations and respected by all who knew her. This tablet was erected by Captain Enoch, 23rd Regiment RWF and the Rev. George Enoch of Wallsworth Hall, Gloucestershire, the only surviving sons of the said John and Anne Enoch, in testimony of those who were bound by the strongest ties, filial duty and affection.'

Lastly within the church there is one more memorial; it is a small brass plate on the front of the large pipe organ that stands in front of the west wall and almost hides the window. On the brass plate, is 'To the glory of God and in memory of the Rev. Prebendary Rhys Jones Lloyd, MA, JP, Rector of this parish 1852-1904. This organ has been erected by parishioners and friends. "Mewn angof ni chei fod." – "You will never be forgotten."'

The rector's 52 years service at Troed-yr-Aur, was quite an achievement. According to Mr Baker-Jones in his book, *Princelings, Privilege and Power,* the Reverend Prebendary was a very "colourful character with theatrical mannerisms, idiosyncratic intonation of the liturgy and quaint garb'. He was also a generous priest who even went so far as to help nonconformists during the troubles over the paying of tithes. Here is an individual who deserved the words on the memorial: 'You will never be forgotten'."

Commemorated in the church at Llangoedmor is the son of the Rev. Rhys Jones Lloyd. On his memorial are the words, 'To the glory of God and in memory of George Evan Lloyd, CB, DSO, Duke of Wellington's West Riding Regiment, who fell when gallantly leading his regiment to attack Boer positions at Rhenoster Kop, Transvaal, on the 20th November 1900. His previous war service with the King's Own Yorkshire Light Infantry – Jowkai

Expedition, 1877, Medal and Clasp, Afghan War, 1878, Ali Musjid Medal and Clasp, Nile Expedition, 1844-45, Commandant, Tangur, Medal and Bronze Star; brevet Major, Sudan, 1885-89, Guinis, Despatches and DSO Sarvas, Despatches and Order of Mejidie. Gramazeh, Toski, Despatches and two Clasps. Dongolo, 1896, Governor of Red Sea Littoral and Suakim District, Despatches and promoted Lieutenant Colonel. South Africa, 1900, in comand of West Riding Regiment, Paardeberg, Poplar Grove, Rheonester, Despatches, Medal, four Clasps and CB.'

What a distinguished Army record and what a tale he would have to tell if he had been given the opportunity to do so. I find the dates on the memorial rather puzzling – to be serving in Egypt in 1844 and killed in action fifty-six years later in South Africa. It leads me to the conclusion that he must have been extremely young when in Egypt and well past military age when he was killed.

As can be seen on the east wall in many churches, on each side of the window there are two marble tablets and inscribed on them are the Ten Commandments. Returning to Troed-yr-Aur, the churchyard is also of interest to the visitor. To the left of the path leading to the church there is a tall, slate gravestone, the slate surrounded by stonework. Both sides of the slate are inscribed, in Welsh, with a great deal of information about members of the Morris family of Penrhos, a residence within the parish. On the side facing the path is inscribed: 'Yma gorwedd gweddillion y Parchedig Dafydd Morris, Penrhos, yn y Plwyf hwn. Pregethwr clodfawr ymhlith trefnyddion Calfinaidd. Un o'r rhai disgleiriaf ei ddawn a grymusaf ei weinidogaeth a ymddangosodd ym more y Diwigiad Methodistaidd. Teithiau yn gyson de a gogledd Cymru. Cyfarfyddai a llawer o amharch ac erlid. Roedd defnynau ei weinidogaeth fel y glaw, a llaweroedd a drodd efe at yr Arglwydd. Galwyd ef i orffwys oddiwrth ei lafur ar 17eg o Fedi 1791, pan oedd ond 47 mlwydd oed. Yma hefyd gorffwysa gweddillion marwol y Parchedig Ebenezer Morris, Blaenywern, plwyf Llangunllo. Mab ydoedd i'r Parchedig Dafydd Morris, a gweinidog perthynol i'r un gyfundrefn crefyddol. Ysbryd rhagorol ei dad a orffwysai arno, a thebygai iddo yn wroldeb ei feddwl ac yn nerth ac awdurdod ei weinidogaeth. Fel dyn yr oedd o dymer hoffus a chyfeillgar, yn serchus yn ei deulu, ac yn gymeradwy ymron ei gydwladwyr. Nerth a chywirdebei farn ynghyd a mwyneiddra ei ysbryd a enillent iddo lywodraeth fawr yn yr eglwysi, a chariad ac edmygedd ei holl frodyr yn y wenidogaeth.

Yn Y Pulpud.

Pan eangwyd ei galon gan yr Arglwydd byddai ei wynepryd yn gorfoli a'i enaid yn cynhyrfu o'i fewn, dywedai ac atddywedai yr un ymadroddion, ac hynny gyda egni chwanegol drachefn a thrachefn, a thrwy enyniad ei ysbryd a grym ei lais ymdorent ar ei wrandawyr megis taranau cryfion. A llawer oedd a deimlent fod Duw yn wir ynddo ef. Amcanai yn ei weinidogaeth at ddeffro y gydwybod, a dwyn pechadur trallodedig at Grist gan gyfarwydd y saint i fuchedd Duwiol. Ac wedi llafurio felly am 37 o flynyddoedd bu farw Awst 15ed 1825 yn 56 mlwydd oed yn serchiadau ei gyfeillion ac ynghanol ei ddefnyddioldeb yn unol a'r hygol (sic) ymunau ei ddymuniad a ddatgan yn ystod ei gystudd diweddaf. "Allan o waith, allan o'r byd."'

Ar yr ochr arall o'r garreg y manylion canlynol, 'Er coffadwriaeth am Mary, annwyl briod y Parchedig Ebenezer Morris, yr hon oedd enwog am ei chymhwyster fel gwraig a mam, ac am ei Duwioldeb fel Cristion. Ei chariad cryf at Iesu Grist a'i achos a barodd iddi gadw ei thŷ yn agored i groesawi gweinidogion y Gair a gweini iddynt gyda'r sirioldeb mwyaf dros mwy na deugain mlynedd. Gellir heb betruso ddywed amdani, "A hi oedd fam yn Israel". Bu farw Mehefin 19eg 1845 yn 76 mlwydd oed.

Er cof hefyd am blant Ebenezer a Mary Morris, sef Anne, bu farw Hydref 15fed 1805 yn 7 mis oed. David, eu mab hynaf, yr hwn a foddodd wrth ymolchi yn afon Dyfi, ger Machynlleth, Awst 18ed 1819 yn 27 mlwydd oed. Dygwyd ei gorff yma i'w gladdu. Anne, a fu farw Mehefin 20fed 1823 yn 16 mlwydd oed. Eleazer, eu pedwerydd mab. Yr hwn a fu farw yn Casnewydd Tachwedd 14eg 1826 yn 21 oed, ac a gladdwyd ym mynwent Y Tabernacl. Ebenezer, eu hail fab, yr hwn a fu farw yn ddisymwyth trwy'r ddaear syrthio arno ar Tachwedd 18fed 1828 yn 28 mlwydd oed. Walter, eu trydydd mab, masnachwr yn Liverpool, a fu farw yn Falmouth ar ei ddychweliad o Ynys Madeira, Mehefin 10fed 1839 yn 39 mlwydd oed. Claddwyd ef mewn mynwent sy rhwng Falmouth a Penryn.'

The details on the face nearest the path refers to a father and son, the Rev. Dafydd Morris and the Rev. Ebenezer Morris. They were both Methodist ministers; the father died 17th September 1791,aged 47 years and Ebenezer, the son, died August 15th 1825, aged 56 years. In the inscription both are praised in glowing terms for their devotion to both the Calvinistic Methodist movement, and also to their Saviour, Jesus Christ.

The father was born at Lledrod, Ceredigion and, in his younger days was a drover. He became a minister at Twrgwyn in the parish of Troed-yr-Aur in 1774 when he was 30 years of age. Not only was he a preacher but also a hymn-writer, and his hymns were published in 1773 under the title, 'Cân y Pererinion Cystuddiedig' – The Song of the Suffering Pilgrim. One of his hymns, 'N'ad im fodlon ar ryw rith o grefydd heb ei grym' – 'I am not satisfied with an illusionary religion that is without power.' is still to be found in present-day hymnals.

Of Ebenezer and Mary Morris's children, the two sons, Ebenezer and Walter, were obviously twins; simple arithmetic shows that they were both born in the year 1800. The details on the stone make it clear that the family suffered much anguish and heartbreak over the years. Daughter Anne died in 1807, aged 7 months, David drowned in the River Dyfi, near Machynlleth in 1819, aged 27 years, Eleazer at Newport in 1826, aged 21 years, Ebenezer killed by a fall of rock and earth in 1828, aged 28 years, and his twin brother died at Falmouth on returning from Madeira in the West Indies in 1839, aged 39 years.

On another gravestone, commemorating a Keturia Davies, there is an 'englyn', that is, a four line verse in strict metre:

> Yn y byd adfyd bob ydfa – a gafodd,
> A gofid o'r mwya.
> Llety'r bedd, a diwedd da
> O'r ing fyd sydd ddihangfa.

The verse makes it clear that the lady in question suffered a great deal while alive and that through dying she escaped from her misery.

On a stone, which now lies on the ground, 'Underneath this stone is the body of Benjamin Thomas who had been a faithful preacher of the Gospel for upwards of 40 years among the people called Methodists. He died April 12th 1790, aged 77 years.'

While looking at a copy of the Parish Registers on

microfilm at the National Library of Wales at Aberystwyth I read the following details about the Bowen family:

Rachel Bowen buried April 18th 1751.
??? son of William Bowen baptised February ? 1751, or it could have been 1753 – entry smudged.
Elizabeth Bowen buried 23rd December 1753.
Anne Bowen buried 14th April 1759.
Evan Bowen buried 23rd April 1759.
Thomas Bowen baptised 25th January 1756.
John Bowen buried 6th December 1756.
Dorothea Bowen daughter of ??? Bowen baptised 13th September 1763.
Elizabeth Bowen buried 15th July 1767.
Mary Bowen buried 27th March 1770.
A John Bowen Warden of the Church in 1759.
A William Bowen, Esq., Warden in 1770.
Thomas Bowen Rector of the Church 1815-16.

Although the search of the registers proved interesting, I was unable to work out from the details in them the names of Dr William Bowen's parents. Some time later I found the answer, thanks to the late Major Francis Jones. In his most interesting book, *Historic Carmarthenshire Homes And Their Families*, he mentions that Dr William Bowen was one of the seven children of William and Rebecca Bowen. There were three sons, Thomas, John and William, and four daughters, Mary Anne, Rebecca, Hester and Elizabeth.

Members of the Bowen family have over the years played a prominent and very important part in the life of the local church. As for the church building itself, it is believed that the first church was probably erected sometime between 800 and 1,000 AD; the present edifice built during the first half of the nineteenth century. Between 1738 and 1903 five rectors served the parish. They were:

Thomas Lloyd, 1738-1776
Tudor Brigstocke, dates unknown
Thomas Bowen, MA, 1792-1842
H. Lewis Davies, Curate-in-Charge, dates unknown
Rhys Jones Lloyd, BA, 1852-1903

The registers, all except those still in use, are now in the National Library at Aberystwyth. During the incumbency of the Rev. Thomas Bowen the silver chalice and paten cover of 1574 were recast, preserving the original form, pattern and inscription, Why this work was necessary is not known, but under the border is the London assay letter for 1828-29 and on the paten knob is the date, 1828. The inscription on the bell is: X POCVLVM * ECLESYE * TRE * DROYRE. 1828. Inscribed on a silver paten: Presented to the Parish of Troedyraur by the Revd, Thomas Bowen, MA, Rector, AD 1839.

Besides Plas Troed-yr-Aur, another two properties within the parish deserve a mention – Gwernant and Pantyrodyn. At one time Gwernant was owned by a family named Lloyd and the property stood on low ground. The next family to live there was the Lloyd Williams family and, at the beginning of the nineteenth century, John Lloyd Williams, Esq., built another house on the summit of a nearby hill. In the early 1800s a Captain Lloyd Williams was serving with the 15th Regiment of North India and with the East India Company. This gave the captain an opportunity to dabble in business ventures from which he made a great deal of money.

Pantyrodyn, standing south of the road between Brongest and Beulah, once belonged to the Lewes family. At the beginning of the twentieth century Pantyrodyn was in the possession of Colonel Lewis of Llanerchaeron, but was sold in 1918. Llanerchaeron has recently been restored by the National Trust.

I now return to the Bowen family of Troed-yr-Aur, and to Dr William Bowen in particular. Further research proved fruitful. On the 7th of May 1999 I received from Dr Lucy Rutherford, Bath Abbey Archivist, a reply to a letter I had sent a few days previously in the hope that she would be able to provide some more information. Her letter gave me the following information: 'We have the registers in which burials in the Abbey were recorded dating from 1813, and I have found an entry for a William Bowen, MD. The details are as follows: "Buried in a wall grave in lead, North Aisle, under own stone. Address, Gay Street, Walcot. Buried April 14th 1815, aged 54 years. Buried by William Marshall, curate. Undertaker Mr George."'

It is said that from a small acorn a large oak tree grows. From a few words in two biographies of the life of Jane Austen and a rectangular, marble tablet on the wall of Bath Abbey, have flowed all the words I have written about the Bowen family of Troed-yr-Aur, Ceredigion. I feel that I have almost come to know members of a family that have long since gone, and especially the doctor described by Jane Austen herself as: 'The good Dr Bowen who in 1804 was frequently at Mrs Austen's (Jane's mother) bedside when she was ill.' And yet, I fully realise that there is far more information that with further research could be found out about the Bowen family.

Time to leave Troed-yr-Aur and travel a few miles along the A475, to the church at Llandysul, whose roots go back as far as the Age of the Saints. In the Episcopal Register of St David's, 1397-1518, the church is mentioned at least twice. The first reference comes under the title, 'A licence of non-residence' and it reads: 'Also on 2 June, in the year and place abovesaid (1400), Master Geoffrey Melton, rector of the parish church of LLANDUSSELL obtained a licence of non-residence for one year, he being in the meantime engaged in the queen's service. And he had letters in the usual form.' The second mention entitled, 'A letter testimonial of the oath of the rector of Llandussell' reads: 'To all to whom the present letters shall come Guy etc., (The Bishop), greeting in Him who came into the world to bear testimony to the truth in regard to the things which were under a cloud. Know ye, therefore, that on search of the registers of Lord John of good memory etc., late bishop of St David's, our immediate predecessor, well and faithfully kept, we have found and by the same register it is shewn (sic) evidently that the discreet man Master Geoffrey Melton, rector of the parish of Llandussell, of our diocese of St David's, personally constituted in the presence of Lord John, Bishop of St David's, etc., on 14 March, 1393, the fifth year of the translation of our said predecessor, at Southam of the diocese of Worcester, took an oath on the holy gospels of God corporally touched by him, purely, spontaneously and simply, to pay faithfully during his term in the said church, a yearly pension of 20 marks due to the chapter of St David's out of his church of LLANDUSSELL aforesaid from time and through time whereof there is no memory of man to the contrary, at the terms in that behalf limited, appointed and accustomed, for the payment to be made; there being present Master Robert Heth, notary public, John Aubrey, John Northam and Robert Barton, witnesses to the premises called and asked. All which things we signify and make known to your university by these presents. In witness of all which things we have caused our seal to be set to these things taken out of the register aforesaid. Dated in our manor of Charleton of the diocese of Rochester 3 December 1400.'

The church, which stands on the valley floor not far from the river Teifi, has a massive fourteenth century tower. The door into the church is at the foot of the west wall of the tower. Until 1783 the edifice had a thatched roof; the nave and aisles have three arcades of three arches that probably date from the thirteenth century. In the Lady Chapel there is an ancient altar stone, and in the church a memorial stone, called the Velvor stone, which dates from the sixth century, and on which there is an Ogam inscription.

Many years ago, on January 12th, which in the pre-Gregorian calendar was New Year's Day, the parishioners of Llandysul and the neighbouring parish of Llanwenog, six miles away, participated in a fast and furious, ball game, without rules the two church porches being the respective goals. This game, which often resulted in quite serious injuries, was replaced by a day set aside for a 'Gymanfa Bwnc' again held on the Old New Year's Day, January 12th. It was established by the Rev. Enoch James, vicar of Llandysul, in 1833. All the Sunday Schools in neighbouring parishes were invited to attend the church at Llandysul for the 'Gymanfa Bwnc'. It was, and still is, a day when the members of the participating Sunday Schools, having prepared a passage from the Scriptures would, in turn, stand in the chancel facing the congregation. The children of each Sunday school recite a selected collect; this is followed by the adults joining in with them to recite the selected passage of Scripture. They are then questioned about the contents of the passage by a guest vicar or rector. Each Sunday School is given half an hour, and after the questioning, they end their session by singing an anthem. This annual festival has continued without a break over three centuries, quite an achievement, without a doubt.

The reason I mention Llandysul Church lies in the fact that, on the gravestone in nearby Capel Dewi Church, is recorded the death of the five children of Brynllwyd who died within four days of each other. Also inscribed at the bottom of the stone is the fact that another five children from the same family had died in infancy and had been buried in Llandysul churchyard. I was curious to read the church's Burial Register. Through the kindness of a friend I was given the opportunity to look through the register covering the years 1813 to 1925, and it proved to be an interesting exercise.

The above-mentioned Rev. Enoch James had written the following verse in the register:

> Daw'r garreg oddidraw,
> A dorrwyd nid a llaw;
> Lle dreigla hon,
> Bydd lawer bron mewn braw,
> Cynhyddu mae fel mynydd mawr,
> Fe gwymp allorau Baal i'r llawr;
> A'r nos ymhell a redodd,
> Agorodd dorau'r wawr.

The verse is rather difficult to understand and, furthermore, the question arises as to why he composed the words and then entered them in the register. In the first two lines he mentions that a stone has come from far away, a stone not cut by hand. Where the stone stops many will experience fear. The verse continues by mentioning that the stone increases in size until it resembles a large mountain. The sixth line tells us that the altars of Baal fall to the ground and, in the last two lines, that the night gives way to the doors of the dawn. Baal is mentioned in ten books of the Bible, beginning with the book of Numbers. In the second book of Chronicles, chapter 23, verse 17, it states: 'Then all the people went to the house of Baal, and broke it down, and broke his altars and images in pieces, and slew Mattan the priest of Baal before the altars.' And in 1 Kings, 18, there is the well-known account of Elijah the prophet challenging four hundred and fifty prophets of Baal on Mount Carmel to place a sacrificed bullock on an altar and then call upon Baal to set fire to it. This they did, but nothing happened. Then Elijah called on God to set fire to the bullock, and Elijah's prayer was answered. So the Rev. Enoch James's verse could possibly be referring to this remarkable event as told in the Bible.

Also in the register can be seen some more entries that are interesting in their own way:

'Elizabeth, widow, of the village of Llandysul, fourth wife of Samuel John Evan Rees, buried December 6th 1817, aged 53.'

'May 29th 1829, Owen Bowen, eldest son of the Rev. H. Bowen, late Vicar of this Parish, aged 30. He lived at Llandysul.'

'September 18th 1829, John Bowen, son of the Rev. H. Bowen, late Vicar of this Parish, aged 21. He lived at Cynwyl Elfed.'

'March 11th 1839, Hannah Williams, MAES-Y-MWNCI, aged 5.'

'Mary Evans, Dolgrogws, buried May 30th 1839, aged 17 years.'

'Anne Evans, Dolgrogws, buried June 2nd 1839, aged4 years'

*The name Dolgrogws is interesting because it refers to a meadow on which there could very well have been a gallows.

One entry mentions a farm called BIRDLIP.

On pages 67 and 68 of the register: we read 'Louisa Margaret James, Vicarage, Llandysul, buried June 8th 1844, aged 41.' (Wife of Vicar, the Rev E. James), and the following words written by the Rev. Thomas Lloyd, Gilfachwen: 'She had been a zealous member of this Church for 23 years. Died in full assurance of eternal life through Christ. She was the mother of twelve children, three died before her and left nine behind; the youngest was only one week old. (She obviously died as a result of childbirth.) She possessed all the qualities of a good wife and tender mother. She was the second daughter of the late Rev. Maurice Evans, Vicar of Llangeler, and was married to the Rev E. James, Vicar of this place, August 12th 1823, having lived that share of time without a cross word between them. When she was converted the following verse was carried with power and force to her soul – St Luke 9 v. 26. The last text she heard was Psalm 32 v. 11, and said the following week before she died to her husband that she had great pleasure from the sermon preached by her husband from the said verse.'

Maurice Atterbury James, Llandysul Vicarage, buried August 23rd 1845, aged 26 – an undergraduate at Jesus College, Oxford. (He was the son of the above-mentioned Louisa Margaret James, and he died just over year after his mother.) Three years later another member of the family died – 'Mary Anne James, Llandysul Vicarage, May 1st 1848, aged 24. "She lived and died at the foot of the Cross of Our Blessed Saviour" – Rev. Thomas Lloyd, Gilfachwen.'

A year later the burial of the Rev. Enoch James is recorded – 'Rev. Enoch James, Vicar of Llandysul, 1813 to 1849, a period of 36 years, buried February 24th 1849, aged 57. Buried by William Powell, Vicar of Llanpumsaint.'

The new Vicar, the Rev. E. V. Morgan, records his first burial service on October 12th 1849.

'Evan Thomas, Tygwyn, buried February 20th 1854, aged 100.' 'David Michael, Cwmpedol, May 10th 1854, aged 75, Margaret Michael, Cwmpedol, May 27th 1854.' Was this a case of the widow dying of a broken heart?

The burial of the Rev. David Jones, Cwm, on October 14th 1857, aged 57, is recorded as having taken place at the new church of Tregroes 'William Michael, of this village, April 14th 1858, aged 9 months; Anne Michael, of this village, April 16th 1858, aged 9 months.' Undoubtedly William and Anne were twins and probably the grandchildren of David and Margaret Michael of Cwmpedol. Another sad event in the life of another family that same year: 'David Jones, Sign Botas, October 1858, aged 2 years; Timothy Jones, Sign Botas, December 25th 1858, aged 3 years.' To hold a funeral on Christmas Day seems a very unusual thing to do almonst as unusual as the name of their home. The deaths of children continue in 1859: 'Sarah Thomas, Parke, February 22nd 1859, aged 2 years; Mary Thomas Parke, March 22nd 1859, aged 13 years.' In the period July 6th to November 15th 1859 9 infants, age range 3 weeks to 5 years, and 5 persons under the age of 38 died, and are recorded in the register.

'David Thomas, Rhydsais, February 16th 1860, aged 4; Mary Thomas, Rhydsais, March 30th 1860, aged 9.'

'Eleanor Davies, Coynant, October 10th 1861, aged 7; Mary Davies, Coynant, April 1st 1861.'

'Elizabeth Davies, Bwlchyfadfa, October 10th 1861, aged 7; Mary Davies, Bwlchyfadfa, October 26th 1861, aged 13.'

'Catherine Charles, Coedfoel, May 16th 1862, no age given; Hannah Charles, May 29th 1862, aged 27.'

'David Thomas, Rhydsais, September 12th 1865, aged 27; John Thomas, Rhydsais, September 19th 1865, aged 4.' In 1860 two children having the same address die within a few days just over a month of each other.

The Rev. Thomas Lloyd, writer of the note about the wife of the Vicar of Llandysul, the Rev. Enoch James, was buried on July 30th 1868, aged 66. His address given as Gilfachwen Isaf.

'James Jenkins, buried at Capel Dewi on March 11th 1870, aged 8 years.' He was the brother of Canon James Jenkins, formerly of Cilygraig, Capel Dewi, who was Vicar of Llangunnor Church for 47 years. Another brother was Vicar of Abergwili, while a third brother was Church Warden at Capel Dewi for 45 years and died in his nineties.

On December 2nd 1874 a brother and sister were buried. They were David and Mary Davies, Porthyronnen. David was 5 years and Mary 2 years of age.

A child with an interesting Anglo-German name of Mortimer Wilhelm Christoph Sprengell, Clifton Terrace, was buried on December 28th 1874, aged 10.

'Hannah Davies, Rhydgaled, May 9th 1893, aged 15; Anne Davies, Rhydgaled, May 17th 1893, aged 1 month.' (Both buried at Capel Dewi.)

On March 30th 1898, a John Evans, aged 60, was buried. He had lived in a house called, according to the entry in the Register, Thesbian House. I am of the opinion that it should have been Thespian House; Thespian a legendary Greek dramatic poet of the sixth century BC. It would be interesting to know why the house had been given the name in the first instance.

On January 21st 1903 William George Jenkins, Vicar since 1868 – a total of 35 years, was buried, aged 74 years.

'Sarah Jones, Llain, Blaencathel, October 12th 1904, aged 83; James Jones, Llain, Blaencathel, October 17th 1904, aged 89 years.' Was this a case of a husband this time dying of a broken heart? They were buried at Capel Dewi.

'Jane Thomas, Cefnperthpiod, December 29th 1905, aged 4 years; James Thomas, Cefnperthpiod, January 9th 1906, aged 6 years.' Both were buried at Capel Dewi.

Between September 1st 1909 and March 21st 1910, of the eight who were buried six were ages 79, 77, 91, 85, 88, 83. Compared with the first seven decades of the nineteenth century the infant mortality rate had dropped considerably. Between 1813 and 1925 a total of 3,200 entries were made in the Burial Register. Of that total some were buried in St John's Church, Capel Dewi, and in St Ffraid's Church, Tregroes; the remainder were buried in Llandysul churchyard.

There were an average of 28 burials a year in the parish between 1813 and 1925. Assuming that there has been a church in the parish since the sixth century – this quite possible – the total burials based on 28 a year is around 42,000.

1813   Burials = 42; 24 were infants.
           % Infants = 57.14; average lifespan = 30yrs.

1815   Burials = 36; 11 were infants.

% Infants = 39.39; average lifespan = 41.14yrs.

1820 Burials = 39; 6 were infants.
      % Infants = 15.38; average lifespan = 45.23yrs.

1825 Burials = 28; 11 were infants.
      % Infants = 39.28; average lifespan = 41.01yrs.

1850 Burials = 30; 12 were infants.
      % Infants = 40; average lifespan = 38.84yrs.

1875 Burials = 27; 10 were infants.
      % Infants = 37.03; average lifespan = 39.42yrs.

1900 Burials = 16; 4 were infants.
      % Infants = 25; average lifespan = 42.12yrs.

1925 Burials = 12; infants were 0.
      % Infants = 0; average lifespan = 71.41yrs.

In the period June 18th to August 10th 1813 out of 8 burials 7 were ages 1yr., 2yrs., 2yrs, 1yr. 6mths., 4yrs., 2 and 5 years. It seems from these figures there must have been a virulent epidemic in the parish during that period.

In 1924 the ages of those buried were 79, 66, 90, 77, 16, 86, 92, 51, 80, 55, 90, 75 years. These figures point to 1924 being rather unusual for longevity. Of the 12 buried, 3 were in their 90s, 2 in their 80s, 3 in heir 70s, 1 aged 60 years, 2 in their 50s, but there was one young person – Margaret Rachel Jones, The Cambrian, died aged only16.

In the register there were some interesting, pleasant and unusual names of dwellings within the area. Among those I noticed were, Maes-y-Mwnci, Birdlip, Dolgrogws, Cyfyng, Castell Nadolig, Bwlchyfadfa, Rhydsais,

Blaencathel, Cefnperthpiod, Glanrhyd-y-pysgod, Pwll-y-gletch, Pantmorwynion, Mandinam, Sign Botas. There must have been very good reasons for these names, and research into their derivation would, I feel sure, result in an interesting and illuminating experience.

Capel Neuadd Lwyd Chapel

As the traveller on the road from Lampeter to Aberaeron nears Aberaeron he or she will see on the right hand side of the road a sign pointing to the left; written on it is Capel Neuadd Lwyd. To the vast majority of people travelling on that road the name Capel Neuadd Lwyd will be of no significance whatsoever, yet from 1746 an event that took place within its walls played a very important part in the religious life of not only Wales but, surprisingly, also of far off Madagascar.

Following the sign, one soon reaches the chapel, a typically shaped nonconformist Welsh chapel. Attached to its back wall are two cottages, these also of a design common to rural Wales.

So let us travel back in time to the first half of the 1700s; a Mr Jones, owner of a smallholding called Neuadd Lwyd, built a small school on his land so that his children could be educated. For a number of years prior to this there were many people living in the area who were members of a nonconformist chapel in Ciliau Aeron. In 1746, having had the consent of the owner, they registered the school as a place of worship, and some time before 1760 a chapel, a daughter church of the mother church at Ciliau Aeron, was established at Neuadd Lwyd. The minister of Ciliau Aeron, supported by a number of young ministers, was the Rev. Phillip Pugh. A few years before Phillip Pugh's death, however, and to his extreme disappointment, some members of chapels in the area became devotees of Arminianism. Arminianism was an idea propounded by the Dutch theologian Arminius, who died in 1609, opposing the teachings of Calvin. They also accepted Pelaginism, a belief put forward by Pelagius, a fourth to fifth century monk, that there was no such thing as original sin. But the members of Neuadd Lwyd held on to their Calvinistic beliefs. This resulted in the members of Neuadd Lwyd breaking away from the mother church at Ciliau Aeron and appointing Calvinistic ministers to attend to their spiritual needs.

The ministers who supported the cause at Neuadd Lwyd came from a wide area – Lewis Lewis from Pencader, John Lewis, Newcastle Emlyn, John Tibbot of Esgairdawe, William Gibbon, Capel Isaac, David Davies, Drefach, later of Swansea, and Henry George of Brynberian. When David Davies left Neuadd Lwyd for Mynyddbach in Swansea, the members of the chapel sent a sharply worded letter to members of Mynyddbach condemning them for taking from them a minister very much loved and respected at Neuadd Lwyd. Surely could it be said, that David Davies, in accepting the invitation to go to Mynyddbach, was as much to blame as those persons who issued the invitation. Anyhow, Mr Davies left in 1795 and soon afterwards Thomas Phillips, a member of the chapel at Pencader, was invited to become minister of Neuadd Lwyd. He was officially installed as minister on April 6th 1796.

When Thomas Phillips became minister there were sixty members at Neuadd Lwyd, but during his ministry the numbers increased to hundreds. Over the years the chapel had to be extended twice following its original construction in 1746, once in 1819 and again in 1906. So large did the membership become during his ministry that branches were set up in a number of surrounding villages and hamlets. Dr Phillips also ran a theological college at Neuadd Lwyd, and his ministry was so successful that his name became known throughout the Principality.

On hearing Dr Phillips preaching on one occasion, two of his students, Thomas Bevan and David Jones, were so moved by his description of the then believed immorality of the islanders of Madagascar that they volunteered to go to the island as missionaries; they were the first Protestant missionaries to the island. The two men and their families left this country towards the end of 1817 and reached Mauritius in 1818, where they left their wives and went on to Madagascar. Before long they returned to fetch their wives and children to live in Madagascar. David Jones and his family went to the island before Thomas Bevan and his family. On arriving in Madagascar Thomas Bevan learnt that David Jones's wife and child had died and that David Jones was also seriously ill. David Jones recovered, but by the end of January 1819 not only had his wife and child died but Thomas Bevan, his wife and child, had also died.

On the outside of the front wall of the chapel there is a tablet on which is inscribed: Addoldy'r Annibynwyr. Adeiladwyd 1746, Ail Adeiladwyd 1819, Adnewyddwyd 1906. (An Independent place of worship. Built 1746, re-built 1819, restored 1906.) Between the chapel and the road there is a monument topped with an angel and, on the plinth below the angel, is inscribed: Cofgolofn i enwogion Neuadd Lwyd. Gweinidogion yr Eglwys – Parch. Thomas Phillips, DD, 1796-1842, enwog fel pregethwr, sylfaenydd eglwysi, athraw coleg, esboniwr ac emynydd. Hunodd Rhagfyr 22ain 1842 yn 70 oed. (A memorial to the famous of Neuadd Lwyd, Ministers of the chapel – Rev. Thomas Phillips, DD, 1796-1842, famous as a preacher, founder of many chapels, college teacher, biblical scholar, hymn-writer. Died December 22nd 1842, aged 70.) Parch William Evans, 1835-1896. Gadarn yn yr Ysgrythur, a gŵr Sanctaidd Duw. Hunodd Rhagfyr 22ain

1896 yn 87 oed. (Rev. William Evans, 1835-1896, well versed in the Scriptures and a Holy man of God. Died December 22nd 1896, 87 years of age.) Parch Thomas Gwilym Evans, 1891-1949, hunodd Medi 10fed 1949. 'Ac efe a wnaeth yr hyn oedd dda ac uniawn gerbron yr Arglwydd ei Dduw.' (Rev. Thomas Gwilym Evans, 1891-1949, died September 10th 1949. 'He did right in the sight of the Lord all his days.') These details tell a remarkable story because it means that only three ministers served the chapel in a period of one hundred and fifty years. Pregethwyr a godwyd yn yr Eglwys hon: Michael Jones, Bala, David Davies, Panteg, John Rowlands, Cwmllynfell, Thomas Lewis, Pwllheli, John Davies, Glandwr, Penfro, Evan Williams, Penycae, John Phillips, Trewen, James Davies, Bwlchyffridd, John Davies, David Evans, Meifod, Maldwyn, David Phillips, Cana, Caerfyrddin, Griffith T. Evans, Penygraig, Benjamin Phillips, Ty'ngwndwn, Francis Evans, Ulverstone, David Evans, Pantycrugiau, Morgan Evans, Oakford. (The above are ministers who were raised in this church.)

Cenhadon cyntaf Madagascar, aelodau o'r Eglwys hon: David Jones a Thomas Bevan a'i briod Mary Bevan. Glaniasant yn yr ynys Awst 18fed 1818. Hunodd Thomas Bevan Ionawr 31ain, a Mary Bevan Chwefror 3ydd 1819, ill dau yn 23ain oed. Hunodd David Jones, ar ol llafurio am 23ain mlynedd, Mai 1af 1841 yn 45 oed. 'A defaid eraill sydd gennyf . . . y rhai hynny hefyd raid i mi eu cyrchu.' (The first missionaries of Madagascar, members of this church: Rev. David Jones and Thomas Bevan and his wife Mary Bevan. They landed on the island August 18th 1818. Thomas Bevan died January 31st, and Mary Bevan February 3rd 1819, both 23 years of age.' David Jones died May 1st 1841 aged 45 years, and had served on the island as a missionary for 23 years. 'And other sheep

I have . . . they also I must bring in.' There is no mention of David Jones's wife and child; they had died on the island of Mauritius within a few weeks of arriving on the island. In the case of the two young missionaries and their families it is a very sad tale indeed.

Dr Thomas Phillips was born on a farm called Scythlyn in the parish of Llanfihangel-ar-Arth Carmarthenshire on March 29th 1772. He was the second son of John and Anne Phillips, and both his father and grandfather were deacons in the chapel in Pencader. It is said that he was a very deep thinker even as a child, and at seven years of age held religious views well beyond his years. He also had a strong leaning towards becoming a preacher at a very young age. At eighteen years of age he was admitted as a full member of the chapel. He had been fortunate enough to have received the benefit of a good education in a school run by a Mr Davies of Castellhowell, and he subsequently studied at the college for intending ministers at Carmarthen for a period of two and a half years.

On March 29th 1798, two years after becoming the minister of Neuadd Lwyd, he married a young lady member of his chapel. She was quite wealthy and this enabled Dr Phillips to expand his horizons and to influence the religious life of the people nationwide. They were blessed with a large family; four of their sons followed their father's footsteps by also becoming preachers.

In the year 1810 the ministers of Cardiganshire decided to establish a preparatory college at Neuadd Lwyd in order to enable young men to go to the college at Carmarthen. A Mr John Maurice was appointed as tutor in the classics and Dr Phillips took charge of theology. In 1831 Dr Phillips was honoured with a doctorate from a college in New Jersey in the United States of America. During the last ten years of his life he faced a great deal of personal sadness. In 1834 his son John, a promising preacher, died, and in 1842 his wife of forty-four years died. On December 22nd of the same year Dr Phillips also died. In a book entitled *Hanes Ymneilltuaeth* (The History of Nonconformity) written by a Mr Morgan of Llanfyllin, he is described: 'as a man who was blessed with a handsome countenance; as a Christian he concentrated on the basics of his religion; as a preacher he excelled in both content and delivery of his sermons, and as a theologian he was on par with the best.'

Thomas Bevan was born in the Neuadd Lwyd area, sometime in 1796. He became a member of the chapel when quite a young man, and was soon preaching in the chapels of the district. He studied at the college, and it was on either August 20th or 21st 1817 that he and David Jones while attending a service in the chapel volunteered for missionary service in Madagascar. David Jones was the son of one of the deacons of Neuadd Lwyd. Like Thomas Bevan he also became a student of Dr Phillips. Within a very short time of reaching Madagascar he lost his wife, child, and his co-worker Thomas Bevan and his family, and was left to carry on the work on his own. In 1822 a David Griffiths joined him and set up a school for the children of the island; among the pupils was the king's son. In 1830 he returned to London for a time, and by the time he returned to the island difficulties instigated by the island's authorities made missionary work impossible, so the two were forced to leave the island for Mauritius. On May 1st 1841 David Jones, died and was buried in a graveyard in Port Louis.

Before leaving this seemingly insignificant chapel, with its immeasurable contribution to the religious life of

Wales, a walk around the graveyard will, I feel certain, prove of interest to the visitor.

In the graveyard there are two most unusual gravestones. They are of a kind I have not seen in any other churchyard or graveyard. Both stones are six feet wide and three feet high, differing from the dimensions of the usual gravestone. To add to the unique dimensions the inscriptions are set out in columns – name of deceased, place of birth, date of birth, where person died, age at death.

One stone records the names of members of the family of a Thomas Evans of Pontbrendu Farm, the other, the family of Thomas Davies, Llwynyrheol.

The details on the stones are set out as follows:

Er coffadwriaeth am Thomas Evans a'i wraig a'i blant, Pontbrendu. (In memory of Thomas Evans, his wife and children, Pontbrendu.)

Enw, Lle Geni, Plwyf Ganwyd. Lle Oed.

Name, Born at Parish, Dof B, Where Age

Thomas Evans Pencnwc Llanarth 1.2.1794 Home 71
Magdalen-gwraig Pontbrendu Llanina 27.11.1821 " –
John Evans-mab Llanarth 2.7.1864 20
Magdalen-merch 18.5.1837 –
Catherine Hannah 15.3.1839 –
Evan-mab 18.7.1839-7mis
John-mab 2.8.1844 –
Maen cofadwriaeth Thomas Davies, Llwynyrheol, a'i wraig a'i blant. (Memorial stone of Thomas Davies, Llwynyrheol, his wife and children.)
Thomas Davies Llwynyrheol Llanarth b12.3.1818 Home

d11.10.01 82 Jane-wife Ty Coch, Dihewyd b11.3.1816
d31.12.01. 85

Hannah Neuadd Lwyd Llanerch Aeron b29.9.1848 d12.2.1870

John Llwynyrheol Llanarth b25.12.1849
d31.12.21-71

Anne b7.5.1852
d20.12.11. 59

Margaret b1.4.1854
d21.12.1859. 5

Elizabeth b12.9.1856 d25.12.1859-3

Mary b28.4.1858

Thomas eu wyr, mab Abraham a Hannah Thomas, Ffynnongoch, b13.4.1868, d17.5.1871 – 3.

Henfynyw and Bettws Bledrws

Leaving the chapel of Neuadd Lwyd we rejoin the Lampeter to Aberaeron road, turning left at the junction, and on to Aberaeron. There we turn left on to the A487 and continue through the resort, and after a climbing out of Aberaeron for approximately two miles, reach the church of Henfynyw which stands on the right hand side of the road.

Tradition has it that Henfynyw was possibly the birthplace of our Patron Saint, St David, and the church is dedicated to him. Not far from the church is Ffynnon Dewi (David's Well). The churchyard is entered through a lych-gate. On the upper part of the gable there is a wooden crucifix and on the cross beam directly above the gate the words from John 11v24, 'Myfi Yw'r Atgyfodiad a'r Bywyd.' (I am the resurrection and the life.) In the National Library are Bishop's Transcripts from 1674 to 1868, and also the Parish Registers: the Baptisms Register 1813-99, Marriages Register 1772-1971, and the Burial Register1839-1939.

In the churchyard are gravestones on which there are interesting inscriptions: Er coffadwriaeth am y Parch. David Evans, yr hwn a fu farw Awst 15fed 1873, yn 55 oed. Bu yn weinidog ffyddlon yn Pantycrugiau am 13 o flynyddoedd a dau fis. Bu hefyd yn pregethu yn gynorthwyol gan y Parch T. Rees yn Capel y Wig, Maenygroes am flynyddoedd lawer.

> Deui mewn tŷ o dywod – gosodwyd
> Is aden y beddrod.
> Mae trwbwl meddwl ei fod
> Bychain o'i eisiau uchod.

Colled i'w fyned i'w fedd
A hiraeth oherwydd ei ddiwedd,
Fe'i . . . achos . . .
Angau glas a'i ing a'i fedd.

The inscription informs us that a Rev. David Evans died on August 15th 1873 aged 55; that he had been a minister at Pantycrugiau for 13 years and 2 months. He also preached with the Rev. T. Rees of Maenygroes. The two verses tell us: Now placed in a house of sand,/Lying buried in a grave./It troubles all thinking of this,/His services still very much needed./His death a great loss, and deeply mourned by all he left behind.

On another stone: 'Also Elizabeth, daughter of John and Eliza Lloyd of Aberaeron, who died at Monachdy Arms December 24th 1883 aged 30 years. The eight-line verse is a warning aimed at the young of Aberaeron:

O ieuenctid Aberaeron,
Ceisiwch heddwch Duw mewn pryd.
Er fod lliwiau rhos a lili
Ar eich gruddiau'n cwrdd ynghyd.
Er mor gryfed ydych heddiw,
Er mor iachus yw eich gwawr,
Gellwch fod fel finnau'n fuan,
Yn llu llestri oer y llawr.

[O young people of Aberaeron,/Make your peace with God in time,/Although your cheeks the colour of the rose and the lily,/In spite of the fact that you are now enjoying good health today,/You, like me, can soon be/Cold vessels in the earth below.]

Yet another verse, this time on a stone on which is

inscribed: Er cof am Lewis Jones, Crogfaen, o'r Plwyf hwn, bu farw Hydref 29ain 1852 yn 78 oed.

> Ei goron a flagurodd hyd ei fedd,
>> Do, ei barch gynyddodd.
> Ei wisg o gnawd mi osgodd,
> Aeth i fyd sydd wrth ei fodd.

A very rough translation reads: His crown blossomed until his demise,/Yes, his respectability increased./His cloak of flesh he cast off./He went to a world that was to his liking.

On a stone slab lying on the ground, and on which there is a rough carving, the following details: Here lyeth the body of Jenkin Thomas of Caehaidd who died July 20th 1771, aged 80 years.

> Dyma'r fan dan garreg fedd
> Gorffwys a fu mewn isel wedd,
> Gan ddisgwyl beunydd am y dydd
> I gael ei rhoi o'i rhwymau'n rhydd.

[Here under a gravestone/He lay in low appearance/ Longing constantly for the day/That from his bonds he is released.]

And on another stone another interesting verse that follows details that read: To the memory of Daniel Evans of Morfa Mawr in the parish of Llansantffraed who departed this life March 7th 1823 aged 55 years, Here also lieth the body of Esther Evans, his dear wife, who died March 1st 1824 aged 44 years. Also the body of Mary Evans, the daughter of Daniel and Esther Evans who died January 16th 1813 aged 1 year.

Daniel yw dyn fu o les –
Ac Esther deg ystwyth gymhares,
A Mair eu mer aeres gyd orwedd – o ryfedd res,

Tri chyfaill fu'n tra chyfarch a'u gilydd.
O galon uniawn – di amod a di amarch
Hyd ddyffryn ac erchwyn arch.

[Daniel a man who proved his usefulness,/And fair Esther his partner,/And with Mary their heir they lie./Three friends that greeted each other,/Of true hearts – always on good terms and honourable/To the valley of death and the protection of the ark (coffin).]

Next stop is the church at Betws Bledrws. Betws Bledrws stands some three miles on the A485, the Lampeter to Tregaron road. Betws is the Welsh word for Bede House, and such a house would in olden days be used for rest and sustenance by pilgrims on their way to holy shrines such as the cathedral at St David's or possibly a monastery such as the one that at one time stood at Strata Florida. As for Bledrws, according to the St David's Diocesan Year Book, he was a saint and the church at Betws Bledrws is dedicated to both St Bledrws and St Michael. The church is part of the Lampeter and Llanddewibrefi group of churches, the group consisting of ten churches. The Parish Registers, dating from 1813 are kept in the National Library and also the Bishop's Transcripts from 1801.

Like the churchyard at Henfynyw, and many other churchyards, some of the inscriptions on the gravestones are quite interesting. A matter of a foot or so from the west wall of the porch a slab lies over a grave on which is inscribed: Here lieth the remains of David Evan Charles, late of this Parish, who departed this life June 10th 1810 aged 8. And then follows a very morbid verse that is intended to draw the reader's attention to the fact that life is ephemeral.

> Yfryfia yn brudd darllenydd llon,
> Rwyf i yn gorwedd dan y garreg hon,
> Gan angau glas yn rwym dan glo
> Lle byddi dithau ar fyr dro.

[Sadly contemplate cheerful reader,/I am lying 'neath this stone,/Tied and locked in death/Where you will also soon be.]

On another stone a verse that reads:

> Caf orwedd yn fy ngwely pridd
> Nes delo dydd y cyfri.
> Daw'r meirw'n fyw i gyd i'r lan;
> Cant yn y man eu barnu.

[I will lie in my bed of earth/Until the coming of the day of reckoning./The dead shall come to life and rise;/ And soon they shall be judged.]

Another two stones are at the east end of the church on which are details with a historical slant: In memory of David J. Morgan, Road Surveyor for Tregaron Union, also contractor and builder of Deri Ormond Tower, who died at Brynmaen, parish of Llanddewibrefi, December 5th 1872 aged 75 years. Also of Evan Morgan, his son, Auctioneer and Valuer, late Caerlwyd, Tregaron, died May 11th 1886, aged 65 years. On the other stone: In a vault lie interred the mortal remains of Daniel Morgan, son of David and Mary Morgan, Brynmaen in this parish of Llanddewibrefi and was born at Denmark in this parish on March 5th 1819 and departed this life at the said Brynmaen 12th September 1838, aged 19 years and six months. (David Morgan, Daniel's father, was the builder of St David's Pillar in this parish).

The tower referred to is a tall, chimney-like structure standing on a hillltop overlooking the church and hamlet. A John Jones inherited Derry Ormond on the death of his father in 1817. He then decided to build a new house and knock down the one his father had lived in. Work on the new house commenced in 1824 and was completed in 1827. About the same time the 200ft. high tower was built on a hilltop on his land. The new house cost £6,211 to build.

During the nineteenth century the installing of pipe organs in mansions became popular, and a fine organ was installed in Derry Ormond. In 1953 when the mansion was demolished, the organ was bought by Major John Francis, an auctioneer and valuer in Carmarthen, who lived in Llangunnor. He presented the organ to the church at Llangunnor, and it is a memorial to his wife.

Llangoedmor

While nearing Cardigan on the A484 from Carmarthen I had on numerous occasions noticed a sign pointing to Llangoedmore. One day in May of 1997 I decided to visit the church there, and the visit proved worthwhile.

Not far from the church stands Plas Llangoedmore, a mansion dating back to the time of Queen Elizabeth. In 1758 a John Lloyd bought the mansion for £2,500; he held the post of Clerk of the Check at HM Dockyard at Plymouth. In 1786 the house changed hands once again when John Lloyd sold it to a David Edward Lewis Lloyd of Dolhaidd near Newcastle Emlyn. Fifteen years later, in 1801, it was bought by a Rev. Benjamin Millingchamp whose father was Customs Officer of Cardigan. Benjamin Millingchamp first attended Edward Richards's school at Ystrad Meurig and was further educated at Oxford. Afterwards he became a priest in the Anglican Church. On becoming a naval chaplain on the ship 'The Superb' he served on the flagship of an Admiral Hughes in the Indian Ocean. He saw action more than once and in 1782 was appointed chaplain of the naval fort at Madras. It was through this appointment that he came into contact with the East India Company, and this association with the company resulted in his making a fortune. He returned to this country in 1797, became Rural Dean of Cemaes, Prebendary of St David's Cathedral and in 1825 Archdeacon of Carmarthen. He died in 1829 and is buried at Llangoedmore. He is remembered inside the church by a memorial that reads: In memory of the Venerable Archdeacon Millingchamp, DD, of Llangoedmore, in this Parish. Archdeacon of Carmarthen, Prebendary of St David's, Rector of Rushall, Wilts, 20 years Chaplain of

Fort George, Madras, and senior Chaplain in the British Navy, died January 12th 1829 aged 73. Also in memory of Sarah, his wife, daughter of Thomas Rawlinson of Grantham, Lincolnshire, died February 20th 1869 aged 95.

'Until the day break and the shadows flee away.'

There are also a number of other memorials on the inside walls of the church. A brass plate is inscribed with: 'In loving memory of Lieut, Col, Herbert Rhys Lloyd, 1st Battalion Somerset Light Infantry and 2nd Battalion Royal Sussex Regiment, died 18th November 1932 aged 74.' The other memorials read as follows: 'Sacred to the memory of Elizabeth Catharine (sic), relict of the late William Mitchell of Cardigan, who expired on the 1st June 1827 aged 63 years after a painful and protracted illness. This monument has been erected by the children of her first marriage with Major James Gower of the Royal Marines as the last mournful token they can give of the love and gratitude which they feel for their dear departed mother. Their first, their fondest and their firmest friend.'

Then a memorial reflecting the very high infant mortality rate of the 1800s: In memory of Gertrude Anne who died May the 2nd. 1833, aged 1 year, and of Annette Rhoda who died on the 22nd of the same month, aged 9 weeks. Daughters of Rowley Lascelles of Pencraig, Esq. 'The Lord gave and the Lord hath taken away. Blessed be the name of the Lord.'

There is much talk today about an influx of people from across the border settling down in Wales; seemingly there is nothing new in this. The Lascelles family of Pencraig, like many other families, moved into Wales during the eighteenth and nineteenth centuries. They had made their money as merchants, bankers and lawyers.

Also in the church are a number of other memorials commemorating owners and families of the landed gentry of the district – their houses Cilbronne, Treforgan, Llwyn Gramws, Plas Llangoedmore. Of the houses mentioned, there are two memorials commemorating members of the Jenkins family of Cilbronne. One of the memorials reads: Sacred to the memory of Griffith Jenkins of Kilbronne (sic) in this parish, Esq., who died October 13th 1781 aged 38 years, and Mary Jenkins, wife of the above Griffith Jenkins, who during widowhood of forty-three years was a most affectionate mother to her five surviving sons; she died September 23rd 1824 aged 81 years. Also of the Rev. John Jenkins, AM, Prebendary of York and vicar of Kerry, Montgomeryshire, eldest son of Griffith and Mary Jenkins, who in every relation of life – whether magistrate, son, husband, father, brother, friend – was most exemplary; he left a mournful widow, and infant son, three brothers, and a very numerous circle of friends to lament his loss. He departed this life November 20th 1829 aged 59. The other memorial to the same family has written on it: In loving memory of Jonathan Jenkins, Esq. of Cilbronne, who was always an example of every good in this parish, who died on the 27th January 1851, in his 77th year. And of his beloved wife Adeliza Jane Jenkins, daughter of Major James Gower of the Royal Marines, who died 10th November 1842 aged 52 years. Also their youngest son, Griffith Richard Jenkins. MD, FRCP, who died at Cardigan on the 13th December 1870 in his 37th year. He served in the Royal Navy in the Russian and China Wars, and subsequently was attached to the British Legation in Japan. His zeal in his profession weakened his health to recruit (sic) when he returned to England, but succumbed after a short illness. Dearly loved and deeply regretted of relatives and friends both at home and abroad. Their remains are interred in the family vault in this churchyard."

It may surprise the visitor to see a memorial to members of a family that lived at Abertrinant, a house near the village of Llanfihangel-y-Creuddyn not far from Aberystwyth and at the opposite end of the county, in a north-south axis, to Llangoedmore. But a little research into the family commemorated on the wall of Llangoedmore church will show that the members mentioned were closely connected to Bronwydd, a mansion not many miles from Llangoedmore. The memorial has this inscription on it: Sacred to the memory of Owen Ford Lloyd, Esq., of Abertrinant, youngest son of Thomas Lloyd, Esq., of Bronwydd, who departed this life the 10th day of November 1812 in the 57th year of his age. He was a kind husband and indulgent father and a sincere benevolent friend to all man-kind. His afflicted widow has caused this mournful tribute of his love to be erected to his memory. In the same vault as their beloved father are deposited the remains of two children who died in infancy. Also of Amelia, his beloved daughter, who exchanged this life for a better on the 5th day of October 1812 in the 6th year of her age. Also in the same vault are deposited the remains of Dorothea Eliza, relict of the above Owen Lloyd, daughter of Thomas Lloyd, Esq. of Abertrinant by the Honourable Elizabeth Dorothea his wife and granddaughter of Wilmot, third Lord Lisburne of Crosswood in this county. She departed this life ---- ---- ---- aged – years. (Details of the date of her death and her age have not been inscribed on the memorial.)

The first of the Lloyd family to live at Bronwydd was

a Rev. Thomas Lloyd – this at the turn of the 1600s. The Owen Lloyd mentioned in the memorial was, as is recorded on it, the son of a descendant of this Rev. Thomas Lloyd - another Thomas Lloyd who lived from 1703 to 1775, and who married Anne Lloyd, daughter of a William Lloyd of Henllys. A barrister, Thomas Lloyd became High Sheriff in 1733 and took on the title of Lord of Cemaes. His son Owen married another Lloyd, Dorothea Eliza Lloyd, she was the daughter of another Thomas Lloyd, who lived at Abertrinant. Dorothea, being the heiress, inherited Abertrinant and thus Owen Lloyd through his marriage to her became owner of Abertrinant. He also attained the rank of Colonel, possibly in the local militia.

As one would expect, there are memorials within the church to people who lived at Plas Llangoedmore; indeed, there are four of them. Again, we come across the name Lloyd: Sacred to the memory of Thomas Lloyd, Esq. of Coedmore, who died the 21st September 1810 aged 51 years, and of Elizabeth, his wife, who died at Richmond in Surrey in her 83rd year, and was buried at Petersham in November 1852. This tablet is erected by their grandchildren Thomas Edward Lloyd, Edmund Lloyd, Walter Lloyd, Esquires, in the year 1857.

Next, a tablet on which is inscribed: Sacred to the memory of Thomas Lloyd, Esq., Lord Lieutenant of the County of Cardiganshire, who died at Coedmore, Cardiganshire, July 12th 1857 in his 64th year. He was a kind and affectionate husband and father, and his loss deeply regretted by his widow and family. This tablet is erected to his memory by his sorrowing wife. (There is no mention of his wife's name, or when she died, and at what age.)

In his book *Historic Cardiganshire and Their Families* the

late Francis Jones mentions that Thomas Lloyd was, in his younger days, a very good and well-known athlete. In 1825 he challenged a Cardigan solicitor named Mr Lucas to a race of 30 miles across the Preseli Hills to Haverfordwest, with £50 for the winner. Thomas Lloyd won the race, reaching Haverfordwest an hour before Mr Lucas.

During his life he held some very important offices. In 1816, at the age of twenty-three was appointed High Sheriff; he was also a Justice of the Peace and Deputy Lieutenant of Cardiganshire. In 1854, three years before his death he was appointed Lord Lieutenant and Custos Rotulorum of the same county.

Thomas Lloyd's wife was a Charlotte Longcroft; she was born in 1799 and died on May 5th 1866. She was part heiress of Llanina estate which was situated a mile north of New Quay, Cardiganshire.

Herbert Vaughan in his book *The South Wales Squires* writes that Thomas Lloyd 'was notorious in a free-and-easy age and society for the number of his bastards, several of whom, when they grew up, served their father in a domestic capacity at Coedmore. He was, however, reckoned generous towards a succession of mistresses, for he granted them all small farms or holdings on the Coedmore estate on long leases at low or nominal rent. His sons born in wedlock did not fare so well. In order to be spared the trouble and expenses of keeping and educating them, the three young Lloyds were put out to work on the outlying farms, and it was only after much entreaty from a neighbour that the eldest son and heir was at last sent to school at Rugby and later allowed to read for the Bar.

The selfish old couple (Thomas Lloyd and his wife) were in the habit of driving regularly once a year in their own chariot to Bristol – to eat turtle! . . . Before starting on this gormandizing pilgrimage, the pair used always to pay a visit to pay a formal call at Llangoedmore on my grandparents (H.M. Vaughan's), who on their departure no doubt wished them "Bon voyage et bon appetit!" Yet the old Squire of Coedmore was popular. He rarely gave anything in charity, but was so affable and pleasant-spoken that his suppliant was wont to depart quite pleased with his late interview in spite of an empty pocket.'

There is no doubt from H.M. Vaughan's account that Thomas and Charlotte Lloyd were without doubt interesting 'characters'.

On a stone slab over a grave to the east of the church is the following inscription:

Sacred to the memory of Thomas Lloyd, Esq., late
Lord Lieutenant and Custos Roculorum of the County of
Cardigan who died 12th of July 1857, aged 64 years.
He was a kind and affectionate husband,
Beloved for the simplicity of his manners and the
benevolence of his heart. Respected for his inflexible
integrity, and his pure unaffected purity.
Thou art gone, but we will not deplore thee
Though darkness is of the tomb.
Thy Saviour has passed through the portals before thee,
The Lamb of God is thy guide and thy groom.

Thou art gone to the grave, but we will not deplore thee,
Whose God was thy ransom, thy guardian and guide.
He took thee, and He will restore thee,
And death hath no sting for the Saviour has died.

Again no mention of his wife on this memorial, like the one inside the church.

If H.M. Vaughan's account of the life of Thomas Lloyd is true, and there is no reason to doubt it, Thomas Lloyd's wife must have been a saint to put up with all his womanising, but as the saying goes, 'love is blind'.

So we move back inside the church and leave the memorial to Thomas Lloyd, the man who told a judge without the slightest blush that the coachman and footman on their coach were both his bastard sons. Now we turn to look at another memorial; on it is inscribed: In memory of Herbert Millingchamp Vaughan, Captain in HM 80th (Perthshire) Light Infantry, eldest son of Colonel Herbert Vaughan (late commanding the same Regiment) of Plas Llangoedmore, Co. of Cardigan and of Sarah his wife.

He fell bravely at the head of his company in the British attack on the Redan before Sevastopol on the 8th September 1855, and died of his wounds on the 12th of the same month in the 27th year of his age. Friends, comrades and brother officers have erected this monument as a mark of their affectionate esteem, and as a tribute to his gallantry.

Captain Vaughan's mother was the daughter and heiress of the Rev. Benjamin Millingchamp. She married the above-mentioned Colonel Herbert Vaughan; the Colonel was the grandson of Edward Vaughan who was the son of the Viscountess of Lisburne and David Lloyd, the agent of Trawsgoed estate. Trawsgoed was situated in Llanafan, and stood on the banks of the river Ystwyth, some seven miles south-east of Aberystwyth. According to Thomas Nicholas, in his book *Annals and Antiquities of the Counties and County Families of Wales*, Volumes 1 and 2, published in 1872, the Vaughan family had lived in Trawsgoed since the 1200s.

Below the memorial to Captain Vaughan there is a

brass plate, stating: To the glory of God and in loving memory of John Percival Vaughan of the Indian Civil Service, second son of John and Julia Anne Vaughan of Plas Llangoedmore in this Parish. Born September 15th 1871, died at Karachi, India, May 31st 1906. 'Until the day break'.

Julia Anne Vaughan, John Percival Vaughan's mother, was the daughter of Thomas Charles Morris of Bryn Myrddin, Abergwili and Cwm, Llansteffan. Her father, Thomas Charles, was a member of a Carmarthen banking family. The original house that stood on the site was called Pen-y-Banc, but the new house built around 1858 was called Bryn Myrddin because Julia Anne Morris' mother thought that the name 'Penny Bank' was most unsuitable.

Cwm, the Morris' other property near Llanstephan, was taken down in the 1860s and a new mansion erected to replace it. Today the mansion is a Cheshire Home.

Another memorial is inscribed thus: In memory of R. Price, Gentleman, of Gelli-wen in this Parish who was Surveyor of the Customs at the port of Cardigan for 24 years. He died December 24th 1827 aged 60 years. 'We must all appear before the judgement seat of Christ'.

Yet another two memorials are to be seen on the inside walls of the church: Sacred to the memory of Evan Davies, Esq., late of Trevorgan (sic) in this Parish who departed this life February 7th 1832 aged 67 years. This monument is erected by his sorrowing widow and daughter as the last mournful tribute of their respect, gratitude and affection for one of the best husbands and father. Margaret, wife of the above Evan Davies, Esq. and daughter of the late Benjamin Millichamp, Esquire, departed this life December 11th 1837 aged 72 years. 'Be ye also ready'.

Interred near this place lies the body of Magdalen, the wife of Thomas Lewis of Llwyn Grawys, Esq., who departed this life the 28th of January in the year of our Lord Jesus Christ 1729 in ye 38th year of her age. Also the body of John, 3rd son of the above Thomas Lewis and Magdalen his wife, who departed this life ye 17th of April 1742 in ye 18th year of her age. Here also interred Elizabeth, widow and eldest daughter of Thomas and Magdalen Lewis, died 21st Aril 1786, Aetat 71.

On this memorial it is the death of the husband, Thomas Lewis, that is not mentioned which may not be all that surprising because in 1735 he married as his second wife, a widow, Catherine Lewis of Llanbedr Velfrey, Pembrokeshire. And yet again in 1757 Thomas Lewis married for the third time, a Jane Owen, heiress of Clunyrynys, Ferwig. In 1753 he purchased the Clynfyw estate from Owen Davies, Receiver-General of Westminster Abbey. Thomas Lewis' son William, born of his second wife, married Margaret Bowen of Pantyderi, Llanfair Nantgwyn.

In the churchyard there is a stone on which is inscribed a couplet:

> Life's but a dream, and all things show it,
> I thought so once, now I know it.

In *The Oxford Book of Quotations* it reads: Life is a jest, and all things show it. The words were written by John Gay (1685-1732) in 'My Own Epitaph'. Gay was the author of The Beggar's Opera as well as Sweet William's Farewell to Black Eye'd Susan. He was a contemporary of Alexander Pope (1688-1744) and Lady Mary Wortley Montague, and the three were members of The Scribblers Club.

In The Beggar's Opera, Gay's masterpiece, he exploited a parallel between politicians and petty crooks, which may have a familiar ring to it when we take into account the charges of sleaze made against some politicians during the last few years.

Lady Montague was the wife of the one-time British Ambassador in Constantinople who, during an outbreak of smallpox in that town, had her son inoculated against the disease, and in 1721, during an outbreak of the same disease in London, had her daughter inoculated; this was well before Edward Jenner's experiments. The method used in the case of Laty Montague's children consisted of transplanting matter from a mildly affected patient to one in need of protection from the disease. This method was fraught with danger, and there was a 2 –3% death rate among those so treated.

It was Edward Jenner, in 1796, who perfected the method but did not publish the result of his experiment until 1798.

During the 1700s, cleanliness was not regarded as important by the populace, even with members of the upper classes, and it is reported that Lady Montague, when someone commented on the dirtiness of her hands, replied, "If you call that dirty, you should see my feet!"

There is one other memorial in the church, to that of Lieut. Col. George Evans Lloyd, CB, DSO who was the son of the incumbent at Troed-yr Aur, the details of which can be seen in the section on the church at Troed-yr-Aur.

So, now, it is time to leave the church at Llangoedmore, the visit having been worthwhile and very interesting. The church itself is dedicated to St Cynllo; it has probably a seventeenth century nave and an eighteenth century chancel, while the windows date from the nineteenth century. A fifth century saint, St

Cynllo, is associated with not only Llangoedmore but also with Rhayader church, the churches at Llanbister, Nantymel and Llangynllo in Powys. In Llangoedmore is a well called Ffynnon Cynllo whose waters are reputed to be good for curing rheumatism.

Now let us travel towards Lampeter and call in the church in the hamlet of Llanwenog. The church is dedicated to a Saint Gwenog who was its virgin founder. Near the church was a Ffynnon Wenog, its water reputed to be good for children with weak backs. There were two other springs in the parish – Ffynnon Ddafras and Ffynnon Meredith.

Thanks to Sir Rhys ap Thomas' patronage, a west tower and a south window were added to the single nave, as well as a south chapel, within which there is a Norman font. Inside the church there are beautiful carvings of the Crucifixion under the east window and also carvings on the pew ends, all based on the design of Mrs Davies-Evans of Highmead, near Llanybydder. The carvings were executed by a Belgian refugee, Joseph Reubens, who came to the district during the first World War. The pew ends are in reality memorials to Saint Gwenog, Hywel ab Owain Gwynedd and the men of the area who were killed in the 1914-18 War. The nearby primary school is also worth a visit; on a mantelpiece in one of the classrooms are carved the heads of another two men who died in that same war.

And now we journey to the hamlet of Llanwnen in order to visit the church, which is dedicated to Saint Lucia. With its thirteenth century chancel and fifteenth century tower it is possible that the south doorway could be Norman but much of the present structure is nineteenth century.

Inscribed in Welsh on a gravestone in the churchyard

is; Er cof am John Davies, Pantyrodyn, plwyf Llanfihangel-ar-Arth, bu farw Chwefror 1af 1875 yn 25ain mlwydd oed.

> Un a fo'n iawn ei fywyd – a gedwir
> Yn gadarn ei wynfyd.
> Ni gyll i fyn ochelyd,
> Na dydd na diwedd byd.

The words of the inscription commemorate a twenty-five year old John Davies of the parish of Llanfihangel-ar-Arth, a parish, incidentally, a number of miles from Llanwnen. He died February 1st 1875; the verse extols his virtues, and that he will be kept in a state of bliss forever and a day.

On another stone, again in Welsh, are details of a woman who died in 1885, aged 88 years, and the following verse:

> Oedd fenyw gall a thyner,
> Yn hoff o eiriau Duw.
> Hi welodd ddyddiau lawer,
> Ond bellach marw yw.

[She was wise and tender/ And loved the Word of God/ She saw many days/ But now she is dead.]

On another gravestone are details relating to a very sad episode in the life of a husband whose wife died in childbirth on April 27th 1885, followed by the deaths of the twins born at that time; one twin died on May 11th and the other on May 13th 1885.

'In memory of Elizabeth Richards, wife of Thomas Richards of Pentre Sion in the parish of Lampeter. She died April 27th 1885, aged 26 years, also Daniel, her son, died May 11th 1885, aged 3 weeks, and Elizabeth, her daughter, died May 13th 1885, aged 3 weeks.

> Yn y gweryd hon y rhoddwyd
> Gwraig rinweddol a dinam.
> A'i dau efell bach a gladdwyd
> Yma'n fuan at eu mam.'

[In this grave this one was placed/ A virtuous and perfect wife/ And her little twins were buried/ Soon along with their mother.]

A circle with its centre some six miles west of Lampeter, and a diameter of around fourteen miles, stretching from Llandysul in the south-west to Llangybi in the north-east, has dotted within it fourteen Unitarian chapels. The chapels are Ciliau, Rhyd-y-gwin, Cribyn, Brondeifi, Cae'ronnen, Capel y Groes, Alltyblaca, Capel y Bryn, Capel y Cwm, Bwlchyfadfa, Capel Newydd Llwynrhydowen, Yr Hen Gapel Llwynrhydowen, Pantydefaid, Capel y Graig.

Members of the Unitarian movement deny the belief held by Christians of God being Three In One – God the Father, God the Son (i.e. Jesus), God the Holy Spirit – The Holy Trinity. The Unitarians believe that He is a loving God the Father and that Jesus was a good man whose teachings, if followed, could lead to a peaceful world in which human beings fulfil His commandment by 'loving one another as He loved everyone'.

It can be said that the beginnings of Unitarianism go back some seventeen hundred years. Not every Christian was ready to accept that Christ was truly the Son of God; this belief was led by a priest of Alexandria in Egypt named Arius. This led to a split and a great deal of controversy among the leaders of the Christian Church. In an attempt to resolve the matter the emperor Constantine called together some three hundred bishops to his palace at Nicea,

An ascetical, moral leader of a Christian community in the area of Alexandria, Arius attracted a large following through his teaching that God was the absolute one and only one, and that Christ is not truly divine. Arius believed that God was unique, alone self-existent and immutable. According to its opponents, especially the bishop Athanasius, Arius' teaching reduced the Son to a demigod, and undermined the Christian concept of redemption since only He who was truly God could be deemed to have reconciled man to the Godhead. What Arius believed became known as Arianism, and it was because of Arius' teaching that Constantine I called the bishops of the Church together at Nicea in the year 325 in order to resolve the problem which endangered Christanity.

At the Council of Nicea Arius was condemned and considered to be a heretic. As a result of the council's decision the emperor then exiled Arius. Influential support from colleagues in Asia Minor and from the emperor Constantine's daughter, succeeded in effecting Arius' return from exile and his readmission into the Church. Shortly before he was to be reconciled, however, Arius collapsed and died while walking in Constantinople.

Although this ended the heresy in the empire, Arianism continued among some tribes in Germany to the end of the seventh century. Today some Unitarians are virtually Arians in that they are unwilling either to reduce Christ to a mere human being or to attribute to him a divine nature identical with God the Father. The Christology of Jehovah's Witnesses, also, is a form of

Arianism, as they look upon Arius as a forerunner of their founder, Taze Russell.

As I have mentioned earlier, Unitarianism established itself in the Teifi valley, and overlooking the road from Llanybydder to Llanwnen, the B4337, stands the chapel of Alltyblaca. Inscribed on a slate on the wall, and above the front doors, are the following details:

Capel Alltyblaca
(Undodiaid)
Adeiladwyd 1740,
Ail-adeiladwyd 1837,
Adnewyddwyd 1892.
John Davies, Gweinidog.

[Alltyblaca Chapel/Unitarians/Built 1740/ Rebuilt 1837/Restored 1892/John Davies/Minister.]

Although most of the Unitarian chapels in the area were formed out of the old Independent congregations, the cause at Alltyblaca arose out of the Baptists meetings at Newcastle Emlyn and Hengoed (now Aberduar in the parish of Llanybydder). It was the influence of Jenkin Jones, the minister of Llwynrhydowen, and the one who ministered to both chapels until 1853, that led to the establishing of the chapel at Alltyblaca.

During the ministry of the Rev. Davies of Castellhywel, Alltyblaca became an important place of pilgrimage to a number of famous worshippers. It is said that Thomas Evans (Tomos Glyn Cothi), a minister and author, often visited Alltyblaca as a young man, having travelled from Brechfa. Thomas Evans maintained that it was hearing what was preached there that encouraged him to set up the first Unitarian Cause in Wales, and also to become its minister, at Cwm Cothi in Carmarthenshire sometime around 1794. Between 1802 and 1804 he was imprisoned in the jail in Carmarthen because he supported the French Revolution. In 1811 he became minister of a chapel at Aberdare, and it was in Aberdare that he died in 1833.

Another regular visitor was Edward Williams (Iolo Morganwg); he visited Alltyblaca in order to receive communion from his friend, the Rev. Davies of Castellhywel. Iolo Morganwg lived from 1747 until 1826, and was a stonemason by trade. A poet and an antiquary, he became interested in neo-Druidism and, while living and working in London, organised in 1792 the first meeting of 'Gorsedd Beirdd Ynys Prydain'. He, like Tomos Glyn Cothi, also spent some time in prison, Cardiff gaol, due to the fact that he had been declared bankrupt. In 1819 he succeeded in introducing the 'Gorsedd' as a ceremony at the Eisteddfod at Carmarthen; this he achieved at a meeting held in the Ivy Bush Hotel in the town. In the grounds of the hotel there used to be a circle of stones similar to the circle that is set up to this day wherever the Royal National Eisteddfod of Wales is held; whether this circle was laid down by Iolo is unknown.

From 1957 to 1974 the chapel's minister was the Rev. Jacob Davies. The Rev. Davies became known throughout Wales as a broadcaster, speaker, adjudicator, poet and humourist.

In the graveyard there are inscriptions that are worth recording. 'Er cof am Parch Thomas Griffiths (Tau Gimel), gweinidog, emynydd ac hanesydd (1818-71).

> Heddgarwr oedd y gwron – a didwyll
> Nodedig ei galon;
> Ganwyd ef yn genad Iôn,
> A'i ddawn oedd wledd i ddynion.

[A lover of peace this man – guileless/Remarkably so his heart/Born a missionary for the Lord/His talent a gift for all men.]

And then a stone on which is inscribed details about a woman who must have endured much heartache: Er cof am Eleanor, gwraig John Jones, No. 1 Llanwnen, yr hon fu farw Gorffennaf 10fed 1882 yn 58 oed. Hefyd am bedwar o'u plant sef, David, Daniel, Eleanor, John. The verse reads:

> Yma gorffwys yn y graean,
> Annwyl fam a phedwar baban,
> Hyd nes rhoddo Duw yr alwad
> Foreu mawr yr atgyfodiad.

[Here lying in the gravel/A dear mother and four babies/Until God gives the call/That great day of resurrection.]

Not far away is the grave of a John Thomas of Penlôn who died in 1842 and on the stone, a verse by a poet named Daniel Ddu:

> Oedd ei fryd ym mhob gwybodaeth,
> Ond yn bennaf mewn cerddoriaeth,
> Gobaith sydd y cân yr awron
> Gerdd ei Dduw yng ngwydd angylion.

[All his mind aimed at knowledge/But most of all at music/The hope is that he is this hour/Singing of God in the presence of the angels.]

Other gravestones have the following inscriptions:

Er cof am Mary gwraig y diweddar David Jones,

Blaencruser, Plwyf Llanwnen, bu farw Medi 18fed 1882 yn 68 oed.

> Roedd fenyw gall, wybodus iawn,
> A'i gwedd yn llawn hawddgarwch,
> Ac hollol rhydd o frad a thwyll
> Yn caru pwyll a heddwch. Dewi Hefin.

[A wise, knowledgable woman/Her appearance full of amiability/And totally lost to treason and deceit/Loving discretion and peace.]

Er cof am y Parch. T. Evans, mab Daniel a Margaret Evans, Lowtre, Plwyf Llanwnen, yr hwn oedd yn weinidog ffyddlon yn eglwys Undododaidd Kingswood yn agos i Birmingham am ddeng mlynedd. Bu farw Medi 21ain 1848 yn 31 oed.

> Daeth rhyw lef fawr gref i'r fro,
> Geilw Iesu i gael Ei was ato.
> Dyn annwyl a'i ddwyn yno
> I ail fyd yn Ei law o.

Commemorated on the stone is the Rev. T, Evans, aged 31, who was a Unitarian minister at Kingswood near Birmingham. and the verse: A loud shout came heard in the country,/Jesus calling His servant to Him/A gentle man he took away/In His hand to a second kingdom.

Er coffadwriaeth am Sarah, priod John Evans, Blaencwrt, o'r Plwyf hwn, yr hon a fu farw Mawrth 10fed 1870 yn 56 oed. Hefyd am John Evans, Maescegydd (sic), gynt o Blaencwrt, yr hwn a fu farw Rhagfyr 14eg 1895 yn 85 mlwydd oed.

Nid dyma'r fan lle mae fy rhan,
A'm trigfan mewn prysurdeb.
Mae'm tŷ a'm amgau
Ar fryniau tragwyddoldeb.

[This is not the place for me/An abode of strife/ My house and enclosure/Are on the eternal hills.]

Er cof am Evan Thomas, Tycanol, Drefach, Plwyf Llanbedr, yr hwn a fu farw Mawrth 3ydd 1873 yn 45 mlwydd oed. Hefyd Margaret, ei wraig, bu farw Awst 23ain 1876 yn 56 oed.

I'r iawn ei fywyd nid yw'r bedd
Ond toll i fyd y nefol hedd.
Llwyr ben ei daith i'r man lle mae
Rhyddhad o bob daearol wae.

[To the good the grave is not/ But a toll paid for the heavenly peace/Journey ends in a place/Of freedom from every woe.]

And finally this couplet:

Byr iawn yw bore einioes,
Byrach pan brynhawn ein hoes.
DJ

Short is morning's life/Shorter still life's afternoon.

And now we leave Alltyblaca and move on to Cwmsychpant.

To get to Cwmsychpant we head for Llanwnen, and where the road meets the A475, turn left and after a few miles, arrive in the hamlet of Cwmsychpant. The Unitarian chapel, called simply, Capel Y Cwm, stands on the right hand side of the road. Of all the Unitarian chapels in the area this is the youngest of them. It was in 1886 that a number of people living in the area started meeting for worship in a room above a shop in the hamlet. In 1906 the chapel was built on land belonging to Pantybildo Farm. Until 1916 the minister was a Rev. John Davies, who was also reponsible for the cause at Alltyblaca and Capel y Bryn. From 1917 to 1929 a Rev. Lewis Williams took charge of the chapel with the Rev. T.O. Williams in charge for the period 1916 to 1917. With the coming of the Rev. S.E. Bowen – 1922-1956 – a service was held in the chapel every Sunday evening, and this continued during the period the Rev. D. Jacob Davies, 1957-74, ministered there; he was followed by the Rev. Griffith Jones.

Among those buried in the graveyard is Professor Evan James Williams, DSc, FRS, a world-renowned figure in the study of atomic rays.

Inscribed on another two gravestones are the following verses:

(Whoever the person was, the following verse, written by a poet who calls himself Cennech, praises his life and character.)

Deil pob erw a dramwyodd
Wawr a hwyr i gadwi'i graen;
Deil pob ffrind a gynorthwyodd
I fawrygu'i fuchedd blaen.
                              Cennech.

[Every acre that he travelled/Dawn or evening he kept in

good condition/Every friend that he assisted/Still glorify his simple morality.]

The next verse points out the irrefutable fact that the person commemorated, like all of us, was nearing the great eternity that the river Jordan is not far away, and that he longs to reach a country that is a far better place than the world we live in.

O ddydd i ddydd, o awr i awr,
Rwyn nesu i'r tragwyddol fyd mawr.
Nid yw'r Iorddonen ddim ymhell,
O am gyrhaeddyd gwlad sy' well.

Pembrokeshire Churches
(& some more churches of the Diocese)

Leaving Ceredigion, we travel on the A487 road to Pembrokeshire. The first call is at Nevern, its church best known for a fine Celtic cross, c1000AD, standing near the south wall, and for the bleeding yew tree to the right of the path which leads into the church. Near the cross is another early Christian stone, the inscription on it in Latin, which dates from around the fifth or sixth century. The inscription is: VITALIANI/EMERETO, both names common during that period. There is an Ogam inscription on the left angle of the face.

The large west tower is of the sixteenth century and the nave and chancel possibly from the fifteenth century. The nave is nearly 18 metres long and the two transepts on each side of the nave are now used as chapels. The two window sills in the transepts are inscribed, one with both Ogam and Latin writing on it: MAGLOCVN FILI CLVTOR (The stone of Maglocunus, son of Clutorius.); the other stone has inscribed on it an interlaced Latin cross which probably dates from the tenth century.

For the majority of visitors, it is the Celtic cross and the yew tree that attracts them to the church. However, there is far more to the church and churchyard than the cross, the two windowsill stones and the tree. In the churchyard there are a number of gravestones whose inscriptions are worth reading.

On one grave there are two stones, one with a Welsh inscription, the other in English. The English inscription reads: 'In memory of the Rev. John Jones, MA, (Tegid), for ten years vicar of this parish, died May 2nd 1852, aged 60 years.' (Tegid was the Rev. Jones' bardic name.) In Welsh:

'"Coffadwriaeth y cyfiawn sy' fendigedig." Isod y gorffwys gweddillion marwol y Parch John Jones, MA, (Tegid), offeiriad, bardd, ysgolor a gwladgarwr ffyddlon, Peryglor y Plwyf Hwn 1842-52, Prebendwr Tŷ Ddewi 1842-52. Ganwyd Chwefror 10fed 1792, bu farw Mai 2 1852. Gosodwyd y golofn hon gan . . . mae ei garreg fedd wreiddiol tu ôl wedi 'sgrifennu yn Saesneg."

The Welsh inscription tells us that the Rev. Jones was vicar of the parish from 1842 until his death in 1852, that he was a poet, scholar, and a faithful lover of his country. He was also a Prebendary of St Davids Cathedral. Born in Bala in 1792, his education started in Bala under the guidance of Robert Williams of Y Pandy, near Bala. This Robert Williams was also a poet and, following his religious conversion, his work consisted mainly of carols and moral outpourings. He is remembered for his famous line: 'Beibl i bawb o bobl y byd.' (A Bible for all the people of the world.)

In 1814 John Jones went to study at Jesus College, Oxford. In 1818 he graduated in mathematics and he was ordained into the church the following year. He was appointed chaplain and precentor of Christ Church, Oxford, and given a living at St Thomas where he set up schools for both boys and girls.

John Jones was undoubtedly a controversial character; he crossed swords with more than one other scholar. In 1841 he returned to his native land and was given the living of Nevern in Pembrokeshire. There he remained until his death in 1852. In 1848 he was one of those appointed to translate 'The Report of the Commission on Education in Wales' into Welsh. The report became known throughout Wales as 'The Treason of the Blue Books' because the contents of the report gave a picture of the Welsh as being backward, uncouth and immoral. One should not be too surprised at what the three commissioners had written in the report; they were monoglot Englishmen and considered all those who could not speak English as completely ignorant.

As well as John Jones' grave the churchyard holds the graves of twenty-three members of the Bowen family of nearby Llwyngwair Mansion, now a hotel, and the surrounding land a caravan park.

The surname Bowen is derived from 'ap Owen', the ap standing for 'son of'. A Sir James ap Owen, a follower of Henry Tudor at the time of the Battle of Bosworth in 1485, bought Llwyngwair at around 1503 from the Cole family. At one time there were 34 bedrooms in the mansion.

Thirteen generations of the family subsequently lived at Llwyngwair and, over the years, were active in public life. The family could boast of seven High Sheriffs, a Lord Lieutenant, deputy lieutenants, magistrates and parliamentary commissioners. During the eighteenth century the Bowen family had leanings towards Methodism, and George Bowen, who lived from 1722 until 1810 became known as 'The Nonconformist Churchman'. Llwyngwair was visited by a number of prominent Methodists, among them John Wesley, Howel Harries, Daniel Rowland and William Williams, Pantycelyn.

The Bowen family graves in Nevern churchyard are enclosed by a low wall and on the north side, forming part of the churchyard boundary, stand four, large, grey slate stones. On these are the following details. Reading from left to right the first stone has inscribed on it: In memory of Leonard Oliver Edward who died at Llwyngwair August 25th 1878, aged 18 weeks, and of James Robert, who died at Ottawa on August 29th 1878, aged 18 years. The grandsons of J.B. Bowen, Esq., MP of

Llwyngwair, and of the above James Bevan Bowen, Harriet, his widow, and Sir George Bevan Bowen, KBE, died July 3rd 1940, Florence, his wife, died September 9th 1935, and of Air Commodore J.B. Bowen, CBE, died August 12th 1969, Noel, his wife, died May 9th 1951.

On the second stone: Interred within these walls James Bowen of Llwyngwair, Esq., John Owen Bowen, Dorothea Lucy Bowen, also, Martha, wife of the above James Bowen, Esq. Blanche Maria Bowen, died at Cheltenham, May 27th 1852, aged 12 years. George Bowen, Esq., of Llwyngwair, Sarah Anne Bowen, George Thomas Bowen, and of Sarah, relict of the above named George Bowen who died 17th September 1874, aged 73 years. Frederick Bowen, Philip H. Bowen, Capt., BA, Martha Margaret Bowen.

Inscribed on the third stone; In memory of Letitia and George, children of the Rev. David Griffiths, Vicar of this Parish, who died in their infancy AD 1794.

> They tasted of life's bitter cup,
> Refused to drink the poison up.
> They turned their little heads aside,
> Disgusted with the taste, and died.

Also interred within these walls the Rev. David Griffiths, Anne, his wife, and Esther their daughter, also Anne, wife of George David Griffiths, Esq., and the above George David Griffiths.

On the fourth stone: Interred within these walls George Bowen, Esq., Esther Bowen, his wife, the Rev. Rice Thomas Bowen, Clerk, George Bowen, Esq., Capt. RN, William Bowen, Esq., sons of George Bowen of Llwyngwair, Esq., Essex Bowen, Esq., Capt. RN, Easter Bowen, Elizabeth Alicia Bowen, Dorothy Rowlands, Jane Bowen.

On the twenty-three small stones within the walls surrounding the graves, there are further details about those members of the family named on the four large, slate stones. On one of the small stones this typical Victorian verse:

> Sisters, mothers, on her grave
> Drop a tear of woman's love.
> Fathers, brothers, softly tread
> Where our gentle Blanche is laid dead.

On the same stone: Also Sarah Anne Bowen, died May 6th 1868, aged 26 years.

George Owen, the antiquarian, described the mansion of Llwyngwair in 1607 in these words: 'Llwyngwair, the mansion house of James Bowen, gentleman . . . the house and demaynes more than half compassed with the river Nevern yielding as well commoditie (sic) fishing as other pleasures. The seat pleasant for wood and water.'

Inside the church, and on the south wall of the south transept which forms the Warren Chapel, is a stone on which is inscribed: 'Underneath lyeth in this vault in hope of joyful resurrection the body of Catherine Warren of Trewern, who departed this life March 5th Anno Domini, 1720, aged 39 years. She was the youngest daughter of Lewis Morgan, Esq., of Wiston, by Anne Lloyd, daughter to James Lloyd, Esq., of Cilrhiw, and co-heiress to her mother. She was the mother to seven children, Anne, Mary and Jane Warren deceased. Four now living, William, John, Anne and Elizabeth Warren. "Envy not my happiness for I am gone before. Prepare to follow me, and live forever more."'

Of Trewern, George Owen, the antiquarian, wrote: 'Trewern, the mansion house of William Warren, Esquire, called in ancient writings Trewernwaelod. It is the ancient inheritance of the said William Warren for diverse hundred years past, how ancient it is not well known.' The first known reference to Trewern is dated 1344; it states, 'Thomas, son and heir of Newburgh granted lands within the precincts of the burgages of Fiscard (sic), called Tŷ Roys, for two years to William Warin ap David Voil.' The Haverfordwest Corporation Deeds, dated 1430, state, 'Joan, formerly wife of Lewis Wareyn of Traverne, widow.'

In his book, *The South Wales Squires*, Herbert M. Vaughan relates an interesting story about one of the residents of Trewern; a Rev. David George, mentioned in the Voters List of 1834 as the tenant of the property. The story tells us that because of the Rev. George's liberal beliefs the landlord ordered him out of Trewern, and he moved to a farm called Brithdir Mawr. The Rev. George served as Mayor of Newport for two years and died on the 15th of May 1892. During his tenancy of Trewern a storm damaged one of the chimneys. A mason was called in to repair the damage and, in order to do the work, he had to climb up the kitchen chimney. He lost his way, and ended up in a secret chamber above the porch. The chamber was filled with treasure – silver plate and other valuables believed to have been hidden in the room at the time of the Reformation, and subsequently forgotten. The account continues by stating that the Rev. gentleman and the mason kept their find a secret and made a pact. From time to time the parson would take up one piece of the treasure to London, sell it, and divide the proceeds with the mason. True or not, the story makes interesting reading.

Leaving Nevern, the journey continues south on the A487 to Fishguard. Most people, on hearing the name Fishguard, think of it as the cross-channel ferry port to

Ireland but the town has a far stronger claim to fame.

The most notable event in Fishguard's history occurred in 1797. A French expeditionary force consisting mainly of convicts was despatched by sea in a ship commanded by an Irish-American named Tate to capture Bristol. A storm arose at sea that forced the ship towards Fishguard, and the so-called soldiers landed at a spot called Carreg Gwastad, near the town. The soldiers began to ravage the surrounding area as local troops prepared to take action against them. Legend has it that, as the French approached the town of Fishguard a crowd of Welsh women, led by a Jemima Nicholas, and dressed in their red shawls, beat the British soldiers to it. The women marched back and fore along the cliff top. The French soldiers mistook the women for red-coated British soldiers and immediately surrendered, and a surrender document to that effect was signed in the Royal Oak Inn that stands in the middle of the town. In the churchyard, a matter of a few yards from the Royal Oak Inn, there is a memorial stone commemorating Jemima Nicholas. Inscribed on it: In memory of Jemima Nicholas of this town, 'a Welsh heroine' who boldly marched to meet the French invaders who landed on our shores in February 1797. She died in the main street July 1832, aged 82 years. At the time of the invasion she was 47 years old, and lived 38 years after the event. Erected by public subscriptions collected at the centenary banquet, July 5th 1897.

This was the last invasion of Britain and, to celebrate the two hundredth anniversary of the event, a number of the ladies of Fishguard made, and put up in the town hall, a beautiful tapestry depicting the scene on that February day in 1797; a modern version of the Bayeux Tapestry.

Another stone in the churchyard have the following words written: Naomi Williams, died May 2nd 1869, age

77, and a verse from the book of Proverbs – chapter 14, verse 32: 'The wicked is driven away in his wickedness, but the righteous hath hope in his death.'

Inside the church there is a gallery at the west end, and there is also a window designed by the artist John Petts.

Some four miles south of Fishguard, and about a mile or two to the east of the A40 Fishguard to Haverfordwest road is the hamlet of Little Newcastle. In the hamlet is a small church dedicated to St Peter and, in the churchyard, a grave, whose occupant after the event of 1797 at Fishguard, was charged with treason. The grave is marked by a simple grey stone and on it is inscribed: 'Here lieth the remains of Thomas John of Summertown, in the parish, who died March 13th 1804, age 38 years. A man of discernment . . . ' – the inscription then becomes illegible.

Thomas John, a non-conformist minister of religion, along with a Samuel Griffith of Pointz Castle, was charged with treason during the last invasion of Britain in 1797, previously described.

The trial of Thomas John and Samuel Griffith took place at Haverfordwest on September 7th 1797. It seems that the charges were completely without foundation and both men were found not guilty, and subsequently released from prison.

Leaving Little Newcastle and returning to the A40, we join the B4331 and head for the village of Mathry, a distance of some four miles. Standing on rising ground above the A487 Fishguard to St David's road is the church, dedicated to the Holy Martyrs.

The 'martyrs' could very well be six brothers who, it is reputed, were rescued from drowning by St Teilo. According to the Book of Llandaf the six then settled at Mathry. Built into the west wall of the churchyard are two

Celtic stones. Inscribed on them is a cross within a circle, a sign that they are of the Age of the Saints – fifth to the eighth centuries AD. Also inside the church is a stone from possibly the same period on which is inscribed: 'mac cudicci filius cartis uus', 'Maccuoicci, son of Caticuus lies here.'

A stone in the churchyard recording the death of a Margaretta Miles, aged 2 years 8 months, has this verse in Welsh:

Hyderwn fod yr eneth hon
Yn awr yn iach yn canu
Ymhell uwchben gofidiau'r byd
Ym mynwes glud yr Iesu.

Translated, it tells of the hope of those who mourned the child that she is now happily singing, far from the troubles of this world, safe in the arms of Jesus.

From Mathry we travel to the south of the county of Pembroke, and about two miles west of Tenby, on the B4318, is the hamlet of Gumfreston. A short distance off the road is the church, dedicated to St Laurence. In the book, *The Oxford Dictionary of Saints* by David Hugh Farmer, four saints of that name are mentioned, so it is difficult to be sure to whom the church is dedicated. There was a St Laurence a deacon and martyr of Rome who died in 258AD, a St Laurence of Brindisi who lived from 1559 until 1619, and was a Capuchin Franciscan, a St Laurence of Canterbury who died in 619AD, and who was an archbishop and came to England with Augustine in 596-7, and finally, a Laurence O'Toole, born in 1128, and archbishop of Dublin from 1162 until his death in 1180. As the church is of Norman origin and the dedication has remained constant down through the ages it is highly improbable that it is dedicated to St Laurence of Brindisi who lived during the 15 and 1600s. The most likely candidate is St Laurence of Rome and traces of a mural, believed to represent events in his life, can be seen on the north wall.

The main part of the church is probably of the thirteenth century while the tower and porch are possibly from the fifteenth century.

The church was a pilgrimage church on the road to St David's. Pilgrims would have been attracted to the church because of the three springs in the churchyard that rise to form a stream which flows out of the churchyard. The water is reputed to have healing powers. The porch has stone benches, a stone vaulted ceiling and an octagonal font built into the wall. Above the door is a niche that at one time must have held a figure, possibly of the Virgin Mary.

Commemorated within the church are members of the Hall family; Sir Benjamin Hall is the most well known since the clock bell of Westminster, 'Big Ben', is named after him. The pulpit and reading desk date from the 1800s; they were part of the restoration carried out when the Rector was a Rev. Gilbert Smith, incumbent from 1837 to 1877. The reverend gentleman was a keen archaeologist, and Edward Laws, in his book *The History of Little England Beyond Wales*, mentions the fact that he and the Rev. Smith took part in an archaeological dig in a cave on Caldey Island. According to Laws, among the bones they discovered were those of lion, mammoth, rhinoceros, horse, hippopotamus, wild boar, Irish elk, red deer and reindeer. Laws also records that the Rector found, in the submerged forest bed at Manorbier, an old raised beach, and that he excavated three ancient graves on the Ridgeway, not far from Tenby.

The chancel window is Victorian, a replacement of a window from Medieval times. Also in the chancel are grave slabs of the Williams family. The single bell in the belfry is one of the oldest in the county; inscribed on it: 'Sca Maria ora pro nobis', 'Holy Mary, pray for us'.

In the south chapel, now used as a vestry, is an early seventeenth century stone slab. It marks the grave of a Katheren Parat, and it is believed she was in some way connected to an owner of Carew Castle in the days of Elizabeth I.

Out in the churchyard, and of interest besides the wells, is the grave of the famous artist Augustus John's father, Edwin John, as well as that of Gilbert Smith, an archaeologist. Another interesting memorial is one of an Italian prisoner-of-war of the 1939-45 War. The stone is unusual in that it includes a photograph of him, as well as his name – Giuseppe Boneiglio, born 192?, died 1965 – something that is common in Europe. After the war he returned to Italy, got married, and then returned to live in Gumfreston, where he died at a comparatively young age.

Leaving Gumfreston we retrace our steps to Carew with its ancient castle, a famous Celtic cross, a water mill worked by the tide ebbing and flowing twice a day, and of course, its church. The Celtic cross is 14ft. high with an intricate design carved on it. It is believed that it dates from the eleventh century. A Latin inscription reads: 'Maredudd the King, son of Edwin'. Tradition has it that Gerald of Windsor was the castle's founder. Of the original castle nothing remains except for possibly 'The Old Tower'. Most of the castle we now see was built around the year 1300 for Sir Nicholas de Carew. Nicholas de Carew was involved in a battle between his soldiers and those of Owain Glyndŵr that forced Owain to fall back on Carmarthen, which he eventually captured. Edward Laws in his book states: 'This fortunate ambuscade (i.e. fortunate for de Carew) no doubt saved Pembrokeshire, and Sir Nicholas Carew had now avenged that disgraceful escapade at Mynydd Hyddnant. We may well believe that the joy bells rang out at Pembroke, Haverford and Tenby.'

The church, dedicated to St Mark, is described as follows: 'A smaller church stood on this site in the twelfth century. The present building dates back to the very beginning of the fourteenth century. All the walls of the internal layout have changed a great deal, notably during the time of Cromwell. There are still marks on the walls to show where the side altars stood. Faint marks can be seen near the altar rails and chancel steps of burials long ago. The very valuable tiles in the sanctuary were taken from the castle when it became unoccupied and fell into disrepair towards the end of the seventeenth century. The tiles are about five hundred years old and the old building in the churchyard was a charnel house. When old graves were disturbed the remains were laid beneath and in the chapel above. Mass was said for the souls of the departed . . . ' The poet Shelley, the English Romantic Poet of the early 1800s in the book *In Defence of Poetry* wrote 'Adonais' a pastoral elegy commemorating the death of John Keats by declaring that while we 'decay/Like corpses in a charnel' the creative spirit of Adonais, despite his physical death 'has outsoared the shadow of our night'.

The bones that were dug up and placed in the charnel house would be taken out on All Saints Day to be burnt and the bone fire has given us the word bonfire.

Inside the church, in the north transept, there is a tomb with carved effigies of Sir John Carew and his wife Dame

213

Elizabeth. Sir John gained possession of the castle for his family in 1622 after a lapse of 142 years. He had the transept in the church built so that he might be buried there. He died in 1637. Also in the church there is a monumental effigy of the afore-mentioned Sir Nicholas Carew.

From Carew we take a minor road for approximately four miles in a south westerly direction to Lamphey. According to Geraldus Cambrensis it was called Lantefei while to Henry II the place was called Lantesy. It goes without saying that Lamphey is a corruption of the original name that possibly was Llantyfei because the church is dedicated to Saints Faith and Tyfei.

Lamphey is the site of one of the seven palaces of the Bishops of St David's; most of the building work took place between the thirteenth and the fifteenth century. In 1546 it became the property of the Earls of Essex, and was used as a family home. A favourite of Queen Elizabeth, Robert Devereux was born and brought up in Lamphey. Following the death of his father, Robert was taken to London by Lord Burghley who entered him in Trinity College, Cambridge. He could not have been well dressed because his tutor wrote to Burghley's secretary: 'His extreme want of apparel, where you yourself was an eye-witness. Other men marvel that his great want is not supplied.' The tutor goes on to list of things that he considered necessary for the earl:

A gown for my Lord's holidays.
2 doublets, 3 pairs of hose, 2 pairs
Of nether socks, a velvet cap, a hat,
A basin and ewer, pots or goblets,
Spoons, plates, saltcellar, candlesticks,
Pots to be given to the College,
Hangings (possibly curtains).

In another document there is a list of furniture supplied to the Earl that came to £7.05. In the same document his Tutor's bill for the period from the Feast of John the Baptist (could be either June 24th – The Nativity of John the Baptist, or August 29th – The Beheading of John the Baptist) that came to £45.50.

During a Christmas vacation, Robert, Earl of Essex, had his first meeting with Queen Elizabeth, and soon became a great success at Court. In July 1581, Essex took his degree of MA and soon afterwards retired to Lamphey.

The palace, through neglect over the years, became a ruin but restoration work has been carried out there during the last few years.

The original fourteenth century church consisted of a single chamber but during restoration work in Victorian days a chancel arch was installed. The piscine and the lancets in the chancel are partly original but the tower and the transepts have no ancient features. The fine Norman font has a circular bowl with an ornamental panelling round the top, scalloped beneath and a cable ornament bending around the circular stem. On a card inside the church there is written a verse entitled, 'The Difference':

I got up early one morning
And reached right into the day.
I had so much to accomplish
That I did not have time to pray.
Problems just tumbled about me,
And heavier came each task,
'Why didn't God help me! I wondered,'
He answered, 'You didn't ask.'
I wanted to see joy and beauty,

215

But the day toiled on grey and bleak.
I wondered why God didn't show me,
He said, 'But you didn't seek.'
I tried to come into God's presence,
I used all my keys at the lock;
God gently and lovingly chided,
'My child, you didn't knock.'
I woke up early this morning,
And paused before entering the day,
I had so much to accomplish
That I had to take time to pray. Amen.

In the churchyard at the east end of the church, a yard or so from the church wall and more or less hidden behind a holly bush, there is a solid iron cross, and inscribed on it: 'In memory of Mary, wife of the Rev. J.B. Byer, aged 85, died 1878.'

From Lamphey we travel to Penally, a village some two miles south west of Tenby. Not far from Penally is Hoyle's Mouth, a cavern associated with Shakespeare's Cymbeline. Shakespeare's play is a comedy in five acts. It is set in pre-Roman times and its main theme is a wager by a husband on the fidelity of his wife. Surprisingly, although the title bears the name of Cymbeline, king of Britain, he plays a small role in the romance. He is depicted as a person prone to ill-temper, easily manipulated by his queen, but at the conclusion proves to be generous.

Act 3, Scene 3, is set in Wales, and Scene 4 set near Milford Haven. In Act 4, Scene 1, the setting is a forest near a cave, Scene 2 and 4 is before the cave. And it is believed that the cave is this very cavern, Hoyle's Mouth, which Edward Laws in his book on south Pembrokeshire, tells us contained the bones of hyena, brown bear, reindeer. Irish elk and boars. However, we are not in Penally to see the cave; we have come to visit the church. It is dedicated to St Nicholas and the nave, chancel and transepts date from the thirteenth century.

St Nicholas is said to have been the originator of the idea of Christmas stockings; tradition has it that he gave three virgins a bag of gold each in order to deter them from becoming prostitutes.

In the Pembroke Record Office can be seen the Parish Registers – baptisms, 1738 to 1885, marriages, 1739 to 1966, burials, 1738 to 1940. During restoration work on the church in 1851, illustrations in distemper were discovered under many coats of whitewash that was used on the walls of churches.

On the north side of the arch dividing the nave from the chancel is a tablet on which is inscribed: To the honour of God and the glorious memory of the sons of John Wynford, Baron, of St David's and . . . , his wife, who gave their lives for their country in the Great War. Colwyn Erasmus Arnold Phillips, Capt. Royal Horse Guards. Born 11th December 1888, killed 13th May 1915 when gallantly leading a squadron of 'The Blues' in a charge near Ypres for which he was mentioned in despatches. Roland Erasmus Phillips, Commissioner of Boy Scouts of east and north-east London. Advisory Commissioner for private schools and Assistant Commissioner for Wales. Captain 9th (Service Battalion) Royal Fusiliers. Born 27th February 1890, killed 7th July 1916 at the head of his company in a charge against the Prussian Guard at Ovilleres. He had already received the Military Cross and had been recommended for the Victoria Cross.

In the church is the tomb of William de Naunton to his wife – circa 1260 to 1290. The tomb consists of a much worn sandstone slab bearing traces of a Calvary Cross, and an inscription around the edge reads: 'William de Naunton et Isamay (san femine) ici Dieu de leur alries yet merci. Amen.'

In the south transept, there is a stone slab-cross sculpted from a very large stone with a wheel- head. Not far from the stone-slab stands part of another cross, probably of the tenth century. Both crosses are patterned with various designs. Housed in the vestry for safekeeping is a small splayed stone that also dates from around the tenth century. On the outside, and built into the north transept wall, is a plain incised cross.

Before visiting the church at Tenby let us make a short journey to St Florence. The church is dedicated to St Florentius and much of the church, nave, chancel, north transept, and tower, date from the thirteenth century. In the churchyard is a stone, a stepped platform, on which stands a pillar topped with a cross. In olden days the vicar or rector, if so inclined, would preach a sermon while standing on the platform. In the County Record Office at Haverfordwest can be seen the Parish Registers – baptisms, 1763 – 1920, marriages, 1755 – 1836, burials, 1763 – 1957. In the National Library at Aberystwyth there are Bishop's Transcripts from 1799 – 1890, and also for the year 1892.

Built into the west wall is a stone plaque on which is inscribed: 'Near this place lieth the body of John Price, late of the parish of St Mary's, Pembroke, who died February 14th 1807, aged 102 years. In the churchyard a row of ten identical gravestones recounting the deaths of members of the Prout family – Martha, 1865; Elizabeth, 1880; George, 1820; Martha, 1873; George, 1867; William, 1875; Richard 1870; Anne, 1856; Anne, 1832; Thomas, 1870. Ten graves with only one body of the same family in each grave, is rather puzzling, especially as they do not even run chronologically.

On another memorial: 'Joanna, wife of Henry Banner, she died at Bristol April 18th 1831, aged 26.

> Weep not for me husband dear;
> I am not dead but sleeping here.
> I was not yours, but Christ's alone –
> He loved me best, and took me home.'

The words of the verse leave us wondering what this woman's true feelings for her husband had been during their time together as man and wife. The sentiment expressed in the verse, especially in the third line: 'I was not yours, but Christ's alone.' is puzzling with the word 'alone' seemingly rather significant.

A stone is built into the east side of the tower upon which a Eunice Robbins, aged 27, who died during the 1800s is remembered. The verse reads:

> Forgive blessed shade the tributary tear
> That mourns my exit from a world like this.
> Forgive the wish that would have kept me here,
> And stayed my progress to the seat of bliss.

I cannot help feeling that this young woman's wish that her life on earth had been longer was not in any way unreasonable.

And now on to Tenby, with its large and very imposing church in the centre of the town. Dedicated to St Mary, it is the largest medieval church in Wales. Except for a part of the tower, and the south doorway that date from the thirteenth century, other parts of the church are from the middle of the fifteenth century to the beginning of the sixteenth century. On top of the tower is a forty-five metre spire. The wooden pulpit, has the date 1634 carved on it, and on the inside walls of the church are a number of memorials, including a very ornate, colourful tomb with the effigies of the husband and wife lying alongside each other on the top of it and seven of their children kneeling around the base. Inscribed on it in Latin, 'Thomas Rees of Scotsborough, Esquire, placed this monument to the tender memory of a worthy wife, Margaret Mercer, deceased in childbirth, who died May 1st in the year of our Lord 1610, after having lived twelve years most faithfully with her husband and having borne ten children, seven of whom still live; she died aged thirty.' This memorial is typical of the design of that period.

On the east wall of the chapel behind the organ is the kneeling figure of a William Risman, a wealthy merchant and Mayor of Tenby, who died in 1633. The figure and the background to it have traces of their original colouring, but the memorial has been mutilated. A local tradition attributes the damage to a Cromwellian trooper's musket shot aimed at what the trooper took to be a living target.

Also commemorated in the church is a famous mathematician and physician of the 1500s. On the memorial is inscribed, 'In memory of Robert Recorde, the eminent mathematician, who was born at Tenby circa 1510. To his genius we call the earliest important English treatise on Algebra, Arithmetic, Astronomy and Geometry. He also invented the sign equality =, now universally adopted by the civilised world. Robert Recorde was court physician to King Edward VI and Queen Mary. He died in London 1558.'

Robert Recorde was appointed a fellow of All Souls College, Oxford, in 1531. If the above dates are correct he was only 21 years of age when the appointment was made. He later taught at the University of Cambridge, and after qualifying as a doctor in 1545, he served, as is mentioned on the memorial, as a physician to the king and queen of his day. Among his writings was a popular book on arithmetic, The Ground of Artes, The Castle of Knowledge in astronomy and Pathewaie to Knowledge, a shortened version of Euclid's Elements. He first proposed the use of the equals sign in the most notable of all his works, The Whetstone of Witte. It is rather surprising to note that he died in prison, especially since the reason for his imprisonment is not known.

A memorial on the south wall records: 'To the memory of John Phillips, eldest son of Sir John Philips of Picton Castle, Bart., by Dame Elizabeth, his wife, born January 2nd 1726, died December 9th 1753.

> On whom indulgent nature shed
> Her noblest gifts and charms,
> Who bloomed with beauty's early spread
> Even from his nurse's arms.
> By parents care with precepts fraught,
> From grace to grace he growed. (sic)
> His life displayed the things they taught
> And the good things they sowed.
> Thy ways, O Lord, beyond the ken
> Of human wisdom lie,
> And vices rage so long in men,
> And youthful virtues die.

Here also lies Edward Phillips, the brother of the said John, born November 1st 1739, died March 18th 1740.'

High up on the east wall is a memorial with the following inscription: 'Morgan Williams, descended from the heiress of Bishop Ferrar, Bishop of St David's, burnt alive by bigots under Queen Mary, was lately Chief of Gantaam and Senior Council at Madras, where on October 27th 1790, aged 49 years, he resigned the President's chair and his Breath together. An employment of a full thirty years chronicles the continual approbation of his conduct, particularly as Chief Commissioner of Circuit in allaying discontents and healing grievances.'

Next to that memorial is another one with the following written on it: 'Sacred to the memory of Captain John Griffiths, for 52 years a respected member of the ancient Corporation of Tenby, and during that period twice mayor. He died 12th June 1826, aged 82. And of his son, John Griffiths, Jnr., who was also Mayor of this town at the time of his much lamented decease, Alderman and Chamberlain, the duties of which he constantly discharged with integrity and zeal. He died May 27th 1827, aged 56. Also of his widow, Mrs Anne Griffiths, mother of the above named son and five other children of whom only two survived their beloved parents. She died 17th July 1831 in the 88th year of her age.'

On the west wall a tablet on which is inscribed: 'This tablet was raised by a few ladies and gentlemen to preserve from oblivion the memory of Peggy Davies, "Bathing Woman" 42 years to the ladies who visited Tenby. Her good humour, respectful attention and gratitude made her employers friends. On 29th September 1809, in the water, she was seized with apoplexy and expired aged 82.'

The Bishop Ferrar mentioned in the memorial commemorating Morgan Williams was Bishop of St David's, and was burnt at the stake in Nott Square, Carmarthen, on March 30th 1555. A bronze memorial giving details of the execution is within the iron railings at the foot of the monument to General Nott. It is believed that it marks the spot where the bishop was martyred. Bishop Ferrar had been appointed bishop of the diocese in 1548, during the reign of the Protestant King Edward VI. In 1553 Mary Tudor, a staunch Catholic, and daughter of Henry VIII, became Queen. In 1554 Bishop Ferrar was deposed from his bishopric accused of heresy and the fact that he was married. Although given an opportunity to renounce Protestantism, he resolutely refused to do so, and as a result was sentenced to death, and subsequently burnt at the stake. On the memorial; in Nott Square is the following inscription: 'The noble army of martyrs praise Thee. Near this spot suffered for the truth, Saturday, March 30th 1555, Dr Robert Ferrar, Bishop of St David's. We shall by God's grace light a candle in England (**), as shall never be put out. Erected by a Protestant of this town.'

Before leaving Tenby Church a look at one more memorial – it is on the north wall. The inscription gives the following details:

MORS MIHI LVCRUM
(Death has nothing, gain or profit)

John Moore of Moorhayes in Com. of Devon, Esq. Aged 58 years, was buried here April 6th Anno Domini 1639, havinge (sic) by Mary, his wife, the daughter of Richard Coffyn of Portlidge in Com. Devon, Esquire, six sonnes (sic) and ten daughters.
He that from home for loue (sic) (love)
Was hither brought.
Is now brought home, this God
For him hath wrought.

About three miles north of Haverfordwest, and just off the A40, is the church of St Michael, Rudbaxton, or as it is sometimes called, Great Rudbaxton. Today the church is with St David, Prendergast, and is a Rectorial benefice.

It is highly likely that the present building stands on the site of an earlier church, a church dedicated to St Madoc, a sixth century saint. He founded the church at Llanmadog on the Gower and, in Brecon, there is the church of Llanfadog.

The church at Rudbaxton was called Ecclesia de Rudepagstona in the twelfth century, and was at one time granted to the Knights Hospitallers. They were deposed by Henry VIII when he carried out his nationwide programme of dissolution of the religious houses.

The Knights Hospitaller of St John of Jerusalem, a religious order of hospitalers was founded in Jerusalem in the eleventh century. The order was founded by Italian merchants from Amalfi to care for sick pilgrims. It acquired wealth and lands and combined the task of tending the sick with waging war on Islam. Today there are 8,000 knights, both male and female, and the Grand Master is the world's highest Roman Catholic lay person. In the 1500s, following their defeat by the forces of Islam, the Holy Roman emperor Charles V gave them the Maltese archipelago in return for, among other things, the annual presentation of a falcon to his victory of Sicily. The Knights then built a new Maltese capital, Valetta, named after Jean Parisot de La Valette, a Grand Master of the Order.

The present church at Rudbaxton dates from the late twelfth or the beginning of the thirteenth century. During the late 1800s the church, like most churches in the country, was restored. The chancel, nave, tower and south porch date from the twelfth to thirteenth centuries and the south aisle and lady chapel were added in the fourteenth century. In the lady chapel there is a stained glass window that is a memorial to William Owen of Withybush and his wife. The Owen family played an important part in the life of the county. A descendant of the William Owen commemorated in the window, Doctor Henry Owen, was High Sheriff of Pembrokeshire in 1902. He was also a notable historian, and the author of *Old Pembrokeshire Families*, and *Gerald the Welshman*.

The church tower, though not castellated, is typical of Pembrokeshire church towers. It comprises two storeys and contains two bells. One of the bells is dated 1610 and inscribed on it are the words: 'Give thankes (sic) to God'. In the porch there is a plain stoup holy water basin – built into the wall.

Inside the church are a number of interesting memorials, the most striking commemorating members of the Howard family. Covering the east wall of the lady chapel it dates from the seventeenth century and is in the form of three panels, depicting five figures. The panel on the north side shows the figure of a man; he is George Howard. He holds a human skull in his left hand and points to it with his right. In the middle panel a husband and wife, James and Joanna Howard, each carrying a skull, and also holding hands. In the third panel Thomas and Mary Howard, children of James and Joanna Howard, and they again are depicted in the same way as their parents. On the panels are the following inscriptions:

To the memory of George Howard
of this Parish, Esq. who departed
this life ye 6th day of May Ano 1665
aged 32 years and lyeth before
this monument.

To the memory of James Howard
of this Parish Esq. who lyeth before
this monument and departed this life
ye 24th day of November Ano 1668
aged 35 years.
Also to the memory of Joanna the wife of
James Howard who erected this monument
for her dear friends and children
with the intent to joyne (sic) partner
to this monument and left this life.

To the memory of Thomas Howard
of this parish Esq. and Mary the son and daughter of
James and Joanna his
wife Howard . Thomas departed this life
ye 7th day of July Ano Dom 1682 and Mary ye first of
January Ano Dom 1685.

A red mark, signifying blood, on the breast of Thomas Howard is said to be due to the fact that he was killed in a duel. It will also be observed that no date is given for the death of James' wife.

On the west wall of the church is a memorial commemorating Lieutenant General Sir Thomas Picton KCBG. On it is a carving showing the head of the general and underneath the following inscription:

To the famous memory of
Lieutenant General Sir Thomas Picton KCBG
Born at Poynston in this Parish and baptized
in this church August 24th 1758.
Fell at Waterloo June 18th 1815.
He lies buried in the Cathedral Church
Of St Paul in London.

General Picton was the seventh of twelve children, but the second son, of Thomas and Cecil Picton of Poyston, near Haverforwest. Born on the 24th of August 1758, he was named after an elder brother who had died the previous November, aged five years. His actual birth took place in a house in the town of Haverfordwest belonging to his mother's friend. This particular house was later called the Dragon Hotel. He was educated at Haverforwest Grammar School and, in 1771, at the age of thirteen, he was gazetted an ensign in his uncle's regiment, the 12th Foot Regiment. From the 12th Foot he went to the 75th Regiment of Foot and, at twenty years of age, obtained his own company. Five years later and stationed with his regiment at Bristol, he was instrumental in suppressing a mutiny, for which he received the thanks of the King. On the disbanding of his regiment he returned to Poynston, living the life of a country gentleman. In 1794 Picton went to the West Indies and was appointed to the 17th Foot Regiment, later joining the 68th Regiment. He took part in the attack on St Lucia, and St Vincent. He later returned to this country, but after three years he was again in the West Indies where he was appointed Governor of Trinidad. While in Trinidad he was accused of signing a warrant for the examination of a slave girl by torture. There were two trials; at the first he was found guilty but, on being granted the second trial was acquitted of cruelty. Nevertheless, he was censured for carelessness. In 1809 he served at Flushing and from there he joined the army fighting the Peninsular War. He fought at Badajoz, Vittoria, and Ciudad Rodrigo. At the end of the Peninsular War he returned to this country and bought the mansion of Iscoed, near Ferryside, for which he paid £30,000; equivalent today's to between two and three million pounds. From the mansion there is a panoramic view of the Tywi estuary but his stay at Iscoed did not last long. In 1815 he was recalled to the army and met his death on the field at Waterloo.

General Picton served under the command of the Duke of Wellington in the Peninsular War and at Waterloo, and Wellington described him in words that were anything but flattering; Wellington described him as 'a rough foul-mouth-devil as ever lived'. On the 3rd of July 1815 Picton was buried in the cemetery of St George's, Hanover Square in London. On the 8th of June 1859 his body was taken from St George's, and ironically, laid to rest in the crypt of St Paul's Cathedral, only a few feet from that of the Duke of Wellington. So whatever the Duke thought of him in life, he is now obliged to have Picton lying close to him, until the final trumpet sounds!

Before we leave the memorial to General Picton here is one other piece of information regarding the intrepid general. Some time around the year 1793 he fought a duel at a quarry near Withybush, against an Irishman named Charles Hassall, a surveyor-cartographer. During the duel Picton suffered a gunshot wound to the throat, which affected his voice, making him sound hoarse.

For a detailed biography of Picton the book by Robert Havard, *Wellington's Welsh General – A Life of Sir Thomas Picton,* published in 1996 by Aurum Press Ltd, London, is a definitive guide.

Also commemorated in the church is another member of the Picton family – John Picton. Inscribed on the memorial: 'In memory of Major General John Picton, late Lieutenant Colonel of the 12th Regiment of Infantry, youngest son of the late Thomas Picton of Poyston in the county of Pembrokeshire, Esquire, who departed this life on the 3rd of June 1815, having served in Flanders and the

East Indies. Possessing the honour of his commanders, the affection of his soldiers.'

John Picton was the brother of the famous General Thomas Picton, and he was baptised in 1761. During an interesting army career he was, on October 28th 1794, mentioned in despatches by the Duke of York. In 1797 he went with his regiment to India and in 1798, while stationed in Madras, he fought a duel with his commanding officer. In the autumn of 1814 he returned to his home at Haverfordwest and in January 1815, aged 53, he died suddenly.

On another memorial: 'In memory of Hannah Scott, mother of Ann, wife of John Phelps, Esq., who died 25th October 1798 AE 70 years, and also of two sons and one daughter of the said John Phelps and Ann his wife.

Ann obit 27th April 1792 AE 5 years.
??? obit 1st May 1792 AE 3 years.

And Edward, an infant, who died 14th September 1792, and Ann, their youngest daughter, who died October 22nd 1810 aged 14 years.

The Phelps, along with the Martin and the Owen families, lived at different times in Withybush, a mansion near Haverfordwest. The first to live there was a Sparks Martin. Born in 1713, he became High Sheriff in 1750. On his death he bequeathed the estate to his sister Elizabeth, who married a John Phelps. This John Phelps took on the name Martin, and the last member of the family was a Rev. C.M. Phelps who had not taken on the surname Martin, and who died in 1907. The George Leader Owen commemorated on a brass plaque was, along with his brother Dr Henry Owen, sons of a William Owen, who had bought the estate.

On the plaque: 'In memory of John Leader Owen of Withybush in this parish, Esq. Born 1st January 1838, died 9th February 1905. LlB Trinity Hall, Cambridge. DL and JP for this county, High Sheriff 1894. He took for many years an active part in the Administration of Public Affairs.'

There is a photograph of William Laud, Archbishop of Canterbury, and a brass plate in the church, and incised on it: 'Born 1573, died 1645, Rector of this Parish'.

William Laud was born in Reading on October 7th 1573, and was the son of a clothier. He attended Reading Grammar School and then went on to St John's College, Oxford. Until he was nearly 50 years of age he was a successful but unspectacular academic and churchman. He soon joined a movement that was in fierce opposition to Puritanism. In 1611 he was appointed a royal chaplain and came to the notice of King James I. He became a dominant voice in church affairs and appointments and, in 1627, was made a Privy Councillor, to be appointed bishop of London a year later. On the death of Archbishop Abbott in 1633, Laud became Archbishop of Canterbury.

In the spring of 1640 Parliament met for the first time in 11 years and by December of that year Laud was under arrest accused of high treason and incarcerated in the Tower of London. Four years later, in 1644, during the Civil War, he was tried and found guilty. On January 10th 1645 he was beheaded.

It is probable that Laud, like many other clerics at that time, was an absentee Rector of Rudbaxton, and did not serve within the parish at all.

A stained glass window commemorates a William Owen of Withybush, and depicted in the window three saints, St Anthony, St Michael and St Leonard.

And so we depart from Rudbaxton church, and head eastwards. The church proved well worth a visit and will be of interest to all historians.

Leaving Rudbaxton we head towards Haverfordwest, and then along the A40 in an easterly direction for approximately seven miles until the sign for Llawhaden appears. It is in Llawhaden we find the next church to visit.

The church is located in a secluded spot alongside the Eastern Cleddau river, and dates from the thirteenth century. During the fourteenth century a new chancel and nave were built. Three sides of the original tower can still be seen attached to the west wall of the tall, imposing tower built between it and the new nave all those centuries ago. In 1862 most of the nave was rebuilt and the south doorway blocked, a west porch and doorway replacing it. In a recess in the south chapel, the original chancel, there is an effigy of a priest. The font is of Norman origin. The church is dedicated to St Aidan, a disciple of St David. St Aidan became Bishop of Ferns in Ireland. Aidan was called Maidor and Moedhog by the Irish and Madog by the Welsh. It is said of Aidan that he bequeathed his staff, bell and reliquary to three monasteries. They can still be seen, the staff in the National Museum of Dublin and the other two items in the Library of Armagh cathedral. Also attributed to him are incredible feats of austerity such as fasting on barley bread and water for seven years and daily reciting 500 psalms – where he found 500 psalms is a mystery as there are only 150 in the Book of Psalms. Another story relates that some men dressed up in rags on the pretence that they were destitute and asked him for his help. Knowing that they were impostors, he gave their clothes to some deserving poor, and sent the impostors away with neither clothes nor alms.

The Parish Registers for the years 1653 to 1980 and the Bishop's Transcripts for the period 1772 to 1883 are in the National Library of Wales.

Of the memorials the following are quite interesting: 'Near this place lies the body of Anne Furlong, (most probably Ferrier) late of Great Vaynor, who departed this life March 10th 1814, aged 60 years. Also of John Furlong, (sic) her husband, who died October 10th 1818, aged 68 years.

> Long days and nights we had great pain,
> To call for cure was all in vain.
> God did know what time was best,
> He eased our pain and gave us rest.
> Go home dear friends, dry up your tears.
> We must lie here 'till Christ appears.
> And at His coming we hope to have
> A joyful rising from the grave.'

According to Major Francis Jones, in his book *Historic Houses of Pembrokeshire*, a house called Vaynor is described as being in the parish of Manordeifi, while Dr Leslie Baker Jones in his book *Princelings, Privilege and Power*, in which he describes the gentry of Tivy-Side in Ceredigion, also mentions Vaynor. As both writers mention the Ferrier family of Vaynor, and there is no mention of a Furlong family, I take it that the name on the memorial perhaps should be Ferrier.

High up on the south wall of the chancel is a memorial on which is inscribed: 'Near this place is deposited the remains of the Rev. William Evans, MA, late Vicar of this parish and translator into English verses of the poems of the Rev. Rhys Prichard, Vicar of Llandovery. In him were combined a gentleman, a scholar and a Christian. He resigned his soul to God in hope of a glorious resurrection through the merits of Christ Jesus on the 28th day of February 1796, aged 75 years. "Here fallen asleep the faithful pastor rise. He is not dead, the righteous never dies."'

Rhys Prichard, often known as 'Yr Hen Ficer' – 'The Old Vicar' – was born in Llandovery, and lived from 1579 to 1644. In 1597 he entered Jesus College, Oxford, and afterwards served for a short period as a cleric in Essex. In 1602 he took over the living of Llandovery, and in 1614 was appointed chaplain to the Earl of Essex. He also held the post of Prebendary of Christ College, Brecon, and was a Chancellor and Canon of St David's.

A Puritan, he did much preaching in west Wales. There are no reports that he sided with either faction side during the Civil War. He became very concerned with the moral standards of his parishioners and, in an attempt to raise the standards, he composed a large number of verses that contained teachings related to this end. In 1681 the verses were published by Simon Hughes under the title *Cannwyll y Cymru* – 'Candles of the Welsh'. The book became as popular with the people of Wales as the Welsh translation of 'Pilgrim's Progress'.

There is a traditional tale about the Vicar's son, Samuel. According to the story, he fell in love with Ellen, the daughter of a mansion that once stood not far from Lampeter, called Maesyfelin. Her four brothers, worried that if the marriage took place they would have to share the inheritance with Samuel, tied him to a horse that dragged him from Lampeter to Llandovery. Needless to say, by the time the horse reached Llandovery, Samuel was dead and the brothers threw his body into the river Tywi. Ellen went mad and died; a few months later the mansion burnt to the ground and the eldest brother murdered his three brothers and then hanged himself.

According to tradition the misfortunes that befell the mansion, Ellen and her brothers, came about because the Vicar had pronounced a curse on Maesyfelin and its occupants.

It is believed that the tale was an attempt by the people of the district to explain the destruction of the mansion by fire and the family's misfortunes.

Another memorial, on the north wall of the chancel, records the following details, also a verse: 'Near this place lie the remains of Thomas Harries of Saint Enox, who departed this life 19th November 1803, aged 32.

> With patience to the last I did submit,
> And murmured not at what the Lord though fit,
> But with a Christian courage did resign
> My soul to God at His appointed time.'

In Major Francis Jones' book on Pembrokeshire homes the house is called St Kennox, and according to Major Jones it was sometimes called St Enochs. He also states that around the 1620s the Rev, Rhys Prichard (Yr Hen Ficer), when Chancellor of St David's, lived in the house.

On a minor road, halfway between Narberth and Amroth is Ludchurch – the Lud in the name a corruption of Llwyd, Welsh for grey. The word Ludchurch is more or less meaningless whereas Eglwys Llwyd (Grey Church) is a correct description of the church.

The church is mostly of the thirteenth century except for the north aisle and the large square tower, both of which belong to the sixteenth century. In the large churchyard there are three interesting memorials. A gravestone commemorating a Thomas Evans who died February 22nd 1835, aged only 36 years has this rather telling verse on it:

Danger stand thick through all the ground
To push us to the tomb,
And fierce disease walk around
To hurry mortals home.

In the churchyard, and more or less in line with the south wall of the chancel, is a stone slab capping a box tomb. On it is inscribed: 'John Henry Martin, buried May 10th 1823 aged 70 years. At the time of his death he was supposed to be the last surviving officer who accompanied Captain Cook on his third voyage around the world.'

Captain Cook conducted three expeditions to the Pacific Ocean (1768-71; 1772-75; 1776-1779).

His travels ranged from the Antarctic ice fields to the Bering Strait and from the coast of North America to Australia and New Zealand.

After much exploration of the Pacific in July 1776, Captain Cook sailed once again on the ship Resolution, accompanied by another ship, the Discovery, in an attempt to find out whether a northwest passage existed around Canada and Alaska or a northeast one around Siberia, between the Pacific and the Atlantic Oceans. This search was unsuccessful, for neither a northwest nor a northeast passage suitable for sailing ships existed. It was this voyage that led to Cook's death. During an altercation with Hawaiians over the stealing of a cutter, Cook was slain on the beach at a place called Kealakekua by the Polynesian natives. And from the inscription on the memorial in Ludchurch churchyard we can gather that it was on this journey that John Henry Martin travelled with Captain Cook. One cannot help but wonder if John Martin was actually an eyewitness to that murderous event. One thing we can be sure of, and that is, that Martin would undoubtedly have a most interesting tale to tell about his days at sea.

In the southeast corner of the churchyard is a memorial that, at first sight, looks more like a short wall than a gravestone. It is about ten feet wide and approximately seven feet high. At one time along its top there were two rows of six-inch square, blue ceramic tiles. The wind and rain have dislodged some of the tiles over the years. Inscribed on the face of the memorial: 'His Honour Wilfred Bough Allen of Cilrhiw, born November 14th 1840, died at Rosemount, Tenby, June 10th 1922. RIP. And his wife, Anne Sophia, born September 13th 1855, died January 11th 1946.'

Cilrhiw is a Georgian mansion between Princes Gate and Treffgarne, approximately four miles from Narberth. It was in the hands of the Allen family from the middle of the 1800s until well into the middle of the last century.

Also in the churchyard, not far from the south wall, is a large, stone, stepped platform. In the top stone there is a round hole and at one time a stone preaching-cross stood upon it.

Back to Ceredigion and Carmarthenshire

On leaving Ludchurch, we head for one last Pembrokeshire church, the church at Llanfyrnach on the border with Carmarthenshire. The church is in the Deanery of St Clears and is dedicated to St Brynach, or as found in some books, St Byrnach He was an early sixth century saint and is also known as Brynach Wyddel ('the Irishman'). However according to the author of *The Oxford Dictionary of Saints,* he was a legendary Welsh king with many saintly children, including numerous daughters and granddaughters; he does not mention a saint Brynach. The daughters and granddaughters names are Gwladus, Arianwen, Bethan, Tanglwst, Mechell, Nefyn, Gwawr, Gwrgon, Eleri, Lleian, Nefydd, Rhiengar, Gwenddydd, Tybie, Eluned, Ceindrych, Gwen, Cenedlon, Cymorth, Clydai, Dwynwen, Ceinwen, Tudfyl, Enfail Hawystl, Callwen, Gwenfyl, Ceingar, Goleuddydd, Meleri, Ellyw, Keneython, Nectan, Mwynwen, Cain, Endeillion, Clether and Morwenna. And to that there are to be added his sons and grandsons, Arthen, Berwyn, Clydwyn, Clydog, Cynog, Gwen, Gwynau, Gwynws, Cyflefyr, Rhain, Dyfnan, Gerwyn Cadog, Mathaiarn, Pasgen, Neffai, Pabliali, Dedyn, Llecheu, Cynbryd, Cynfran, Hychan, Dyfrig, Cynin, Dogfan, Rhawin, Rhun, Clydog, Caian, Dingad. Here we have a veritable tribe, not the 'Tribe of Israel' but the 'Tribe of Brychan'.

Some of the names are familiar because there are churches in the diocese dedicated to them, for instance, Tybie in Llandybie, Lleian in Gorslas, Cain in Llangain, Llangeinor and Llangynnwr, Arthen in Cefnarthen near

Llandovery, and Dingad, also in Llandovery.

The church, with its square tower, stands in a secluded spot surrounded by trees, and is some distance from the village. In its small, more or less round churchyard, there is a slate gravestone that stands under a yew tree, a few yards to the north of the church door. On it in Welsh: 'Coffa am Elizabeth, John, Phoebe a Thomas, plant Lewis a Sarah Phillips o Nant-y-Groes, y rhai a hunasant yn y flwyddyn 1824 fel y canlyn, John, Ebrill 3ydd yn 20 mlwydd oed, Thomas, y 9fed yn 10 mlwydd oed, Phoebe, yr 20fed yn 12 mlwydd oed, Elizabeth, Mai 31ain yn 26 mlwydd oed.

> O ieuenctid pwyllwch ronyn.
> Hyd yma trowch eich cam
> I weld lle'r i'n yn gorwedd
> O afael tad a mam.

Ac hefyd am y dywededig Lewis Phillips, yr hwn fu farw Mai 20fed 1833 yn 69 oed ynghyd a Sarah Phillips, ei wraig, yr hon a fu farw Awst 22 1831 yn 81 mlwydd oed.' (NB. Age difference.)

'Y mae Duw'n ffyddlon, a thrwyddo ef y'ch galwyd chwi i gymdeithas ei Fab ef, Iesu Grist ein Harglwydd ni.'

Once again an example of a tragedy that families in the 1800s were often faced with. In the churchyard of Capel Dewi near Llandysul is the gravestone that recounts the death in 1875 of five children from one family within four days; here in Llanfyrnach churchyard a similar story, this time four children, ages 20, 10, 12 and 26 from one family dying between April 3rd and May 31st in 1824. In Capel Dewi the children died from scarletina maligna, and one cannot help but wonder which disease was responsible for the death of the four children of

Lewis and Sarah Phillips of Llanfyrnach. It could very well be the same because scarletina maligna was, as mentioned earlier, responsible for more deaths among children in the 1800s than any other disease.

On another memorial in the churchyard another child is remembered: 'Er cof am David, mab William ac Elizabeth Lewis, Landigwined, plwyf . . . , bu farw Mawrth 17eg 1858 yn 6 mlwydd oed.

> Oes gwpan gofid wrth ei fin,
> Fe'i profodd Grodd i'w ben.
> Gwell ganddo flas y nefol win
> A'r wledd tu draw i'r llen.'

And now we travel in a southerly direction, for about five miles along a narrow country lane to the village of Llanboidy. Standing in the centre of the village is the church and, like the one at Llanfyrnach, dedicated to St Brychan. Although the chancel and north chapel were rebuilt in the 1800s there is in the nave a blocked thirteenth century doorway, while in the east wall of the chancel there is a fifteenth century shield depicting the Dynevor family arms. The shield came from Whitland Abbey. An ancient incised slab lies in the south wall.

The narrow path leading to the church door has two, well proportioned, evergreen trees on each side. On the west wall, a few feet below the bell cote, is a blue-faced clock and on the south side of the porch two wooden poles, about six feet high, capped by a wooden saddle roof from which hangs a large bell. In the churchyard there are some memorials worthy of note. On one the following words: In loving memory of Dr Vaughan Daniel Williams Bowen-Jones, MRCS, LRCP, Glanyrafon, Llanboidy, died January 3rd 1930 aged 80 years, who practised in this village for over 50 years. 'Peace, perfect peace'.

On another gravestone: 'Anna Phillips, died November 28th 1850 aged 70 years.

> Vain words on tombs
> Are often spent,
> But good name
> Is a monument.'

An inscription in Welsh reads: 'Er cof am Benjamin Thomas, Ty'rhenrhos, o'r plwyf hwn, hunodd Hydref 9fed 1868 yn 78 oed.

> Yr Iôr bua rhoi bywyd,
> Einioes gyda iechyd.
> Hawl a fedd i alw o fyd
> Man y mynno mewn munud.'

And, finally, in Llanboidy churchyard there is one other very interesting memorial. It stands on the south side of the church and towards the east end of the churchyard boundary. It is in the shape of a tall rectangular slab, incised with a cross, on which a carving of a woman draped in a flowing gown rests. On the top face of the plinth, at the base of the memorial: 'Walter Rice Howell Powell, MP Born April 4th 1819, died June 25th 1889.' On the west face of the plinth:

> George Powell Roch, Captain Pembrokeshire
> Yeomanry, attached to the RSLI. Killed in
> action in Flanders March 21st 1916, aged 49 years.

Walter Rice Howell Powell was named after his father,

who died in 1834, and the family home was Maesgwyn, a mansion within the parish. The mansion, unfortunately, like many other large houses, is now a ruin. He became a JP and DL, and also High Sheriff in 1849. Between 1880 and 1885, and 1886 until his death in 1889 he was a Member of Parliament. A man of short stature, he was known locally as 'y dyn bach' (small man), but his height did not deter him from becoming a keen sportsman, a breeder of horses, and Master of Foxhounds.

The memorial is the work of Sir Goscombe John (1860-1952). Born in Cardiff, he was commissioned to carve the heads of many famous Welshmen such as David Lloyd George, T.E. Ellis and Sir John Williams. He also carved the memorial to the composers of the Welsh national anthem, the James brothers, Evan and James.

Four miles to the north west of Llanboidy, is the church of St Gwynio at Llanwinio. For a church situated in such an isolated, rural setting with only a few houses nearby, one is struck by the extent of the churchyard, which is surprisingly large. Its Parish Registers cover the years 1767 to baptisms – 1812; marriages – 1967; burials – 1910. The registers can be seen in the Carmarthen Record Office. The Bishop's Transcripts, kept in the National Library in Aberystwyth, date back to 1672, the last transcript covering the years 1730 to 1877.

St Gwynio, who lived in the middle of the sixth century was martyred by the Irish not far from where the church now stands, the place where he was killed known as Cil Sant. A reference to a long past curate of the church can be seen in an old document which also states: 'We hear by report of ye country he is defamed and scandalised by one Catherine Vychan, a vile and wicked woman and common strumpet, and by report mother of five or six bastard children and regards not to whom she fathers them.'

In the churchyard there is a gravestone with the following inscription: 'Er cyfeirio llygad y byw gweled y man y gorwedd gweddillion y diweddar Jonah Edwards, Cwmbach, gweinidog gyda'r Methodistiaid Calfinaidd, yr hwn a gymerwyd oddiwrth ei waith at ei wobr Mawrth 6ed 1871 yn 67 mlwydd oed, wedi bod yn pregethu'r efengyl am agos i ddeugain mlynedd yn ddi-fwlch. Ei dystiolaeth ychydig funudau cyn iddo farw oedd:

'Mae na achos i'r gwir Gristion dystio hyd yn od pan yn marw.'

> Ni frysia'r hwn a gredo,
> Mynd at Iesu oedd fy nghri.
> Am iddo fy ngharu – am beth nis gwn i.
> Ond hwn mi a hwn yw hyn
> Na thrig Ef mewn llawnder
> A'm gadael yn llwm.

The reader of the inscription is asked to look to the spot where the remains of Jonah Edwards, a Calvinistic Methodist minister's remains lie buried, who was taken away from his work on March 6th 1871, aged 67 years. He had preached the Gospel for nearly 40 years and his last words as he lay dying were: 'There is every reason for the true Christian to testify even unto death.'

The next church we visit is that at Llandyfriog which is about two miles from Newcastle Emlyn, on the A475 road to Lampeter. The church, grouped with the churches at Newcastle Emlyn, Troed-yr-Aur and Brongwyn, is dedicated to St Tyfriog, who some scholars say was the son of Nudd; a king and a saint who is said to have founded Llysfronydd, known as Llysworney, in the Vale of Glamorgan. The church at Llandyfriog, with its squat square tower topped by a steeple, stands in a secluded spot some way off the main road, and is surrounded by a large churchyard. The Parish Registers date from 1725 and the Bishop's Transcripts from 1676; they can now be seen at the National Library.

A rector of Llandyfriog, the Rev. Samuel Williams (1660-1722), was also a copyist and his most important work was to copy Welsh manuscripts, many of them now also in the National Library. His son was the Rev. Moses Williams who is remembered as an antiquary. He worked for a time at the Ashmolean Museum.

In the churchyard are two memorials of interest. A few yards from the west wall is the grave of a Thomas Heslop who was killed while fighting a duel against John Beynon, reportedly the last duel fought in Wales. It came about as the result of an argument between the two men regarding the morals of a barmaid at the Salutation Inn, Newcastle Emlyn. On the gravestone is inscribed: 'Alas poor Heslop.' An obelisk in the churchyard commemorates David Emlyn Evans who died in 1913. A musician, he composed the two hymn-tunes 'Trewen' and 'Eirinwg'.

On the walls inside the church members of the Fitzwiliam family of Cilgwyn are remembered.

The Fitzwilliams were descended from Admiral Richard Braithwaite, the Admiral having served in the Royal Navy alongside Thomas Lloyd who had died in 1801. In his will Lloyd bequeathed Cilgwyn to the Admiral, much to the displeasure of the Lloyds of Coedmore.

On the south wall a memorial of speckled brown marble on which three brothers of the Fitzwilliam family are remembered. The inscription reads: 'Richard Braithwaite Lloyd Fitzwilliam, Lieutenant in her late

Majesty's Royal Indian Marine. Born 28th August 1873, died of fever August 24th 1902. Buried in the Parish of Llandyfriog.

Francis Crompton Lloyd Fitzwilliam, Lieutenant, Royal Navy. Born 3rd August 1870, drowned on duty trying to save the lives of others 29th January 1898. Buried at Bermuda.

William Loggie Lloyd Fitzwilliam, L/Cpl., Voluntary Company, Argyll and Southern Highlanders. Born 5th August 1879, died of enteric fever on the day he landed in England, 20th of May 1901, after serving 1 year 9 months in the South African War (1899-1902). Buried in this Parish. All of Cilgwyn, Cardiganshire.

"Peace, peace, to those far and near" says the Lord. "And I will heal them." Isaiah 57 v 19.

In memory of three brothers who died in the service of their country. This memorial is erected by their seven surviving brothers and three sisters.'

Enteric fever is better known as typhoid, an infectious disease caused by the bacterium Salmonella typhi. The bacterium usually enters the body through the ingestion of contaminated food or water and multiplies in the lymphoid tissue. It first enters the blood stream within 24 to 72 hours.

One of the most famous instances of carrier-borne disease in medical history was the early twentieth century case of Typhoid Mary.

Mary Mallon, to give her proper name, was born in 1870 and died November 11th 1938 in North Brother Island, New York.

Mary was first recognised as a carrier of the typhoid bacteria during an epidemic of typhoid fever in 1904 that spread through a part of New York, where she worked as a cook. By the time the source of the disease had been discovered, Mary had disappeared. She continued to work as a cook, moving from household to household, until 1907, when she was found working in a house in Manhattan.

Once again she fled but George Soper, a sanitary engineer finally tracked her down and, again, she was detained until 1910.

Four years later, Soper was again looking for Mary when another epidemic broke out at a sanatorium in New Jersey and at Sloane Maternity Hospital in Manhattan, New York. She was at last found in Westchester County, New York, and returned to North Brother Island, where she remained for the rest of her life. She suffered a stroke in 1932 and, six years later, died. Although she was attributed with causing fifty-one original cases of typhoid and three deaths, she herself was totally immune to the disease.

Why the anecdote, albeit an interesting one, you may ask? Well it was that dreaded disease, now curable through the use of antibiotics, that caused the death of William Loggie Lloyd Fitzwilliam.

Having digressed, for which I apologise, let us return and look at other memorials to the Cilgwyn family in Llandyfriog Church.

On the north wall, and facing the door into the church, a memorial on which is written: 'In loving memory of Major John Kendrick Lloyd Fitzwilliam, MC, Order of St Stanislaus (Russia), RHA, 8th son of Charles and Margaret Fitzwilliam of Cilgwyn, killed in action in France near Arras, August 30th 1918, aged 33 years. Buried at Vin-en-Artois.

"Pro Patria Mori."'

Also on the north wall are four white marble tablets in a one, two one pattern. On the top tablet: 'Sacred to the memory of Benjamin Edward Hall, Esq. JP, DL, son of the late Edward Hall, Esq. MD, of Henrietta Street, Covent Garden. Born 24th January 1776, died 4th December 1848 in the 74th year of his age, and Jane Maria, his wife, daughter of Admiral Richard Braithwaite of Warcop, Westmoreland and Cilgwyn, Cardiganshire. Born 14th November 1773, died December 7th 1853.'

The second tablet: 'In this vault are deposited the remains of Richard Braithwaite Hall, Royal Navy, second son of Edward Hall, Esq. of this Parish, and Jane Maria, his wife, and grandson of Admiral Braithwaite of Greenwich. Born July 27th 1808, unfortunately drowned near Jersey, March 30th 1828.'

The next tablet alongside the second one has on it: 'Sacred to the memory of Sarah Elizabeth Gertrude Lloyd, whose remains are deposited in Llangoedmore Church, Cardiganshire. Born 10th November 1810, died 3rd August 1811, in the 26th year of her age. Only daughter of Benjamin Edward Hall, Esq., and wife of Oliver Lloyd of Cardigan. Also to the memory of William James Benjamin Hall, Esq. of Bryntirion, Pembrokeshire, SW, youngest son of Benjamin Edward Hall, Esq. Born 14th February 1813, died 14th March 1840 in the 38th year of his age.'

And the tablet at the bottom reads: 'Sacred to the memory of Georgina, youngest daughter of the late Richard Braithwaite, Esq., Admiral of the White, and Urica Eleonora, his wife. Ob November 23rd 1848. AEt 41. Also her maternal aunt, Gertrude, relict of Arthur Barber, Esq. of Chester, and daughter of George Loggie, Esq., Swedish Consul at Algeria, and Jane, his wife. Ob August 16th 1819. AEt 73.'

Beneath the four tablets is another tablet on which is inscribed: 'These four tablets were by request removed in

1885 from St Mary's Churchyard, Paddington.'

The St Stanislaus mentioned in connection with Maj. John Fitzwilliam was both a bishop and a martyr and lived from 1030 to 1079. Following ordination as a priest he was given a canonry at Cracow in Poland. A bitter quarrel with the king eventually led to his death. It is said that Stanislaus had threatened to excommunicate the king because of his acts of injustice and violence. The king decided that he should be killed, and on the refusal of the king's guards to kill the bishop the king himself killed him with his own sword. Stansilaus was canonised in 1253.

From Llandyfriog we head for the coast and soon arrive at Llanarth, a matter of only four miles from New Quay. The church at Llanarth stands alongside a very narrow, winding lane off the A487. Dedicated to St David, the west tower dates from the fifteenth century, while the nave and chancel have medieval walls. The church is grouped with three other churches – St Cynon, Capel Cynon; St David, Talgarreg and St Mark, Gwenlli. The Parish Registers, deposited in the National Library, cover the years, 1688 to 1855 (baptisms), 1688 to 1969 (marriages) and 1688 to 1864 (burials). The Bishop's Transcripts are from 1674 to 1892.

The stained glass window in the east wall, and above the altar, has three lancets, the left lancet depicting St David, the middle lancet, Jesus, and the third, St Deiniol. Inscribed on it: 'To the Glory of God and Sacred to the memory of the Rt Rev. Daniel Lewis Lloyd, DD, Bishop of Bangor, 1890 – 1898.' Prior to becoming Bishop of Bangor, Daniel Lewis Lloyd had held the posts of Headmaster of Friars School, Bangor and Christ College, Brecon. It is understandable that St Deiniol is depicted in the window; the cathedral at Bangor is dedicated to him. It is said that

St Deiniol, having died in 572, is one of the 20,000 saints buried on Bardsey Island (Ynys Enlli). Along with Dyfrig, Deiniol was instrumental in David taking part in the Synod of Brefi in 545AD.

A stained glass window in the south wall depicts St George, and is in memory of Daniel Rowland Lewis Lloyd, Henry Chester Lewis Lloyd and Richard Lionel Ravenshaw.

In the churchyard there is a gravestone on which there is an intriguing baby's name. The Welsh inscription reads: 'Serchus gof am Thomas Davies, gynt o Pensarnau, yr hwn fu farw Rhagfyr 21ain. 1841 yn 80 mlwydd oed. Hefyd am Jane, ei annwyl briod, yr hon a fu farw Mawrth 24ain. 1854 yn 79 mlwydd oed, ac am faban i Thomas ac M. Davies, "Prince Llywelyn", yr hwn fu farw Ionawr 26ain. 1863 yn 3 diwrnod oed.' According to the above Thomas and M. Davies died in 1841 and 1854 respectively and a boy named 'Prince Llywelyn' in 1863, aged 3 days. To name a boy 'Prince Llywelyn' is rather a strange thing to do, but, we live in a strange world; it has been known for parents to name a boy after a football team -yes, eleven Christian names for one child.

Leaving Llanarth, and travelling on the A487 for nine miles we reach the village of Llanon, or as named in the Diocesan Year Book, Llansantffraed. The church, dedicated to St Bridget, is grouped with three other churches – Dewi Sant, Nebo, St Padarn, Llanbadarn Trefeglwys and St Restitutus, Llanrhystud.

The church has a single nineteenth century chamber with box pews and a fifteenth century west tower. Among the many memorials in the churchyard is the following which tells a very sad tale indeed: To remember with love Richard Andrew, died June 7th 1995, aged 26 years. Also Dominic Millet, died October 2nd 1995, aged

34 years. Adored sons of the Rev. John Raymond Jenkins. 'A wise son maketh a glad father.'

Also there is an unusual stone built into the south wall of the church. Inscribed on it are details of a person, if the epitaph is to be believed who was blessed with, a truly saintly character: 'Here lyeth the body of Lewis Davies, late of Perth-y-Gwenyn, Gent. deceased, who left behind him a gentle and good character in every part of a private life; namely a good Christian, sincere friend, affectionate husband, indulgent father, peaceable neighbour, and a charitable benefactor of the poor and needy; in short he was one of the principal inhabitants of this Parish, and a very useful member thereof, which caused his death to be much lamented by his family and also regretted by all who had the pleasure of his acquaintance. He resigned his soul to God, after a short illness, in hopes (sic) of a joyful resurrection, on Monday, the 18th day of April 1747 in the 52nd year of his age. He is now at rest, and the peace of God be with his soul. Amen.'

A few feet to the left of the memorial to Lewis Davies is another old stone built into the church wall. The inscription reads: Here lyeth the earthy (sic) remains of Alban Thomas, late of this Parish, who departed this life February 20th 1741-2 (sic) in the 57th year of his age. Also the body of Catherine Herbert, wife of the said Alban Thomas, but last of Morgan Herbert, Gent. She died May 31st 1756, age 66 years. Here likewise lie the bodies of Elizabeth, Evan and Mary Thomas, children of the above Alban Thomas and Catherine Herbert who died in their infancy.

It is highly likely that the Morgan Herbert mentioned above was a descendant of the Herbert family of Hafod, once a large and imposing mansion not far from Pont-rhyd-fendigaid, but now unfortunately no longer standing – it was completely destroyed in August 1958 by being blown up with dynamite. The Herberts, through numerous generations, alternately named their elder sons Morgan and Richard.

Inscribed on a slate on the west end of a large box-shaped tomb the following words:

It was pleasure to our ears,
A Sovereign balm for every want,
A cordial for our fears.

Salvation is our happy rest,
Salvation is our home.
Let salvation be included
Upon our silent tomb.

Dyma'r fan lle caf rhoi hun,
Mhlith y meirw heb wae nag ing.
Mewn tŷ o glai dan ddaear glyd
'Mhell o swn daearol fyd.

On the south side of the tomb: 'Er cof am blant John ac Elizabeth Jones, Botre, gynt Llwynteg, y rhai a buont farw fel y canlyn. Elizabeth, Hydref 5ed 1871, yn 22ain oed, Daniel Lewis, Awst 12fed 1876, yn 22ain oed; yn 1843 merch ar ei genedigaeth, hefyd pedwar eraill o'u plant a fuont farw ac a gladdwyd ym mynwent Nantcwnlle. Am ei manylion gwel eu beddfeini yno.'

As we head towards Carmarthen a brief visit to the churchyard at Lampeter. On the left hand side of the path leading to what is an imposing edifice are, in excess of fifty small memorial stones standing in rows; the stones are approximately twelve to eighteen inches high, twelve inches wide, with rounded tops. Inscribed on them are initials only, some with two lots of initials. These stones signify the graves of people who resided and subsequently died in the local workhouse that once stood in the town. Study of the burial registers for the years 1695-1805 and 1813-1968, now deposited in the National Library, might prove an interesting exercise and may throw light on the inmates of the workhouse at that time, now interred in those graves.

Eastwards on the A40

Our first call is at the church of Llanfair-ar-y-Bryn that stands on the northern outskirts of the ancient town of Llandovery. The church is dedicated to St Mary and is grouped with the churches of St Michael, Cilycwm, St Barnabas, Rhandirmwyn, and St Paulinus, Ystrad-ffin.

Standing on the site of a Roman fort, there are Norman windows in both the north and south wall of the church. Other parts of the church date from the thirteenth, fourteenth and fifteenth centuries. Over the years many alterations have been carried out. The first ecclesiastical building on the site was a monastic cell founded in the first half of the 1100s by Richard Fitzpons, a Norman baron. Not many years later, c.1180, the monastic cell was dissolved, and at about the same time the Welsh, in order to rid themselves of a Church set up by the Norman enemy, burned the roof. It was not until the thirteenth century that the rebuilding commenced, including the tower. Changes to the edifice were again carried out in the fifteenth century when a rood screen and a loft were added. Along with many churches up and down the land, considerable alterations were made to the church in the 1880s. In the outside walls can be seen red bricks and tiles, first used by the Romans in their forts.

There are five stained glass windows in the church. The east window dates from 1922 and depicts two important, historical figures, William Williams, Pantycelyn and Vicar Pritchard. William Williams is remembered mainly as a hymn-writer, having written about one thousand Welsh and English hymns, but he was also one of the leaders of the Methodist movement, along with Howell Harries and Daniel Rowlands.

Originally ordained as a priest in the Anglican Church, he was refused priest's orders, and spent the remainder of his life as an itinerant preacher, averaging about three thousand miles a year while travelling the country in this capacity. He is known throughout Wales as 'Y Pêr Ganiedydd' (The Sweet Singer). The inscriptions on the two outer lights of the window are: 'His candle goeth not out' and the opening line of possibly the best known of all his hymns, 'Guide me, O Thou Great Redeemer'. On the 29th of April 1717 he was baptized at the original red sandstone font. A desk in the vestry is said to have belonged to him. He died in 1791, and is buried in the churchyard, his gravestone of red marble standing above his grave on the north side of the church. Inscribed on his gravestone: 'Sacred to the memory of the Rev. William Williams, Pantycelyn, in this Parish, author of several works in prose and verse. He waits the coming of the morning star, which shall usher in the glories of the first resurrection, and at the sound of the Archangel's trumpet, the sleeping dust shall be animated, and death for ever shall be swallowed up in victory. Born 1717, died January 11th 1791, aged 74 years.

Heb saeth, heb fraw, heb ofn, heb ofid ac heb boen,
Yn canu o flaen yr orsedd ogoniant Duw a'r Oen.
Yng nghanol myrdd, myrddiynau yn canu oll heb drai,
Yr anthem ydyw cariad, a'r cariad i barhau.'

On the south face of the stone: 'Also Mary, the beloved wife of the above William Williams, died June 11th 1799, aged 76 years. Also the Rev. William Williams, Clerk, St Clements, Truro, Cornwall, eldest son of the above Wm. Williams, died 30th November 1818, aged 74 years. Also the Rev. John Williams of Pantycelyn, youngest son of the above William Williams, died 15th June 1828, aged 74 years.

"A sinner saved."'

Also in the east window – the centre light – the words: 'Am weddi a'i pherthnasau', and a verse written by Vicar Pritchard:

Clod a gallu, diolch moliant,
Parch, anrhydedd a gogoniant,
A fo i Roddwr pob daioni,
Sydd mor fwyn yn gwrando'n gweddi.

In 1602 Vicar Rhys Pritchard had been instituted to the church of Llandingad with the chapelry of Llanfair-ar-y-bryn. Llandingad Church, stands on the southern outskirts of Llandovery.

A brief outline of the Vicar's life has already been given.

In the north wall of the chancel are another two stained glass windows. One is in memory of the Rev. Edmondes Owens, Vicar of Llandovery from 1911 to 1922. Depicted is St David. The second window is in memory of Canon Worthington Poole-Hughes. The window, depicting The Good Shepherd and dating from 1931, is the work of Kemp. Canon Hughes was Warden of Llandovery College and the window was donated by his family.

On the opposite wall of the chancel can be seen two windows by the artist John Petts – Câr Di (Love Thou), (The Leper Window), 1972. The content of the window is Pett's summary of the teachings of Christ. The other window, again by John Petts, was given by Major and Mrs Stewart of Llanfair House in memory of their son,

Captain John Logan Stewart, GSO 44th Division, Dunkirk, 1940.

There are more windows in the nave. In the south wall is a window in memory of Naval Surgeon Daniel Sunders, the window given by the officers of HMS Conqueror and Royal Marines Battalion, Japan 1865. The window depicts Christ The Healer. Also in the south wall, a window that is a combination of both Norman and Saxon architecture with a Roman tile to be seen in the arch.

In the west wall is a window in memory of another member of the Stewart family. It commemorates Major William Edmond Logan Stewart and Mrs Mary Adele Morland Stewart; the window was given by their daughter Mary Elizabeth Halliday.

Within the church is a pulpit designed by W.D. Caroe, a well-known church architect. It dates from 1922. The organ is pre-1800, and made by Henry Bevington. The altar is of carved oak and dates from the Stuart period. In 1535 there were four bells; two of them were re-cast in 1902, the cost paid for by Mrs Magdalene Morris of Coomb, Llangynog who, before her marriage, was a member of the Gwynne family of Glanbrân.

Glanbrân, now a ruin, stood about a mile from the hamlet of Cynghordy. It had been the property of the Gwynne family for fourteen generations. In 1777 a Roderick Gwynne erected a new mansion, which was sold in 1875 to an industrialist by the name of Isaac Haley from Huddersfield. Following his death it was bought in 1929 by brothers named Gibbins from Glamorgan.

On the west wall of the porch, there is a memorial on which is inscribed: 'Sacred to the memory of Mr Thomas Jones of Ystradwalter, who died September 3rd 1762, and also Mrs Elizabeth Jones, relict of the above Thomas

Jones, she died August 10th 1767. It may be truly said that they were pious, just, humane and benevolent, and that they contributed largely in proportion of their ability relief of their necessitous neighbours. This monument was erected at the expense of their affectionate son, the Rev. Mr Jones, Rector of Knapton, Vicar of Paston, and the Headmaster of the Free Grammar School at North Walham in Norfolk. They both died at the age of 63.'

Ystradwalter stands about two miles north-east of the church and its origins date back to the 1500s. A Howell ap Rhydderch of Ystradwalter married Gwenllian, the daughter of Sir Rhys ap Thomas, KG. In 1596 Dwnn called at Ystradwalter and David Powell, grandson of Howell and Gwenllian, signed the family provenance for him. By the end of the nineteenth century the house was owned by the Pryse-Rice family of Llwynybrain.

Leaving Llandovery, we continue on the A40 and, roughly three miles along the road, we see a sign pointing to Cefnarthen; it is well worth a visit as there is a interesting chapel there: It was in the chapel at Cefnarthen that William Williams Pantycelyn's father went to worship, where he was a deacon, and where William Williams also attended as a child and as a young man.

As soon as the visitor decides to follow the sign to Cefnarthen he or she may begin to have doubts as to whether it is wise to do so as the road, or to be more accurate, the lane, leading to the chapel is very narrow. It winds its way between a steep, wooded bank on one side and a precipitous slope down to a stream on the other side. But the scenery compensates and cancels out any regrets one may have for making the detour and, although the journey to the chapel seems unending, the sight of the chapel, standing not many yards from the gurgling stream that flows into much larger river Tywi, is well worth the effort. The location of the chapel is idyllic and the surrounding countryside and enveloping peace makes the journey worthwhile; here is a veritable heaven on earth. However it has not always been thus as the stream, trees and surrounding fields could recount a time of extreme danger and persecution in years gone by.

Walking around the chapel and the graveyard, one feels a strong sense of history and also of spirituality. If only the stones in the building could talk, what an interesting tale they would be able to recount.

On the front wall of the chapel is a rectangular tablet on which is inscribed in Welsh: 'Er cof am y Parchedig Rhys Prydderch, Ystradwalter, 1620-1699. Un o arwyr y ffydd Gristnogol cynulleidfa Ogof Castell Craig yr Wyddon, 1662-1689. Awdur "Gemau Doethineb".' Translated, it tells us: 'In memory of the Reverend Rhys Prydderch, Ystradwalter, 1620-1699. One of the heroes of the Christian faith, shepherd of the flock of the Cave of Castle on the Rock of Wyddon, 1662-1689. Author of "Gems of Wisdom".'

Those few words on that simple tablet take us back to a very difficult and turbulent time in the religious history of our nation. They were the days when freedom to worship according to one's conscience was not allowed, and those brave enough to defy the Establishment's insistence that all were to worship in the official church of the state were in danger of imprisonment or worse. Such people were forced to worship in secret locations, and the words on the tablet tell us that the founders of the chapel at Cefnarthen, prior to the building of the chapel, worshipped in secret in a nearby cave.

Not far from the village of Pencader, Christians of that area also worshipped in a cave at Cwmhwplin, and it is traditionally believed that before Capel Seion in Drefach, Llanelli was built in 1712 the inabitants of the district worshipped under an oak tree on the land of Clôs Farm that stands halfway between Drefach and Pontyberem. We should be so grateful that we have the freedom today to worship as we desire and we should not forget the sacrifice and suffering of such people as the founders of Cefnarthen chapel.

One of these was a Jenkin Jones, Llanddetty Hall, Brecs. who, as a minister and preacher, was responsible for winning the first converts to the cause. It is interesting to note that in Major Francis's book, *Historic Carmarthenshire Homes*, a Colonel Jenkin Jones of Llanddety Hall married a Barbara Mansel of Mudlescombe, and he died in 1689. Could this be the same Jenkin Jones, or was the preacher the colonel's son, or connected in some other way?

Following the restoration of the monarchy by King Charles II, Jenkin Jones and members of his congregation were arrested and imprisoned in the jail at Carmarthen for one month.

The Independent chapel of Cefnarthen is one of the oldest chapels in the Principality and, as already mentioned, the first adherents to the cause came about through the efforts of Jenkin Jones, who was preaching in the locality even before the outbreak of the Civil War in 1642. The cave where the first worshippers gathered is within a short distance of the chapel; it can still be seen, although the entrance has a lot of stones and earth restricting entry. Immediately following the passing of the Act of Tolerance, the chapel was erected for worship in 1689 with Rees Prydderch its first minister. Before becoming a minister, sometime between 1662 and 1670, he was a schoolmaster. At the same time he ministered to the people of the area in secret and was not publicly ordained until 1688.

Among those who attended Rees Prydderch's school was a William Evans, who later became the first teacher at the Academy, later called the Presbyterian College when it moved to Carmarthen in 1704 The Academy was, at the time, situated in Priory Street. William Evans also taught under the auspices of the SPCK, and was a minister to a small number of people that met in a house in Priory Street.

Of interest is the fact that Rees Prydderch was born, ordained and died on January 25th – the Feast Day of St Paul. Shortly before his death, a certain Roger Williams assisted him in his ministry at the chapel and it is believed that Roger Williams was one of the founder members. He died in May 1730, having been a minister at Cefnarthen and Merthyr Tydfil for a total of thirty years.

Following Roger Williams's death, three ministers came in quick succession to be responsible for the chapel – a David Williams, ordained in June 1731, a John Williams who, according to chapel records, officiated at a communion service on October 31st 1731. By October the following year, a David Thomas was the minister and he stayed there until December 2nd 1739.

It is generally believed that David and John Williams were the sons of Roger Williams, and it is also believed that it was during their ministries that Arminianism was accepted by some members of the chapel. It was a doctrine propounded by a Dutch theologian called Arminius, who died in 1609. Arminius opposed the views of Calvin, especially that of predestination, i.e., God's appointment for eternity of some members of the human race to salvation and eternal life. In other words Calvin believed that everything is fore-ordained by God. This led to a split occurring among the members and the followers of Calvinism left to worship in the chapel at Glynypentan.

Among those who were followers of Calvinism were John and Dorothy Williams of Cefncoed; they were William Williams, Pantycelyn's parents. John Williams died in 1742, aged 86, and was blind for the last six years of his life. Dorothy and William Williams, nine years after moving to worship at Glynypentan, gave land for the building of a chapel at Pentretygwyn, which was built in 1749.

As a result of the split that had taken place among members at Cefnarthen the cause at the chapel weakened considerably. But on August 19th 1772, the two factions having resolved their differences, a special service was held in the chapel to celebrate the reunification of the members which was attended by a number of ministers.

Another tablet is to be seen on the outer side of one of the walls; it reads: 'In memory of the pious Rev. Peter Jenkins of Penrhiw, in this Parish, Minister of the Gospel at Drychoed for 45 years and at Gwynfe who died July 19th 1821, aged 72 years.'

As the visitor can see, the chapel is in an excellent state of repair, and when one considers that the first hymn was sung, the first prayer intoned and the first sermon preached in the chapel over three hundred years ago, it is upliffting to know that the cause is still on-going.

Before leaving Cefnarthen I believe that another of the chapel's ministers deserves a mention for the work he did in Cefnarthen, and also in two other chapels.

His name was Edward Jones, and he was born at Blaenyglyn, near Cefnarthen, on February 26th 1811. He was the youngest of three children and received very little formal education as a child because there was no day school near his home, and his parents were not in a financial position to send him away to school. He was indebted to the Sunday School for the education that he did receive, as it was there that he learnt to read, and the only book available to him was The Bible. His mastery of the skill of reading led him to learn long passages from The Bible by heart. He was also a very curious boy, who wanted to learn as much as possible about the world around him.

At fourteen years of age he was apprenticed to a David Humphreys, a cobbler. In 1829 a religious revival broke out in the district and, although many of his contemporaries attended the services, Edward Jones kept away because he felt his dedication to the cause was lacking. But eventually he did attend a service and, as a result, decided to submit himself to his Saviour, Jesus Christ. Very soon afterwards, fellow worshippers tried to get him to preach but he refused their request to do so.

In 1830 he went to work in Tredegar as a cobbler and, while there, he lived a very frugal life, thus able to save ten shillings (50p) a week. In 1831 he returned to his home to follow his trade, and it was during that year he agreed to start preaching. Two years later he started as a pupil at a school at Rhydybont, and applied himself to his studies with the result that he learnt English, Latin and Greek. By 1836 the money he had saved while working as a cobbler ran out and he had to leave the school. He then set up his own school at Esgairdawe but, a year later, he received a call from the members of the chapels at Bethel, Pentre and Cefnarthen to be their minister. He was twenty-six years of age when he was ordained as minister of the three chapels in May 1837.

Immediately following his ordination he worked extremely hard, preaching and as a caring shepherd of his members. He soon became a noted preacher, and was very much in demand throughout south Wales. In 1840 he spent a month as minister of Tabernacle chapel in Liverpool, a chapel in the throes of a revival at the time. On returning to his own chapels he succeeded in starting a revival in the area and, as a result, the number of members of the three chapels totalled more than two hundred and fifty. During the first twenty-five weeks of 1841 he preached one hundred and forty sermons – nearly six sermons a week.

His superhuman efforts affected his health and, unfortunately, sleeping in a damp bed resulted in his contracting tuberculosis. On December 15th 1841, at only thirty years of age, he died.

Edward Jones was of a small stature but he possessed a big personality. He was also of a gentle, friendly nature and had a clever, clear mind. Although careless with regards to dress, he was extremely precise in all his work. Thousands had reason to be grateful to Edward Jones for introducing them to the Gospel and, even over one hundred and fifty years later, we should not forget him or all those like him for maintaining, often under difficult conditions, the flame of Christianity burning in our land.

From Cefnarthen we head back to the A40, turn left, and travel in the direction of Brecon. After about five miles we arrive at Llywel. The church can be seen from the A40 and it is only a matter of a hundred yards or so to the left of the main road.

The church, which dates from around 1400 is dedicated to St David, and has a large crenelated tower. It is 65ft. high and has 70 steps leading to the watchman's tower at the top. The chancel and nave are mostly of late fifteenth and early sixteenth centuries – 1480 to 1520, and the church door is also of the fifteenth century.

The font in present use dates from 1869 but, in the

vestry there is a pre-Norman font over a thousand years old which was discovered in the churchyard in the 1860s. On the vestry wall can be seen the Llywel Stocks that were made in 1798, replacing the stocks and whipping post made in 1771. In a case in the wall behind the present font is a bell that once belonged to a town crier.

Inside the church are two ancient stones; the Llywel Stone and the Aberhydfer Stone. The actual Llywel Stone is now in the British Museum, the one in the church being a plaster replica. The original stone is of circa 500AD and has Ogham symbols inscribed on it.

In the year 1500 the church would have had a rood loft above the chancel arch. It would have been from the loft that the lessons were read and the occasional sermon preached. In 1869 the rood loft was removed, resulting in the chancel arch coming into full view. A screen presented to the church in 1925 separates the chancel from the nave; it is supported by four main posts. On these are carved Aaron's rod and foliage. The transom rails on both sides have carvings of vine leaves and grapes on them.

Symbols of the class distinction of yesteryear can be seen – the choir stalls are of oak while the pews in the nave are of pitch pine. The altar has carved decorative panels on it. The middle panel depicts the Lamb of God and on the north side a fig tree, a vine, corn, the Chalcedonian lily and the passion flower. On the third panel an oak tree on which can be seen a bird in its nest, this a reference to the 3rd verse of the 84th Psalm: 'Even the sparrow has found a home, and the swallow where she may have her young – a place near your altar, O Lord Almighty, my King and my God.'

In the south wall of the Sanctuary, there is a tomb recess dating from the fifteenth century; the effigy that once was on it has disappeared – anything to do with

Cromwell, I wonder? Under the chancel floor is a vault that is reached by stone steps from outside the church, the entrance to which is located by a stone in the wall. It is reported that, following the last person to be buried in the vault, the grill leading into it was locked and the key thrown back into the vault.

On the walls of the chancel there are two interesting tablets: 'Here lieth the body of Sibyl, wife of Howell Morgan, Esq., the daughter of Thomas Jeffreys of Cefnrhosan in Llywel, Gent. He (i.e. Howell Morgan) had issue, Morgan, Thomas and Elizabeth. She (i.e. Sibyl) died the first day of January 1600.' This memorial has on it the oldest inscription that I have seen during my visits to churches, chapels and churchyards.

The second memorial, again dating from the 1600s, is inscribed: 'Here lies the body of . . . Charles, Esq., whom he had issue Jeffrey, Thomas John, Howell, Watkin. Roger, Anne. He died 10th February, Anno Domini, 1642.' (This gentleman died the year the Civil War broke out between the forces of King Charles I and those of Parliament, led by Oliver Cromwell.) 'John and Roger died issueless in London. Jeffrey and Thomas, of whom no issue, now lieth buried here, which Watkin married Gwenllian, daughter and heiress to Evan Bowen, Cwm-y-Dŵr, of whom he had issue Edward, Evan, Jeffrey, and John, and died March 10th Anno Domini, 1648. The two last, Jeffrey and John, settled in London.'

On the north wall of the church, in Welsh: 'Er coffadwriaeth am David Owen, "Brutus", golygydd Yr Haul am dri deg a hanner o flynyddoedd, awdur Brutisiana ac &; bu farw dydd Mawrth, 16eg o Ionawr 1866 yn 71 oed.

O Brutus, fedrus fedrwr,
Marw a fu un mor fawr fel awdwr.
Ni wel Gwalia un gŵr
Byth mo'i fath hyd fyth.

Gosodwyd y cofadail hwn gan ei holl gyfeillion.'

David Owen was born in the village of Llanpumsaint.
Born in 1795, he was a man of many talents; a preacher,
schoolmaster, and as mentioned in the memorial, the
editor of an Anglican journal entitled Yr Haul (The Sun).
Originally of the Independent persuasion, he later joined
the Baptists and was ordained as a Baptist minister.
Involved in fraud, he was forced out of the Baptist
denomination and went back to his original
denomination. He published seventeen books, including
several biographies. He settled down in a hamlet called
Pentre-tŷ-Gwyn not far from Llandovery, and he is also
commemorated on a tablet set into the outer wall of a
forecourt wall outside a chapel in that hamlet.

For David Owen to take the pseudonym Brutus shows
clearly that he was well versed in the history of ancient
Greece. The original Brutus is said to have had a vision
while on a visit to the Temple of Diana, on the island of
Leogetia, that he would, one day, discover a land in the
west and what he had seen in the vision was later realised
when he and a friend landed at Totnes in Britain the
country which was later named after him.

Continuing eastwards along the A40, the road takes us
through Trecastle, Sennybridge, and on to Brecon with its
cathedral and, standing in the town square, church of St
Mary.

Around the year 1100 the cathedral was founded as a
priory and, in 1923, it was designated as the Cathedral for

the Diocese of Brecon and Swansea. Between the years 1201 and the 1300s, rebuilding took place with the construction of a presbytery, transepts and a nave. During the sixteeenth century the Duke of Buckingham sponsored the heightening of the central tower.

The font, dating from about 1140, has a Latin inscription and has carvings of beasts, birds and interlace on it. In the cathedral can be seen the effigies of Walter and Christina Awbrey, dated 1312, another four inscribed sixteenth century slabs, effigies of Sir David Williams and his wife dated 1613, a fourteenth century memorial in the Harvard chapel and a wooden female figure from the 1550s. There are also quite a number of other memorials within this grand edifice.

The church of St Mary was originally a chapel-of-ease to the Priory Church. During the thirteenth and fourteenth centuries it was enlarged, and several of the fourteenth century windows remain. In the east wall is a fifteenth century window. Again, the Duke of Buckingham had work carried out in this church, as he had in the cathedral; he added the very tall tower at the west end of the church.

Approximately five miles as the crow flies, and to the east of the town of Brecon, is the village of Llangors and, not far from the village, is Llangors Lake. My first visit to the village and its lake was in the mid-1940s when I was stationed at the military camp, Derring Lines, that is on the outskirts of Brecon. Part of the infantry training was sailing in canvas covered, flimsy boats on the lake.

This time, I am in the village to visit the church and, fortunately, it was open. It was a Saturday, and there was much activity within the church; the vicar, his wife and members of the church were there preparing for the first service to be held on the Sunday following renovation work that had lasted for six months, at a cost of £150,000.

The church is dedicated to St Paulinus. He is said to have been the son of a Nudd Hael, and his mother Tonwy, daughter of Llewddyn Luydog. It is also said that he had eight brothers and lived, according to Dobble, an authority on Welsh saints, at Llandingat (Llandovery).

David Hugh Farmer, in the book *The Oxford Dictionary of Saints*, states that Paulinus is better known as Pol (Paul-de-Leon) and that he originally came from Wales but that, in the 6th century, he moved to Britanny and worked as a bishop in the area that is named after him. Farmer goes on to state that Paulinus was a hermit and a disciple of St Illtud. He built a monastery at Ploudalmezau and died aged 94. It is also said of Paulinus that, when living in Wales, he founded a monastery at Llanddeusant. His feast day was on March 12 and he is well established in Britanny and the Loire valley in France.

The church's large, square tower, the nave, south aisle and ribbed barrel roof date from the late fifteenth century but there is some older masonry in the north wall of the nave. The font is circa 1300 and the organ dates back to the seventeenth century. Inside the church can be seen fragments of early Christian stones.

Leaving Llangorse we head back towards Carmarthen and, a few miles to the east of Llandovery, on the left hand side of the A40, is a memorial that is neither in a church nor in a churchyard. The memorial is in the form of an obelisk surrounded by railings. The inscription on the pillar reads: 'This pillar is called "Mail Coach Pillar", and erected as a caution to mail coach drivers to keep from intoxication, and in memory of the Gloucester to Carmarthen Mail Coach which was driven by Edward Jenkins on the 19th day of December in the year 1835, and he was intoxicated at the time. He drove the Mail on the wrong side of the road, and going at full speed or gallop met a cart and permitted the leader (leading horse) to turn right, and went down over the precipice of 121 feet, and at the bottom near the river came against an ash tree, and the coach was dashed into several pieces. Col. Gwyn of Glan Bran Park, Daniel Jones, Esq. of Penybont and a person of the name of Edwards were outside and David Lloyd Harries, Esq. of Llandovery, Solicitor, and a lad of the name Kenrick were inside passengers of the Mail at the time, and John Compton, Guard. I have heard say that where there is a will there is a way; one person cannot assist many but many can assist a few as this pillar will show as suggested, designed and erected by J. Bull, Inspector of Mail Coaches with the aid of thirteen pounds, sixteen shillings and sixpence received from the 41 subscribers in the year 1841. The work of the pillar was executed by John Jones, Marble and Stonemason, Llanddarog near Carmarthen, repainted and restored by postal officials 1930.'

It is obvious from this memorial that the problem of drink-driving precedes the age of the motor vehicle, and that the end result is, unfortunately, the same.

Returning on the A40 towards the west, we leave it at Llandeilo and take the road to Ammanford and the Amman Valley. In the churchyard of Christ Church, Cwmaman, and on its north side, is a most interesting memorial. It depicts an angel supporting the recumbent figure of a young girl dressed in the uniform of the ATS – the women's army of the 1939-45 War. The workmanship of the carving is of a very high standard, and the inscription tells a very sad tale:

To the memory of
Mollie,
Despatch Rider (ATS) attached to the
6th Welch Regiment,
beloved daughter of
Handel and Miriam Davies, Swansea,
late London House, Garnant,
died on active service February 13th 1940
in her 19th year.

After reading the inscription the visitor is left wondering how this young girl, came to join up at such a young age, when the official call up age was 21, how she became a despatch rider – usually a man's duty in those days – and what was the cause of her death. It should become immediately obvious to the reader that she was of an adventurous temperament. Tracing the life-story of this young girl would undoubtedly produce an interesting story.

From Cwmaman the next step of the journey leads us to the churchyard of St John's Church in Skewen. Some of the memorials have, written on them, some interesting verses that once again show the faith and certainty of the Victorian and Edwardian era.

'In loving memory of David, loving son of Thomas and Elizabeth Lloyd who departed this life January 9th 1907 in his 18th year.

> A flower grew by Jesse's rod,
> Its fragrance was full of God,
> The odour still we have today,
> But God the flower took away.'

In loving memory of Susan, wife of William Curtis of

Pentreffynnon, who died December 1st 1907 aged 50 years.

> Year by year, Oh! how we miss her,
> None but broken hearts can tell.
> We have lost her, Christ has found her,
> Jesus hath done all things well.'

'Sarah Harries, wife of Charles Harries of Skewen, died December 15th 1915 aged 39 years.

> A loving wife, true and kind
> She was to me in heart and mind.
> A careful mother too as well,
> When she on earth with us did dwell.'

'In loving memory of Joshua, elder son of Griffith and Elizabeth Williams of Swansea, and grandson of the late Francis Taylor of Neath Abbey, Chief Engineer of the S.S. Ruabon, lost off the Smalls Lighthouse January 29th 1884 aged 30 years.

> He has anchored his soul in the haven of rest,
> Ile sails the wide sea no more.
> The compass may sweep o'er the wild storm deep,
> He's safe where the storms come no more.'

And then a grave with an imposing granite Celtic cross at its west end while the grave itself is covered with a granite stone on which is inscribed: 'In memory of the Rt. Hon. Sir Samuel Thomas Evans, GCB, born at Skewen 1859, Member of Parliament for mid-Glam, 1890-1910, Solicitor General, 1908-1910, President of the Probate, Divorce and Admiralty Division of the High Court of

Justice from 1910 to his death in 1918.'

A quite lengthy biography of Sir Samuel Thomas in *Who's Who* reads: 'Evans, Rt. Hon., Sir Samuel Thomas Evans, GCB 1916, Kt. 1908, PC 1910, King's Council, President of the British Crimes Court since the outbreak of the War. Born 4th May 1859, son of John Evans, Skewen, Neath. Married in 1887 Rachel who died 1889, daughter of William Thomas of Skewen. Second wife married 1905, Blanche, youngest daughter of the late Charles Rule, Cincinnati, USA, one son and one daughter. Educated at Aberystwyth University College, University of London, JP Glamorgan, Pembrokeshire, Breconshire. Honorary Freeman of the County Borough of Swansea and the Borough of Neath. He was Honorary Fellow of Jesus College, Oxford, Honorary LLD, University of Wales, Barrister of Middle Temple. The last QC appointed in 1901 (Queen Victoria died that year). Bencher and Trustee of the Middle Temple 1908, Recorder of Swansea 1906-08, Solicitor General 1908-1910. MP (Liberal) Glamorganshire (Mid Division) 1890-1910. Address, 11 Lancaster Gate, London W and 9 Sussex Square, Brighton. Clubs; Athaneum, United Services, Reform and Garrick.'

The journey from Skewen to the Gower is a short one, and it is in order to visit two churches in that beautiful part of Wales that we go there. The first of the two churches stands in the village of Cheriton. Cheriton is a small village situated on the Burry Pill stream near Llanmadog. Like Llanmadog it is dominated by the 550 foot Llanmadog Hill. To the south-east is Ryer's Down at 372 feet high and to the north is North Hill Tor with its prominent limestone scar overlooking Landimore Marsh and the Loughor estuary.

The early, practically unaltered, thirteenth century

church is one of the smallest on the Gower Peninsula and displays many interesting features. In the porch there is an ancient carved stone. Also included is a good south door, fine arches, a piscina (a stone basin for carrying away water used in rinsing the chalice and other church plate), a rood loft staircase (a rood loft is a gallery on top of a screen between the chancel and nave), and two very old fonts – one Norman and the other Saxon. The older font is not used any longer. The strong battlement tower has a saddleback roof. A former rector, the Rev. John David Davies, was well known as a historian on the Gower area and he was also a skilled wood-carver. His work can be seen in the choir stalls, altar rail, altar and chest.

In the churchyard is the grave of a seven-year old girl named Gwenith Jones. Born on October 6th 1920, she died March 2nd 1928, and at the bottom of the inscription giving the relevant details an inscription in German: 'Dem Auge Fern – Dem Herzen Nah'. Roughly translated it is 'To the eye far away or distant – To the heart near or close'.

It would be very interesting to know why there is a German saying inscribed on the grave of a seven-year old Welsh child buried in a churchyard in an anglicised part of Wales; there must be a logical explanation for this. For example, could it be connected with another grave, that of Ernest Jones who was a psychoanalyst of note. It is said that he was instrumental in assisting Sigmund Freud to escape to the west from Austria following the Nazi occupation of that country in 1938.

From Cheriton it is only a short run to the second of the two churches, the church at Llanrhidian with its ancient, square tower, which is very similar to the one at Cheriton. In the porch there is an ancient stone known as

'The Leper Stone' that has carvings of human beings and animals on it. No one has managed to decipher the inscription. Although the nave has been rebuilt, there could possibly be some thirteenth century masonry in the chancel.

On the outside of the south wall, there are two memorials, their inscriptions worth recording. On one there are details about a Robert Hary who died in 1646. He had been married twice and from the two wives he had nine children. Then the following inscription with its interesting spelling.

'Here lyeth my lifeless corps bereaved of living breath,
Not slaine by sinne which is the cause of death,
But by decree which God hath said All Men Shall Dy,
And Come to Judgement to know how they shall try.
And now Heavenly God That living breath
Thougavest Me
That mortalle life and soul I yield and give againe to Thee
My corps to earth for short time I doie give,
My soule unto my saviour Christ eternally to live.'

A few feet away from the Hary memorial is a stone commemorating Agnes, wife of Samuel Morris, who died a hundred years after Robert Hary, in November 1746, aged 27 years.

Death with its dart hath pierced my heart
Whilst I was in my prime.
My husband dear, your grief forbear,
'Twas God's appointed time.
My tender husband dear, now cease to weep,
Death to the Saints is but an early sleep.
Go on Thro' Grace, in God's appointed way,

Then joyful shall we meet on the great day.
At the expense of Samuel Morris.

Inscribed on another stone: 'Underneath lie the remains of John Dunn, son of John and Mary Dunn, of this parish, who departed this life the 25th of April 1798, aged 25 years and 9 months.

Our flesh slumber in the ground,
Till the last trumpet's joyful sound.
Then burst the Chain with sweet surprise,
And in our Saviour's image rise.

Also Mary Dunn who departed this life 25th of April 1804, aged 72 years. Also John Dunn who departed this life ye 25th day of January 1806, aged 87 years. Also near this place lie the remains of Elizabeth, the widow of Thomas Austin, sister of the above John Dunn, died September 1st 1788, aged 78 years.'

The Dunns must have dreaded the 25th day of the month – although the years differ, the father died on the 25th day of January, and the mother and son on the 25th day of April.

On a flat stone lying on the ground a few yards from the west wall is recorded a most unusual surname: 'In memory of Solomon Bydder, of this village, mariner, who departed this life 27th June 1790, Aetat 50 years. Also John Bydder, mariner, son of the said Solomon Bydder by Mary his wife, who died 25th July 1812, Aetat 44 years.'

And lastly, a large slate memorial slab on which is inscribed: 'In memory of Sarah, wife of William Tall of this parish, died 29th September 1853, aged 70 years.' Then a few inches below just the two words: 'Also the'. It is obvious that an inscription recording the death of

William Tall should have been entered after his death, but as often happened, none of the surviving members of the family, assuming there were some, saw to it that the work was carried out.

And so our journey around south western Wales comes to an end. As can be seen from the title of the book, its contents only give a glimpse of the amount of interesting information that is still out there to be gathered and collated. This work contains facts and anecdotes that refer to only a few of the hundreds of churches, churchyards and memorials that are in Wales. Each one of them has something to interest the visitor, and I urge you to embark on your own journeys of discovery.

Index / *Mynegai*

Churches, Chapels and Churchyards.
Eglwysi, Capeli a Mynwentydd.

Gumfreston	St. Laurence	210
Henfynyw	St. David	174
Lampeter	St. Peter	250
Lamphey	SS. Faith & Tyfei	214
Laugharne	St. Martin	95
Little Newcastle	St. Peter	209
Llanarth	St. David	247
Llanarthne	St. David	41
Llanboidy	St. Brynach	239
Llandawke	St. Margaret	97
Llanddarog	St. Twrog	36
Llanddowror	St. Teilo	101
Llandyfaelog	St. Maelog	73
Llandyfriog	St. Tyfriog	242
Llandysul	St. Tysul	155
Llanegwad	St. Egwad	63
Llanfair-ar-y-Bryn	St. Mary	252
Llanfihangel Abercywyn	St. Michael	84
Llanfyrnach	St. Brynach	237
Llangathen	St. Cathen	51
Llangeler	St. Celer	136
Llangoedmor (e)	St. Cynllo	184
Llangors (e)	St. Paulinus	266
Llangunnor	St. Cynnwr	28
Llanllwch	St. Mary	18
Llanllwni	SS Luke & Llonio	134
Llanon (Llansantffraed)	St. David	248
Llanpumsaint	Pum Sant	115
Llanrhidian	SS. Illtyd & Rhidian	272
Llansadurnen	St. Sadyrnin	110
Llanstephan	St. Steffan	111